*Yale Studies in English*

Yale Studies in English publishes books on English, American, and Anglophone literature developed in and by the Yale University community. Founded in 1898 by Albert Stanburrough Cook, the original series continued into the 1970s, producing such titles as *The Poetry of Meditation* by Louis Martz, *Shelley's Mythmaking* by Harold Bloom, *The Cankered Muse* by Alvin Kernan, *The Hero of the Waverly Novels* by Alexander Welsh, *John Skelton's Poetry* by Stanley Fish, and *Sir Walter Ralegh: The Renaissance Man and His Roles* by Stephen Greenblatt. With the goal of encouraging publications by emerging scholars alongside the work of established colleagues, the series has been revived for the twenty-first century with the support of a grant from the Andrew W. Mellon Foundation and in partnership with Yale University Press.

PAUL H. FRY

# Wordsworth and the Poetry of What We Are

*Yale University Press*
*New Haven &*
*London*

Published with assistance from the Louis Stern Memorial Fund.

Set in Sabon by Keystone Typesetting, Inc.
Printed in the United States of America.

Library of Congress Cataloging-in-Publication Data

Fry, Paul H.
    Wordsworth and the poetry of what we are / Paul H. Fry.
        p. cm. — (Yale studies in English)
    Includes bibliographical references and index.
    ISBN 978-0-300-12648-8 (cloth : alk. paper)
    1. Wordsworth, William, 1770–1850 — Criticism and interpretation.
2. Wordsworth, William, 1770–1850 — Philosophy. 3. Coleridge, Samuel Taylor,
1772–1834 — Philosophy. 4. Philosophy, English — 19th century. 5. Philosophical
anthropology in literature. 6. Philosophy of nature in literature. 7. Philosophy in
literature. 8. Nature in literature. I. Title.
PR5892.P5F79 2008
821'.7 — dc22
2007046556

A catalogue record for this book is available from the British Library.

The paper in this book meets the guidelines for permanence and durability of the
Committee on Production Guidelines for Book Longevity of the Council on
Library Resources.

10 9 8 7 6 5 4 3 2 1

To the memory of my parents, Jess and Ann Fry,
Wordsworthian lives in their diurnal course

# Contents

# Preface

Introducing a reprint of the 1835 edition of Wordsworth's *Guide to the Lakes*, the Malvern Public Librarian nicely says that Wordsworth's "great prefaces . . . strive, with characteristic humility, to seek out the hiding-places of his power." Not just the prefaces, of course, and not just his own power: Wordsworth had a way of sensing the power hidden in all poetry, and never stopped writing about it. At the same time, however, he believed that his own peculiar power, like that of a handful of predecessors, was original, and that his originality was what mattered. In this book it is my wish to bring the hiding-places of Wordsworth's original power to light in the poetry that was written as early as 1787 and as late as 1817.

My title alludes to the impassioned declaration of purpose in the "Prospectus to *The Recluse*." Having passed in review the great myths of traditional poetry, especially Milton's, Wordsworth claims that his own poetry will encourage "the discerning intellect of Man" to find such myths implied, or entailed, as "[a] simple produce of the common day." Raising his pitch still higher, he proposes to "chant . . . the spousal verse" of mind and nature, using "words / Which speak of nothing more than what we are." I shall add a word about the continuation of this passage below, but for the moment I want to call attention to a choice of words in which the theme of my book can be found. Wordsworth might have said "*who* we are." Agreed, "nothing more than who we are" is a still odder expression than the one he uses, and it is important to see why. The modern "who" would just be coming into use as an honorific term celebrating the exaltation of the Human achieved by enlightenment thought, and we should expect "who" — and for that matter "what" too understood as a placeholder for the same idea — to be preceded by an expression of expanded scope rather than by the curtailment of "nothing more than." So why the curtailment? And why the depersonification, or reification, of the human as a thing in itself, as "what we are"? And above all, why the intense enthusiasm attached to phrases that another poet might well find depressing? The answer, I shall claim, is that Wordsworth discovers the revelation of being itself in the nonhumanity that "we" share with the nonhuman universe, and that this revelation is the hiding-place of his power.

Hoping to achieve a measure of pedagogical continuity, I have drawn in part from notes for a graduate seminar that was once devoted exclusively to Wordsworth. Typically such a course is called "Wordsworth and Coleridge," but for a while I stubbornly held out against the stereo approach, only to discover in the long run that it best served my own ends. Conceding defeat, I came to devote several weeks of the seminar to Coleridge's major poems and a reprise of the main ideas that we had unavoidably discussed all along because Wordsworth came to understand his own vocation in large part by disagreeing with them. In this book I place his disagreement in sharper relief than has been customary, and argue that it surfaced from the very beginning of his friendship and collaboration with Coleridge. Just as Shelley's career is a quest for a hero that is not Byronic, so Wordsworth's seeks an imagination that is not "an esemplastic power," and a means of access to actuality that is not anthropocentric. Every book has a foil: late capitalism (by means of which in a very different book I could have explained Wordsworth's alienation into thinghood as unhappy reification); tenured radicals; perfidious Albion; whatever it may be. The foil here, affectionately and respectfully treated, is Coleridge.

We are always complaining that the work of our colleagues is "undertheorized." Although my other focus as a teacher is literary theory, I am made uncomfortable by the demand for the elaboration in each and every publication or conference paper of a methodology, in itself not at all necessarily theoretical, which is under compulsion to be "engaged" with the very latest shifts of "debate." It is always ill-advised not to know what's going on, yet it seems equally ill-advised to snuggle so quickly into emerging paradigms, armed with the unshakable — and psychoanalytically predestined — article of faith that yesterday's thought was bad and today's is good and maybe the day before yesterday's was good after all. In romantic studies today, the three most exciting new frameworks, each rethinking without challenging or displacing the dominant historicist and feminist work of the past twenty years (to which the first part of Chapter 1 is a response), are "green criticism," cognitive science, and media or systems theory. To the first of these as it is applied to Wordsworth, I offer a modest challenge in Chapter 4, and by the other two somewhat interrelated approaches I remain for the most part uninfluenced even while I learn from them on the sidelines.

My own orientation, which I hope soon to see rehabilitated as a matter of the day before yesterday, is broadly phenomenological. The reader is likely to discern influences as varied as Hegel, certain parts of Freud, and Heidegger. This tradition in part explains the depth of my admiration for Geoffrey Hartman's Wordsworth criticism, but the way in which I diverge from these modes of thought may explain my divergence from Hartman as well. My favorite page in *The Phenomenology of Mind* is the first, where Hegel identifies the basis of consciousness in "sense certainty," and while I am caught up by the inner necessity of everything that follows in Hegel, I remain nevertheless a radical empiricist, and therefore belong more squarely to what I may be the first to call the "Cambridge School" of Wordsworth criticism than to the Yale School. It is amazing (or perhaps not so amazing) how few of the most imaginative Wordsworthians share with Wordsworth his fundamental intellectual framework, his adherence to the monist empirical tradition that passes from Locke through David Hartley. As any reader of Hartley knows, there is nothing in this way of thinking to preclude religious convictions, whether they be the intermittent pantheism of Wordsworth in the 1790s or the settled orthodoxies of his later years; nor do the intimations of a spiritual plane on which nearly all Wordsworth criticism has focused require the grounding in transcendental idealism that Wordsworth in his Coleridgean moments seems to accept. The Lockeian tradition is the one inherited by the non-Wordsworthian, quirkily Coleridgean I. A. Richards (whose career can be understood as an attempt to reconcile Pavlov, Hartley's descendent, with Plato), but it is taken over with far less interest in saving idealism by the critics and scholars who were Richards's students and followers at Cambridge: William Empson, Basil Willey, and Hugh Sykes Davies. Mediated in part by J. H. Prynne, this set of attitudes resurfaces, I think, in the difficult and exciting new book by Simon Jarvis, *Wordsworth's Philosophic Song* (2007).

In the long run, I will be found to have touched upon theoretical issues of many kinds, especially in relation to the linguistic turn that "Yale" (including Cleanth Brooks) and "Cambridge" (Empson and Davies in any case; and see Jonathan Wordsworth's excellent "Twenty Wordsworth" in *The Wordsworth Circle* for 2000) have in common. But there is one issue over which I should pause here, because it is in just this one respect that my approach is at least in

some sense truly undertheorized. I mean the intractable problem of inten-
tionalism. My whole emphasis on the nonhuman, insignificance, and the un-
differentiated will probably seem counterintuitive, and will likewise seem anti-
thetical to what Wordsworth purports to say in many of his best-known
passages of poetry and prose. Safest perhaps if I were then just blithely to say
that I don't care what Wordsworth intended, I only want to bring out a kind of
undersong that I can document in his "text." That position would at least be
consistent. But I am no less eager than any other critic to convince the reader
that Wordsworth intended the meanings I find in him, and I ransack both
poetry and prose to find Wordsworth agreeing with me — to put it as self-
critically as possible. That's a vulnerability, to be sure, perhaps manifest in my
case but also, as I see it, an inescapable problem even for those critics to whom
judicious objectivity is an end in itself. (Even the most painstaking textual
scholars, the Cornell Wordsworth editors and the followers of John Alban
Finch, together with hermeneutically more daring scholars like Kenneth John-
ston, all of whom have done so much to clarify Wordsworth's compositional
processes, are still making him up as they go along.) The problem is exacer-
bated by the fact that I have no model of a psychoanalytic or political uncon-
scious to fall back on; there is no "ontic unconscious" that I know of unless it is
hinted at in Freud's *Beyond the Pleasure Principle.* So I cannot speak of what
Wordsworth "unconsciously intended," but I do sometimes border on doing
so, and what remains undertheorized in my work is my inability to anchor
such moments in a definite intentional concept. I cannot on the other hand
avoid using a selectively evidentiary approach to argue that Wordsworth did
intend ("consciously"? "in part"? "at some level"?) that which I suppose his
poetry to mean, even though I shall frequently acknowledge all the occasions
on which, at the very least, he "intends to intend" something different, if
indeed he does not definitely *mean* something different. What I shall for the
most part be found saying is that even on those occasions what is original in
his work is "still present" if viewed at the right angle, and that way of putting it
I do think justified.

Yes, "nothing more than what we are" is a theme that is supposed to "arouse
the sensual from their sleep / Of death," though I am not sure how or why; and
yes, when in "Tintern Abbey" we are "laid asleep in body" we also become "a
living soul," though I am not sure how or why. My point remains, though: if
Wordsworth had said "*who* we are" he would have laid an intelligible ground-
work for transcendence, or at least for anthropocentrism; and if he had been a
little less insistently *medical* in remarking that when we are laid asleep in body
the "motion of our *human* blood" is "[a]lmost suspended" he would have laid
an intelligible groundwork for becoming a living soul. The "human" in each

case remains squarely on the side of what we are now, and offers no bridge to this or that saving hypothesis about what we may become, and in any case there is no clear evidence in Wordsworth's most characteristic poetry that any such hypothesis is required, except insofar as saving the appearances for public consumption and even for private conscience is required. And there I am forced to leave the matter. Readers convinced that the themes I have emphasized are necessary in order to explain what is otherwise inexplicable in Wordsworth may be willing to agree that my "evidence" keeps the problem of intention at arm's length without harm just *because* it is convincing.

The first chapter introduces the themes of the book, especially as one can find them in Wordsworth's prose, but with forays into the poems. After situating my emphasis in relation to ideas of the political or politicized Wordsworth, I turn to Wordsworth's critique of differentiation and of Coleridge's theory of the imagination as a "shaping spirit," suggesting that Wordsworth himself sees the imagination — if that is what it is — as the openness of the mind to the revelation of unity. The next two chapters concern Wordsworth's self-understanding in relation to characteristic views of him among his contemporaries, especially Jeffrey and Coleridge, sharpening the focus of the book's argument by explaining, as precisely as possible, the underlying premises (insights as well as misunderstandings) that shape his reception. The fourth chapter opens with a panoramic view of the history of Wordsworth criticism, the guiding thread here being the question whether he was or was not a "nature poet," whatever that designation has been taken successively to mean. The remaining five chapters are roughly but not rigorously chronological, and work primarily through readings of exemplary poems. The fifth, sixth, and ninth move from the earliest poems (Chapter 5) to lyric and narrative poems ranging from the *Lyrical Ballads* era to the odes of 1817 that revisit the four great crisis lyrics of 1798–1805. The seventh chapter reads *The Prelude* — "The Poem to Coleridge" — as a sustained, vacillating, yet ultimately decisive revision of Coleridge's influence. The eighth approaches *The Excursion* as a critique of the Wanderer, rejecting visionary idealism as the appropriate medium of religious understanding and announcing an essentially unrevised yet diminished, more circumscribed vocation for the poet. A brief afterword revisits the old argument charging Wordsworth with "primitivism" in relation to the ontology of the actual that has been my theme.

# Acknowledgments

No one can read much of my work without recognizing my debt to Geoffrey Hartman, and now that I presume to write a book about Wordsworth, well, my deepest debts of all are those that clarified my disagreements. Other colleagues to whom I am grateful for conversation and insight are Leslie Brisman and especially Christopher Miller, who read the whole manuscript and commented most helpfully. Special thanks to Joseph Roach, who has made excellent suggestions, kindly used part of his Mellon Research Grant to restart the Yale Studies in English series with this book, and withal has been a constant source of encouragement. Still at Yale, I want as always to thank my wife and faculty colleague Brigitte Peucker, my best and most patient sounding board. Of the many students from whose challenging insights I've benefited in recent years, I single out Eric Lindstrom, Helmut Illbrook, Michaela Bronstein, Steve Tedeschi, David Gorin, Ana Nersessian, and Jeremy Kessler.

Turning elsewhere in the field, I think first of my gratitude to old friends, Marshall Brown and Henry Weinfield foremost among them. I am also grateful for exchanges in recent years with David Simpson. For a Harvard event that allowed me to present a version of my first chapter, I thank the convener Ann Rowland (an earlier student), as well as Alison Hickey (another still earlier), Laura Quinney, and Bruce Graver. For the Coleridge chapter I am especially indebted to the enforced labors of Ross Murfin, who in effect finished the book I had put together for the series of which he was General Editor. For hard work and introductory comments on a version of Chapter 5 in the volume mentioned below, I thank Helen Regueiro Elam and Frances Ferguson.

I read different fragments of Chapter 6 on two different occasions, both of them *hommages* to great scholars. The first was at a symposium in honor of Johannes Anderegg, and I want to thank Johannes for this and for all our conversations over the years. The second was at a special section of the 2006 NASSR in Montreal in celebration of Geoffrey Hartman. I want to steal this chance to acknowledge those who made it productive and congenial: my fellow panelists Ian Balfour, Anne-Lise Francois, Kevis Goodman, again Laura Quinney, Marc Redfield, Joshua Wilner, and Geoffrey himself; those whom I met there, especially Marilyn Gaull; and the chance to renew old acquaintance with Alan Bewell, Christoph Bode, Andy Elfenbein, and William Flesch.

Thanks finally to two friends who have moved out of the craft and on to more momentous doings: Dick Brodhead, who has more Wordsworth memorized to better purpose than anyone I know (the list includes those who are not Americanists or university presidents), and Tom Hyde, who knows what I'm up to.

I am grateful too for the two readers' reports solicited by the Yale University Press, and to editor John Kulka for his shepherding through of the manuscript. Thanks also to John's successor Jennifer Banks and her assistant Joe Calamia, to Margaret Otzel and Joyce Ippolito for their careful manuscript and production editing, and to Alden Ferro, Karen Stickler, and Mary Valencia for putting the book in the reader's hands. Versions of Chapters 2, 3, and 4 have appeared elsewhere as follows:

"Wordsworth in the 'Rime'" appeared in *"The Rime of the Ancient Mariner,"* ed. Paul H. Fry, *Case Studies in Contemporary Criticism* (Boston: Bedford/St. Martin's, 1999).

"Jeffreyism, Byron's Wordsworth, and the Nonhuman" appeared in *British Romanticism and the "Edinburgh Review,"* ed. Massimiliano Demata and Duncan Wu (London: Palgrave Macmillan, 2002).

"Green to the Very Door? The Natural Wordsworth" appeared first in *Studies in Romanticism* 35 (1996), and then in *The Wordsworthian Enlightenment: Romantic Poetry and the Ecology of Reading,* ed. Helen Regueiro Elam and Frances Ferguson (Baltimore: Johns Hopkins University Press, 2005).

Two brief fragments of "Hoof After Hoof" appeared in *Dazwischen: Zum transitorischen Denken in Literatur- und Kulturwissenschaft,* ed. Andreas Härter, Edith Anna Kunz, and Heiner Weidmann (Göttingen: Vandenhoeck & Ruprecht, 2003), and as part of "Progresses of Poetry," in *The Wordsworth Circle* 37 (2006).

# Introduction: Wordsworth's Originality

## "Politics"

This introductory chapter begins with a section that will not at first seem introductory. Before explaining my approach to Wordsworth, that is, this section explains instead why my approach for the most part avoids issues related to history and politics. It is an "apology" of the sort that seems necessary in today's academic climate, but it is also a sincere admission that these topics interest me more, and engage more of my attention, than may appear at times elsewhere. Powerful revisionary thinking about Wordsworth along political and historical lines has dominated the classroom and the academic press for the past twenty years, but it is not just this exemplary work that demonstrates the considerable explanatory power of "historicism" (new or old). It is just foolish to deny that as soon as any competent reader begins to use these tools, new vistas come into view and the old familiar landscape looks strikingly different. Sometimes this sort of emphasis is simply out of scale despite its measure of insight, but then so is any sort of emphasis that proves flat-footed or exposes a tin ear. With this conceded, however, the discussion of Wordsworth's politics that follows in this section is meant to suggest, in general qualification of such approaches, that there is an *intrinsic* breach of scale, not just occasional overkill, in politicizing his oeuvre. His poetry is indeed politically motivated in all sorts of conscious and unconscious ways; yet it also has a far more radical, pressing, and original motive, which is ontological — or rather, as I shall call it, "ontic." In clearing space for the possibility that politics (like other governing ideas) falls silent, as it were, while lyric is still talking, still trying to get said what it has uniquely to say, I shall have begun introducing the topic of this book after all.

Citing for my section heading the title of the poem of 1939 that Yeats wanted to have printed last in his collected edition, "Politics," will seem grossly ill-considered today. In debate with a recent political exhortation by Thomas Mann, Yeats composes his last word to the world:

> How can I, that girl standing there,
> My attention fix
> On Roman or on Russian
> Or on Spanish politics[?][1]

By today's standards, or indeed one would hope by anyone's at any time, he could scarcely have said anything more obnoxious. Doddering old Yeats was on virility hormones and proud of it, apparently proud also no longer to be the effete being who wrote "Easter 1916," the greatest modern political poem in English. He may in addition have been insulting Mann, as the bisexuality of the author of *Death in Venice* was widely suspected. And above all, Yeats had the temerity to say, on the brink of war, amid rumors of genocide and the clash of two bloody, paranoid, yet politically seductive tyrannies (and with the Troubles of 1916 by no means abated at home), that some things in life are so fundamental that they make politics seem superficial, a dry subject matter around which there swirls, endlessly and tediously, a lot of inflexible talk. Today, in a maelstrom of comparably appalling political events, the reader finds me alluding to that silly poem by Yeats, whose heartfelt commitment to the political right in his later years is in fact signaled by this very idea, popular if not universal on the right — the idea, namely, that politics isn't everything.

To be sure, this last view is yet more characteristic of the Center. Moving to extremes in either direction normally involves organizing and understanding life in political terms, which is to say, in a single set of terms; but there is still an asymmetry between right and left to be observed, one that will advance me toward my argument. Yeats's notion that other things are more fundamental than politics simply isn't available to the left, whose materialist premise is perforce that all the conditions that shape and enable "life" just are its political economy. Sex itself is politics, and so is the genealogy of everyone's thinking on any subject whatever. This is not necessarily the view of politics on the right, though it quite often is, because, at least as the left understands the matter, for many on the right politics seems more superficial than custom and folkways, "the way things are," and the very mention of politics arouses dark fears of intellectualized, system-driven change. Of course this position is easily de-mystified as, precisely, the "politics" of conservatism; and the quietistic right itself demystifies it quickly enough when it comes time to vote.

But one realizes, in mulling over such tokens of thought, that in tracing this path one has arrived at the writings of two figures whose politicized quietism haunts the political imagination of academic humanists, chiefly on the left, today: Burke and Wordsworth. As James Chandler has shown, if the Burkean keyword "custom" is for Wordsworth a "second nature,"[2] it betokens the way the social fabric just is (as nature itself just is), prior to and underlying the intervention of meliorist political agendas that will inevitably *tear* this fabric. Today we find this blindness to history nearly incredible; but for such histor-ically well-versed writers as Burke and Wordsworth, it is a deliberate blind-ness, blind not to the grand sweep of history but to historical *process*, couched in the choice of a certain inaugural event—the Magna Carta, Church Estab-lishment, the Glorious Revolution—which constitutes, like the Battle of Jena for Hegel or the achieved classless society for Marx, the "end of history." "History" from this chosen event forward *becomes* custom, with class rela-tions fixed in place and rationalized as a timeless agrarian regime of charity and mutual benefit. This entropic state of things must be preserved, if neces-sary, by political means, "politics" being then those merely secondary and reflective schemes that either reinforce or threaten custom.

These observations may imply, I hope, a valid, immediately recognizable account of the "later" Wordsworth: Tory place-holder, tireless canvasser against Reform and Catholic emancipation, author of Ecclesiastical Sonnets, sonnets in defense of capital punishment, the Wanderer's celebration of British imperialism (planting custom like the oar of Odysseus "on every shore"), and all the rest of it. The debate still rages, to be sure, with wonderfully vivifying results for Wordsworth and Coleridge scholarship, concerning the actual date of what E. P. Thompson, echoing Byron and his contemporaries, calls Words-worth's "apostasy." Such dating is made more difficult if one believes with Thompson that the government crackdown on oratory and pamphleteering in 1796 and 1797 drove radical opinions into hiding without at first necessarily changing them.[3] Conventional views on the date of Wordsworth's apostasy range from 1797 or 1798 to 1806, with the majority finding the most decisive transitional signs between 1802 and 1804, the progress of French affairs being the normally cited catalyst, together with simple weariness at playing what Coleridge called (distressingly early on in a letter placating his reactionary brother) "the squeaking baby-trumpet of sedition."[4] There have also been much earlier dates proposed, however, dates not in themselves compelling if one thinks simply of Wordsworth's announced political and social views, most notably the incendiary Llandaff Letter of 1793, but which nevertheless prompt a challenging question to which my point of departure in the present book is related.

This question will also return us to Yeats, enabling us to see a little farther into his carelessly phrased opinion, perhaps farther than he did. (After all, this is the same person who had already said, in a much better poem, that he had heard the hysterical women say they were sick of the palette and fiddle-bow.) The question then is, are we on firm ground if we suppose an early date when Wordsworth was still driven by politics, accepting the idea that politics is the basis and structure of existence, a date which was then supplanted by the notion that politics is only a reasoned attitude — alongside art and far less important than religion — toward the true basis and structure of existence, which is custom? I don't mean to suggest that this question is easy to answer. One is tempted to say, with those who doubt his early radicalism, that there was never a time when he was not, *in potentia,* an agrarian conservative, having been merely misled, temporarily, about the political implications of his rural vision. On the other hand, however, we know that there were personal resentments making his early mistrust of the ruling class and social inequality in general an important part of his lived experience, and these, together with his friendships in radical circles, caused him to be, temporarily, something like a political animal. (Even this argument implies that there are people, un-afflicted or unaware of or indifferent to affliction, who may not be political animals — which is never to say that such people don't have political opinions, even strong ones.) Much depends, as all agree, on how one reads *Salisbury Plain* in its various drafts, *The Borderers, The Old Cumberland Beggar,* and *The Ruined Cottage.*

Were I not about to attempt a turn of thought that moves outside of the terms of this debate, I would certainly be obliged to offer a reading of these interesting poems in my turn. I would prefer, however, as one who takes the view that Wordsworth was never radically politicized (although at least in 1793 he was without a doubt politically radical), to consider his friendship with Michel Beaupuy as it is described in *The Prelude.* Beaupuy, we can infer, was a politicized being through and through, "one devoted," who "fashioned his life" on that of ancient republicans trained in philosophy (1805, IX, 407, 428). I take it that that was one reason why, as a *rara avis,* he fascinated Wordsworth, himself not unduly dismayed at least on political grounds to be caught up in a love affair with a Royalist, or in any case with a person who had in common with him the obvious fact that she was not a politicized being through and through either (although she became one at a later date). Wordsworth listened with fascination to Beaupuy's political rhapsodies, but willingly gives the impression that he saw himself conversing in peripatetic groves rather than arming his mind in political trenches, until he was brought up short — and that is my point: he was aroused from a discursive reverie — when Beaupuy pointed to "a hunger-bitten girl" drifting along with a heifer and vacantly absorbed in knitting (*not Yeats's girl!*), and said " 'Tis against *that* / That we are fighting' " (1850, IX, 517–18). Carried away by emotion, Wordsworth then first discovered in himself a committed revolutionary partisan. Wordsworth in this moment of *The Prelude* thus focuses upon himself, I would argue, a psychological study in contagious enthusiasm, the undersong of which is that some people are politicized by instinct, some only by circumstance, if even then.

Why is Beaupuy's reaction to the girl pivotal? Because Wordsworth knows that, free from the infectiousness of the moment, he would have seen the girl in a different way, though not Yeats's way either. He has already commemorated her in 1799, and he was five years old when he saw her: "more near, / A girl who bore a pitcher on her head / And seemed with difficult steps to force her way / Against the blowing wind" (XI, 304–07). "Spots of Time" criticism is by this time nothing if not fanciful, and this girl has in fact been sexualized as though she were Yeats's, her garments vexed by the wind having become see-through in the adult poet's screen memory, or at least revealing; but surely that is not the point. True, she is aestheticized. One sees her in a genre painting, perhaps with a biblical or political theme, where admittedly *à la* David or especially Delacroix something might be made of the body under the garments. She is also quite consciously de-politicized, as though in answer to Beaupuy's girl: although she is engaged in labor and probably a peasant, her hardship is pointedly caused by the weather (one is not inclined to call it allegorical weather) and not by social circumstances. But it is not in these registers that she made her deepest impression on Wordsworth. The aesthetic and the anti-political are but mediations of what is neither: the famous "visionary dreariness" of which she forms an element with the naked pool, the pitcher, the beacon on the summit, and the site of the hanged man. She is an object among objects, one with all things (especially the dead) precisely in the negation of her social being that the composition of the scene, and the acuteness of its solitude, forces upon her. By contrast, the "heartless mood of solitude" in which Beaupuy's wayfarer knits is completely political; she is despondent, society is heartless, she is outcast and forgotten, hence alone. None of the ideas keyed by such words in the Beaupuy passage have their usual Wordsworthian value; hence the focus of the scene in the Loire Valley, guided by

Beaupuy, is inequality, not equality. Equality for Wordsworth (oneness, unity) was never a political idea. Fostered amid rocks and stones and trees, he saw equality in this largely mineral world as the ontic unity of all things, including human things. That was his central and most radical insight, and it is the subject of this book.

Though it is not political, this insight certainly has, or briefly had, a political dimension, which Hazlitt recognized in calling Wordsworth a "leveling" poet.[5] Hazlitt, in *The Spirit of the Age* and in *Lectures on the English Poets,* noticed the virtual nonhumanity of Wordsworth's characters in *Lyrical Ballads* and elsewhere — some of them social outcasts but just as many very old, very young, or very stupid — and saw that they were "marginals," as Alan Bewell calls them,[6] at the outermost edges of the human community, defining that community by delimiting it. Politically speaking, one might say that if I am essentially a thing there is certainly no natural reason why other humans *qua* things should be superior to me; in just that respect we are created equal, and if I am a marginal, an Alzheimer's victim or a village idiot, I have a great deal to teach those who may be "central" (politicians, aristocrats, poets) about the pretentiousness of rationality, "that false secondary power / By which we multiply distinctions" (1850, II, 216–17), which is necessarily blind to the indivisibility of the actual: "The cocks did crow, tu-whoo, tu-whoo, / And the sun did shine so cold," as the Idiot Boy teaches. Those portentous collapses of difference by the simple-minded are what drove Wordsworth's first readers wild with indignation and provoked all their defensive mockery: they knew they were being told that difference itself is error. Yet this definition of equality is not ultimately political, even in the poetry of 1793–96, but ontological.[7] Wordsworth's republican views notwithstanding, this definition can easily have superimposed upon it the most reactionary defense of hierarchy because, in Rousseau as in Wordsworth, social being is itself precisely the differentiation, the hypothesis of *meum* and *tuum,* that supplants the unity of natural being. Taken all in all, the notion of ontological equality is a "dreary" insight, as Wordsworth startlingly said in describing the scene in which the girl with the pitcher appeared, and perhaps indeed it is tinged by the feeling of guilt at having betrayed any possible conception of himself as a political agent, which is the theme of David Bromwich, or tinged possibly by the repression of history, with all its telling signposts, which is the theme of Alan Liu.[8] Possibly it is this guilt, too, that prevents Wordsworth from confronting or even admitting the implications of his insight. About that too there will be much to say.

Wordsworth's poetic vision, then, does not retreat from politics to custom because from the beginning neither politics *nor* custom is its most authentic, original focus. To make the argument I want to make, therefore, when I turn once and for all to the work in Chapter 5 I shall begin not with the poetry of 1793–96 but with the juvenilia of 1789–92. Even if custom is not politics, it is still the basis for a politics, and while it may be a second nature, it is still (proudly) historical and regional, having nothing directly to do with the nature of being or beings — though it may, like the girl with the pitcher, lend itself to the rural genre scenery in which that nature discloses itself most readily to the attentive eye. In my view, this is a fairly circumspect way of putting the argument of the "Preface to *Lyrical Ballads*," especially its paltering with the word "common": common to all (the poet is a man speaking to men), yet more vivid among the common people — with the politicized sense of unenclosed grazing space somewhere nearby, closer than the baronial halls of older ballads but still not focal, as in "Simon Lee." The ontic, unsemantic self-identity of things, underlying and no doubt fostering the imaginary timelessness of custom: this is Wordsworth's true theme, constantly touched upon yet shied away from, masked at various times in more acceptable — but less original — pantheist, quietist, and idealist registers.

Biographical evidence can serve this emphasis as readily as it serves the political emphasis, and can perhaps even qualify the latter. The political Wordsworth can be constructed out of evidence from France, from his experience among the London dissenting societies, and from the Alfoxden circle (Thelwall, Coleridge, Poole, et al.) that attracted the attention of the Pitt government. It was long the fashion to make fun of the bungling "Spy Nosy" (the government agent Walsh) and his misconceptions about the poets' research for Coleridge's *The Brook,* and now the fashion has swung to the opposite extreme of saying that the orators and pamphleteers Thelwall and Coleridge were quite understandably under surveillance, however mistaken Pitt's homeland security forces may have been to suppose that they were seeking out good landing places for French invaders. (No one to my knowledge has yet suggested that they actually were doing that.) I agree certainly that the spy's presence was not absurd, and agree likewise that Wordsworth and his sister were thrown out of Alfoxden because of the company they kept, as we now insist, rather more than for keeping company with each other, disturbing as that too must have seemed. But here Beaupuy again becomes relevant. That was a political friendship, with political discussion its very marrow and the shaping of political opinion its end in view. Is it simply a sign that apostasy has already set in that the Alfoxden circle talked for the most part, according their constant, invariant recollections, about philosophy and poetry?

Many would say yes. Thompson, again, argues that radicals like Thelwall, fresh from prison and knowing themselves to be watched, just lost their nerve and started thinking about cultivating their gardens. Thelwall thought of himself as an activist in bookish retirement, not on the run, with Liswyn Farm his Sabine retreat. In "Anecdote for Fathers," Wordsworth regards Thelwall's Welsh retreat as an alternative *locus amoenus*. Opium, metaphysics, and domestic irritations began creeping up on Coleridge all at once during this period. Wordsworth was still fretting, as he always had been, about what to do with himself more continuously than about what to do for humanity. Although it was an idyllic time, in short, one just cannot say that it was a political idyll. Its ferment, an Alan Liu or perhaps a Thompson might argue, was a concentrated energy arising from the very strain of repressing politics. Possibly so, but what is downplayed in any such account is that Wordsworth and Dorothy Wordsworth and Coleridge (here I think Thelwall, though a poet, and certainly Poole can be set aside) were completely caught up in the intensity and excitement of their conversations and elated above all by the novelty of the poetry that began to emerge.

In *The Prelude*, Wordsworth remembers talking politics with Beaupuy, philosophy and poetry with Coleridge and Dorothy. Thelwall and Poole are not mentioned. What was exciting in Nether Stowey, what was worth remembering, was what seemed *new*: a new rationale for poetry about which Wordsworth and Coleridge would later crucially disagree, and perhaps (as I will argue) even then disagreed, but which galvanized them in their poetry itself and in conversation. Politics remained a worthy and heartfelt topic, one imagines, even if one hears little about it; but it could never be pressingly *new* because the principles of political philosophy, republican or otherwise, were all rooted in venerable traditions — as the comparably peripatetic conversations with Beaupuy, not in themselves sufficient for politicization, had already shown. If in the Alfoxden period there are already signs of political revisionism, as I would agree, any such change is not a conscious primary concern but is subordinate to the novelty of an emergent poetics. This is not necessarily to say, though, that a new vocation for poetry perforce entails a new politics. As I have said, one can be happily mistaken about the politics of custom, for example. Alternatively, the ontic theme that becomes fundamental for Wordsworth could possibly remain — though in his case it does not — an implied radical politics, with the social to be understood only *as* the natural, much as it is in today's radical ecologies that accord equal rights to all bio-species. In this sense and in many others, Wordsworth's is an only partly de-politicized materialism. His new theme is, in any case, "radical," a new radicalism that drives Wordsworth forward with more energy than any other kind because it is his own, and affords him, as Coleridge recognized even in disagreement, his unique place in the history of poetic insight. Henceforth in this book, for the reasons here given, I will have relatively little to say about politics or political implications in Wordsworth. I shall be talking instead, as critics at times perhaps too unwarily talked a generation ago, about the old Alfoxden topic: poetry in its complex and often surprising relation to philosophy and religion, which is to say, the anthropological function of poetry.

## Widest Commonalty

Wordsworth, I shall claim, was always acutely aware of something he could not say; "not say," that is, in two senses. The first sense is that he could not bring himself to say, could not even allow himself fully to recognize and accept what everything in his poems and much in his prose cries out that he in some sense knew; and not only knew but at least obscurely saw to lie at the heart of his poetic originality: *poetry discloses the unity constituted by and as the being, apart from meaning and apart even from difference, of all human and nonhuman things.* He could not say this outright, even in youth (when perhaps nothing other than the censure—even the censorship—of others might have prevented him), owing to all the religious, political, and social assumptions based on hierarchy and discrimination that seemed like natural boundaries to the scope of intellect. We always just take for granted that poetry is supposed to reconfigure the diversity of life, to place distinction in relief, to forge unity anew rather than disclose its preexistence; and no one has ever expressed these suppositions more eloquently than Coleridge, the difficulty of acknowledging his complete disagreement with whom is part of what obscures Wordsworth's originality from his own view, and becomes a recurrent theme of this book.

The second sense in which Wordsworth could not say what he seems always driven to say amounts simply to the linguistic imperative that reinforces the first sense. In-difference is in fact the one thing that neither poetry nor language itself *can* say or even indicate, however fervent and unmasked the wish to do so may be. Hence it is neither wholly a failure of nerve nor in any sense a weakness of technique that prevents Wordsworth from quite saying what he wants to say. He is able to compensate for this impossibility, however, by making us see the limits of semeiosis (here pretending to enlist Coleridge on his side): "No officious slave / Art thou" of "that false secondary power / By which we multiply distinctions" (*The Prelude*, 1850, II, 215–17).

In the last two chapters of this book I argue that the original insight of Wordsworth's youthful poetry, while largely hidden amid later priorities, never wholly disappeared and in certain ways became clearer. In the long run he did believe that more than one kind of power—not just the power of imaginative sympathy but also the power of vested authority—crucially matters in the makeup of a social being. But imaginative sympathy, which I shall be attempting to describe in a new way, remains the ground of all true feeling, including even the feeling that confers value on the niceties of social and ecclesiastical discrimination. Wordsworth's poetry assumes the task of extending imaginative sympathy in "widest commonalty" ("Prospectus" to *The Recluse,* 18), promoting a fellow-feeling with all modes of being, not just social being, based on what they have in common — to put it with appropriate simplicity. This common denominator I propose to call the nonhuman, arguing that in Wordsworth's view the human is to be understood most radically as the perception of the nonhuman in human identity itself: in the infant, somnolent, idiotic, senile, *and* socially deprived states of being human, together with the intimation of death and corpsehood. This view of the nonhuman human in its "marginal" conditions — noted early by Lamb and Hazlitt — does not preclude the "spiritual" view, with its equal emphasis on the nonhuman, except that for even the early Wordsworth (whether or not he was the "semi-atheist" Coleridge thought him to be in 1796),[9] the more readily available terms for the commonalty of all things suggest pantheism, hence veil the more unusual form of the insight. Thus, for example, one finds what William Empson called the "muddle" of "Tintern Abbey": the sense sublime of something far more deeply interfused, etc., which teeters between pantheism and the monistic materialism that shapes the logic if not the rhetoric of the Lockeian tradition.[10]

For the later Wordsworth, nonhuman things needed perforce to be excluded from religious devotion, with its focus on human salvation; he was embarrassed before many years passed at having called himself a "worshipper of nature" in "Tintern Abbey."[11] The natural and social worlds alike, despite being as vividly and sometimes hauntingly appreciated as ever in his later poems, came to be evoked primarily, though still not exclusively, in quest of symbols for human eschatology. Nature became once again, or seemed to become, the traditional Book of Nature, legible as the Bible is legible, which the poetry of Wordsworth's Great Decade had plainly repudiated;[12] and in the awkwardness of reconciling this pious purpose with his enduring awareness of what I call the minerality of being we can locate his "poetic decline" — although, in the interest of arresting this decline, I shall conclude this book by attaching as much interest as possible to certain poems of 1817.

Some of the more up-to-the-minute readers who encountered this approach to Wordsworth in my *Defense of Poetry* and elsewhere[13] found a similarity to the work of Giorgio Agamben, with his emphasis on the alienation of speech — inaugurating subjectivity simply by saying "I" — from the "psychosomatic" state of the "bare life," or "infant being."[14] I am bound to say, yes, something like this is what I want to talk about, although I cannot agree (nor, I think, would the Emile Benvéniste whom Agamben follows here [ibid., 5–6]) that the first person singular is any more important than the copula or for that matter any of the other deictics in alienating speech from the phenomenal ipseity of things. (One of the points I hope to make most forcefully is that Wordsworth was not, *pace* Hazlitt and Keats, a radically subjective poet.) Nor do I think — and here I distance myself not only from Agamben but from theorists of the linguistic turn — that the prison house of language is a space within which the circumspect rigors of commentary need be confined, agreeing with Words-worth that words are "not vehicles but powers to kill or animate" (*CL* 5, 185),[15] and that the "prison house" (Intimations Ode) has more than one padlock. Nor, finally, can I be wholly comfortable with the jargon of authentic experience that enables Agamben's recuperation of social and political issues from his own denudations: his modulation of sheer indifference, that is, to-ward a benign onto-theological *agape* teased out of the very term for indif-ference: *quodlibet* — "whatever," construed as what is wanted or desired.[16] As Wordsworth knew well in giving equal attention to ordinary events and ordi-nary birds and flowers (a focal project in the poems of 1802 especially), and despite his apparently Heideggerian embrace of rusticity in the "Preface," any preference of one event to another, one place to another, in short one object to another, aestheticizes one's milieu and merely substitutes one hierarchy for another — necessarily for a social being but perniciously for one's human grasp of the nonhuman.

In my view, Wordsworth more than any other poet, critic, or theorist before or since understood why the lyric moment of poetic expression, as opposed to the dramatic and narrative moments, exists. He was an anthropologist of (lyric) poetry, the purpose of whose poems was to explain why poetry exists. It has been of great interest recently to observe speculative literary theory turn-ing back to the eighteenth-century origin-of-language tradition Wordsworth had in his bones,[17] ceasing to ask what poetry is (poetics) and asking instead why poetry exists (literary anthropology). The leader in this turn of thought was Wolfgang Iser; but Iser always took for granted, I think unwarily, that literature is fiction. The "as if" of fiction on his view gives the reader or hearer a double perspective that enables feeling around the edges of selfhood toward otherness.[18] What is lacking in this account, even in its application to fiction, is the quixotic effort to evoke the Barthesian "*effet de réel.*"

Telling stories is what language is tailored to do (speech, again, is irreducibly fictive), and certainly stories consciously known to be fictive are useful for identity-formation and socialization — useful, that is, within the pale of the human *qua* human, the social world in which Wordsworth's six years' darling of a pygmy size cons another part. Thus far into an anthropology of consciously fictive literature Aristotle in refutation of Plato's entire social philosophy first carried us, although he prudently admitted that he had no one term for such a loose category. But Wordsworth, who decried "incident" in poetry throughout his life and whose most un-Aristotelian moment in the "Preface" is his subordination of action to character (see *Criticism*, 73), did not want to tell stories. He knew they were unavoidable, but for him they were almost a necessary evil, decidedly a means and not an end. This is clearest in his various attempts to explain the purpose of *The White Doe of Rylstone*, a poem he valued far more highly than we do: he keeps saying that insofar as the characters in this misleadingly Scott-like narrative choose to act, they fail, and insofar as their focus is contemplative they are transfigured—the human (Emily) and the animal (the white doe) being released together into the same luminous order of being. Hence Wordsworth's choice of epigraph for that poem, the passage on the transitoriness of action from the then-unpublished *Borderers*. For Wordsworth, the lyric moment does not reshape existence, it names being. It tries to do, in short, what language cannot do.

Where the imagination discloses unity, language signifies difference. For Wordsworth, the challenge then was to bend language out of its purpose and toward the purpose of poetry; this should go far to explain the extreme, seemingly indefensible realism, so obviously absurd in the fictionalist Coleridge's eyes, of his attack on "poetic diction" in behalf of "the real language of men." No, spoken language isn't like that, Coleridge explained in the *Biographia;* it always builds on linguistic models (if only the Bible and the eloquence of the local vicar and barber), never springs from the soil. But Wordsworth had only meant that this undoubted truth is a great pity, and that an original poetry can at least hope to gesture in the direction of actuality.

Here a qualifier is in order, one that Wordsworth may have communicated to Isabella Fenwick in order to reconcile his apparent naïveté on this score with Coleridge's critique. Because language is indeed a power, it helps the imagination respond to the world with fitting intensity. To speak of things in themselves is not at all to reduce them to a taxonomic exhibit (to kill is also to classify; we murder to dissect):

> pictures of animals & other productions of nature as seen in conservatories, menageries & museums &c—would do little for the national mind, nay they would be rather injurious to it, if the imagination were excluded by the presence of the object, more or less out of a state of nature; If it were not that we learn to talk & think of the Lion & the Eagle, the Palm tree & even the Cedar from the impassioned introduction of them so frequently into Holy Scripture & by Great Poets,[19]

— there would then be, he concludes, no benefit in merely looking at objects. Objects, that is, as individuated entities, a lion as opposed to — by which one ought to mean as inimical to, as excluding — an eagle. The imagination is needed, as a "feeling," to merge them with other objects even as, and precisely because, the linguistic aspect of imagination, in just this sense a "power," makes their identity glow.

It is only with this understanding that Wordsworth's pronouncement at the beginning of the "Essay, Supplementary" to the 1815 "Preface" will appear not to militate against the present argument. "The appropriate business of poetry," he says, "is to treat of things not as they *are,* but as they *appear;* not as they exist in themselves, but as they *seem* to exist to the *senses,* and to the *passions*" (*Criticism,* 192). This sounds like a full concession that poetry is properly fictive, a story about things. It is only an injunction, however, against seeing things as distinct from each other, "as they are" in the sense that of course no two points can occupy the same place and time and no two leaves are the same. The way things "seem," the way they exist for the senses and passions, of course does involve all the humanizing turns of thought that Ruskin called the Pathetic Fallacy and de Man, prosopopoeia; but it also entails, to the contrary, what I am calling the nonhuman in the human. The awareness that the widest commonalty of things is their common objecthood belongs only to and within human consciousness — as does, for that matter, the profoundly imaginative premise in Kantian ethics that objects must be acknowledged and allowed to exist in and for themselves. The most difficult part of the Fenwick passage quoted above is "more or less out of a state of nature," which I am not sure I understand. In this context, it could mean, perhaps, that without the imagination consciousness merges with the state of nature it reflects, and fails to think the nonhuman because it has become the nonhuman.

## *Imagination?*

An axiom: for Coleridge, imagination makes things one, it is fictive, a shaping spirit; for Wordsworth (if one here brackets the largely Coleridgean "Preface" of 1815), imagination discovers things to be one, it is revelatory. Wordsworth will not come right out and generalize to this effect, even though, for example, the experience described in all the great Spots of Time except — apparently — Simplon, Snowdon, and the suddenly idealist effort to explain the Spots themselves in Book 11, make it quite plain that, far from being "lord and master" (1805 *Prelude,* XI, 271), the mind perceives, in such moments, that "the utmost we can know / Both of ourselves and of the universe" (ibid., VII, 619–20) is nothing but a label we attach to a blind object. In plain prose, Wordsworth confines this negative way of defining the imagination to a sub-category. Speaking of "The Daffodils" in a note to the 1815 edition (together with two other poems, "The Reverie of Poor Susan" and "The Power of Music"), he says: "The subject of these Stanzas is rather an elementary feeling and simple impression (approaching to the nature of an ocular spectrum) upon the imaginative faculty, than an *exertion* of it" (*Criticism*, 109n.). At moments like these, the imagination can hardly be called a faculty at all; it is simply an auraticization of impressions. The case can be made that Words-worth really has no theory of the "creative" imagination at all. How could he have one, if a poet according to him is a man speaking to men, not differing in kind but only in degree?

Many of Wordsworth's poems (especially those composed in 1814, some to be included among the newly so-designated poems of Imagination—other-wise unremarkable poems like "Cora Linn," "The Brownie's Cell," and above all "Effusion in the Pleasure Ground . . .") reflect on the contrast between the fancy's fussy and delusive preoccupation with differentiation and the imagina-tion's serene indifference. I shall conclude this introduction by showing how the reductive power (and power reduction) of the imagination is represented in the Skating episode of *The Prelude,* but wish to pause here at a sonnet that reflects on the arbitrariness of object preference:

> With ships the sea was sprinkled far and nigh,
> Like stars in heaven, and joyously it showed;
> Some lying fast at anchor in the road,
> Some veering up and down, one knew not why.
> A goodly vessel did I then espy
> Come like a giant from a haven broad;
> And lustily along the bay she strode,
> Her tackling rich, and of apparel high.
> This Ship was naught to me, nor I to her,
> Yet I pursued her with a lover's look;
> This Ship to all the rest did I prefer:
> When will she turn, and whither? She will brook
> No tarrying; where She comes the winds must stir:
> On went She, and due north her journey took.

In this poem written sometime between May 1802 and March 1804—to which perhaps Keats owes a few cadences of "On First Looking Into Chapman's Ho-mer"—Wordsworth shows that there is no necessary reason to form attach-ments in a visual field, or even to invest any one focal point with special significance. The sea is sprinkled with ships as the sky is sprinkled with stars — and as this poem, be it noted, is sprinkled with monosyllables of equal length; ships, like stars, appear different from one another on closer inspection, but one cannot honestly attach significance to this variety of appearances without techniques of expert classification (the astronomer's or harbormaster's) that poetry typically avoids.[20] Then fancy intervenes, bringing her usual baggage: giants escaped from the tinsel of romance, together with the easy cross-gendering of an object once it is personified. This is all confessed in the charming tone of a children's hornbook ("This Ship to all the rest did I prefer: / When will she turn, and whither?"); and by an equally charming transference of the child's omnipotence of thought the privileged object is made all-powerful ("where She comes the winds must stir").

And then, in the sort of understated close that Wordsworth controls beautifully (like most skilled sonneteers, he sees the form as a miniature of epic, which often imitates the anticlimactic last lines of Homer: this line is perhaps closest to the last line of *Paradise Regained,* with its sudden human foreshortening of the divine), the speaker backs away from all the accumulating giganticism and admits that, like a star, to him the ship is just a compass reference. That it goes due north? Well, it is pointed toward the Straits of Mull, if you can get that into the poem. One could also speak of a northering of imagination, an attenuation, chilling, emptying out. But that sense of diminishment in going north may be mistaken, as the ship could be going back ("a giant from a haven broad") to the Giant's Causeway, a place Wordsworth worked into his later poems quite often. Probably it is best to say, then, that the ship thus glorified, no longer merely similar to a star, is on its way to becoming the North Star, the guiding star that keeps travelers on their course, a symbol of the human compulsion — in the absence of iron's nonhuman magnetism — to organize the world by accepting the pull of an arbitrary attraction.

Alongside a reading of this kind, here is Wordsworth's reading of this sonnet in a letter of 1807 to Lady Beaumont, who had been reporting the criticisms of others, among them her sister Mrs. Fermor, who thought this sonnet beneath him: "I see you have many battles to fight for me," wrote Wordsworth, and then set grimly to work. His interpretation, which is a page and half long and impressively skilled, bends my reading above toward the idea that there is something innate in certain objects that makes them worthy of our attention, that awakens our responsiveness precisely as a matter of what can be half created and half perceived. He cites in his defense the passage about the succession of Hesperus as a focal point by the even more dominant moon in *Paradise Lost* 4 (ll. 605–09). The reading builds from there. However, prior to this moment Wordsworth has set the interpretive scene, as it were, in a way that cannot, or at least need not, necessarily be built upon: "There is scarcely one of my Poems which does not aim to direct the attention to some moral sentiment, or to some general principle, or law of thought, or of our intellectual constitution" (*CL* 2, 148). Certainly this is true, and one should consider how totally unlike any poetic intention preceding it (except indeed that of Coleridge) this statement of purpose is — and how far from "moods of my own mind." Regardless whether he was struggling to find a new niche for a calling that was being squeezed out by the novelist and other sorts of prose writer — as recent emphases on the romantic poet's "profession" would have it — Wordsworth remained "passionate for the instruction of reason" (*Criticism*, 195). He continues:

> For instance in the present case, who is there that has not felt that the mind can have no rest among a multitude of objects, of which it either cannot make one whole [something it is striving to do, evidently, but one may ask: why should it?], or from which it cannot single out one individual, whereupon may be concentrated the attention divided among or distracted by a multitude? After a certain time we must select one image or object, which must put the rest out of view wholly, or must subordinate them to itself while it stands forth as a Head.

There is nothing in this last sentence about the creativity-compelling power of the object selected. "In nature every thing is distinct," as he says elsewhere, "yet nothing defined into absolute independent singleness" (*Criticism*, 207). In the present passage Wordsworth says only that we "must" select something; it is a "law of the mind" that we do so, and that that something (this is what Agamben calls the *quodlibet,* the "whatever") henceforth becomes, not *the* Head, as it would be were it selected for its intrinsic value, but *a* Head, just arbitrarily set in place.

I think that "a" is a very telling article. Apart from intermittent glimpses like this one, Wordsworth brushes past the insight that constitutes the originality of his work. Consider his reading of the sonnet's opening lines. Calling attention to the subtlety of lines 2 and 4, he points out that the first phase of feeling in the indiscriminate spectator, "a kind of dreamy indifference," is reflected in "Joyously it showed," but that this happiness gives way to the "comparative listlessness or apathy" of "Some veering up and down, one knew not why." In other words, he wants to say, the mind is driven to be actively discriminating by the eventual tedium of indifference. Yet the familiar terms he uses in the poem suggest that the moods accompanying indiscrimination are themselves so varied, ranging from the "joy" of an intimation to the "visionary dreariness" of a Spot, that in themselves they can furnish an entirely self-sufficient emotional range for the ontically receptive consciousness. The sense that one needs to discriminate, thereby forming hierarchies of value and rank, comes from the false secondary power.

Wordsworth sometimes writes "imagination" when he apparently means "fancy," oddly enough when you consider how often he had heard Coleridge talk about the difference, yet no one can confuse his drift — as when, thematizing the human imputation of significance to things, he writes of the *White Doe* a year later that objects in the poem like the banner and the doe "produced their influences and effects not by powers naturally inherent in them, but such as they were endowed with by the Imagination of the human minds on whom they operated" (*CL* 2, 222). This instability in his use of the term would appear merely careless, except that there is really no term in his lexicon that is harder to pin down, I think because of the complex and, at most, slight evasion of insight I have wanted to emphasize. He would probably say, if pressed, that fancy discriminates in sheer self-exuberance (his own connoisseurship of the picturesque being a case in point) whereas the imagination discriminates for the sake of a higher unity. Well and good: Who could wish to deprive the imagination of all the powers Coleridge ascribes to it?

The sense of having undervalued the imagination (which, in my view, he must obscurely feel) seems to motivate his decision to expand the "poems of imagination" category for the 1845 edition: "Limiting the class as I had done before seemed to imply, and to the uncandid or observing did so, that the faculty which is the primum mobile in Poetry had little to do, in the estimation of the author, with Pieces not arranged under that head" (*CL* 7 [III, 4], 708). But is there not also implied here the simpler sense that all of his poems, having all the same purpose, have likewise the same mode of inspiration?

As a case in point, it is a standard complaint about our perception of particular objects that henceforth nothing is left to the imagination, and that is what we take Wordsworth to mean in saying that the actual sight of Mont Blanc made it "a soulless image on the eye" (1805 *Prelude* VI, 454). Similarly, when he says of first seeing Rome in a Fenwick note on a late sonnet ("Is this, ye Gods, the Capitolian hill?" 1840), "Sight is at first a sad enemy to imagination" (*Fenwick, 71*), he means to confirm the poem's pious determination to compensate for sensory disappointment by fixing the imagination on unchanging things. (Note, however, what the function of imagination even in this sonnet would be were the religious message neutralized, leaving the immutability of being alone as a proper object.) But his qualification of this commonplace recalls us to the earlier and less ideologically stable sonnet on the ship: "not so much in respect to the impression made at the moment when it is first seen & looked at as a whole; for then the imagination may be invigorated & the mind's eye quickened to perceive as much as that of the [the editor suggests 'senses' to fill the lacuna here]" (*Fenwick,* 71). So "first" is not first. Writ small, this resembles Hegel saying on the first page of the *Phenomenology* that "sense-certainty" is the first impression of consciousness, then devoting his book to a grand dialectical fiction about the self-splitting of consciousness. Why not learn more from what is first?

Wordsworth's privileged moment of poetic perception (call it the imagination, since he does) does not confer, is not meant to confer, meaning on things. The Wordsworthian imagination always serves to show that things (all things, including God and eternity) are one, not that things are significant.[21] In the 1815 "Preface," he famously explains the composite image of the Leech Gatherer as an instance of the way the imagination "modif[ies]" conjoined images, in this case stone, sea-beast, old man, and cloud, the last of which (we are to conclude with Wordsworth's coy encouragement) unifies the whole on the plane of immaterial ideality:

> The stone is endowed with something of the power of life to approximate it to the sea-beast; and the sea-beast stripped of some of its vital qualities to assimilate it to the stone; which intermediate image is thus treated for the purpose of bringing the original image, that of the stone, to an nearer resemblance to the figure and condition of the aged Man; who is divested of so much of the indications of life and motion as to bring him to the point where the two objects unite and coalesce in a just comparison. After what has been said, the image of the cloud need not be commented on. (*Criticism,* 182–83)

There is no distortion at all in this description (once again Wordsworth's admirable precision as a reader is at work), but it does leave more unsaid (interesting that it speaks of something being unsaid) than it acknowledges. The poet's imaginative act is as plastic and sculptural as you please, augmenting and chipping away, but the effect of its work is not, as in Coleridge, a form but a disclosure — the form being, as Wordsworth hints, as evanescent as a cloud. And what the similes surrounding the Leech Gatherer disclose is the outmodedness of a hierarchical master-concept then still current, the Great Chain of Being. Stone, beast, man (marginal man, senescent and impoverished), and cloud are not linked in a chain of ascent, although the metonymic movement of the passage of course cannot be bracketed, but as an all-encompassing network of affinities, interchangeable with each other in the profound indifference of the moment.

No wonder the embarrassed poet cannot concentrate on the Leech Gatherer's human power of speech. What matters, what makes the old man in his nonhuman, mineral stillness a *Denkmal,* is that he is appears within a single suffusing mode of existence, excluding only the social mode (Dorothy's journal record of the encounter had stressed that he was in fact a beggar)[22] because that is the only mode in which the nonhuman fails to appear. He is "the leech-gatherer on the lonely moor," and no more. He does not quite have the social agency of a worker, for example, although in the poem he gains "an honest maintenance." Leeches are now rare, he says in a passage disapproved of by Coleridge as "matter-of-fact" (precisely!); and his stirring the pond with his staff curiously literalizes the concept of going through the motions. His gathering is rather an aspect of his being, as he draws even the vermicular and the aqueous into the poet's unified field.

## Wordsworth's Originality

Ontologically, then, even though not politically, Wordsworth is a great leveler, making the chain of being a unified, continuous field of being. Herein lies his "originality"—a word I must now try to justify, following Geoffrey Hartman in this pursuit, who declares: "The only way to respond to the forceful criticism of Wordsworth's time [and, of course, of our own] is to face the question it raised: is there anything radically new in his thinking?"[23] We know how deeply he believed himself to be original, how he protested on more than one occasion "that every author, as far as he is great and at the same time *original*, has had the task of *creating* the taste by which he is to be enjoyed" (*Criticism*, 210; cf. *CL* 2, 150). We have not, however, thought as carefully as we might about just what his originality consists in. It certainly has little enough to do with whether or not poems like the *Lyrical Ballads* had been written before, despite the excitement that topic generated for a while—unless of course what one means by "like" is made a good deal more subtle than Robert Mayo, Charles Ryskamp, and today's more Foucauldian aficionados of the archive have been able to make it.[24] It cannot be, furthermore, that he was a "nature poet" or an Anglican poet or even that he thought of poetry as teaching. As Arnold said rightly, he had no "philosophy" to impart. He could only have written *The Recluse* if he had been Coleridge. He knew this all along, and when Coleridge failed to supply ideas on returning from Malta the fate of the poem was sealed. Not that he could never have gotten Coleridge's philosophy into poetry without help, as is sometimes said; he simply could never enter into it, as a system, for the reason my argument here is meant to explain.

The great romanticists of the "Yale School" have stressed Wordsworth's apocalyptic imagination, his transfer to the psyche of what Milton did for the Christian covenant. This comes much closer; but, with Wordsworth's undoubted encouragement, it is a view of his accomplishment that substitutes

Revelation (keynoted in the Gorge of Gondo) for revelation. I have already discussed the way in which language itself virtually forces Wordsworth into religious displacements of ontic feeling, and in this respect I think Hartman, Bloom, and Weiskel follow his language, insofar as it can be his, too scrupulously. To say that Wordsworth confers a religious or at the very least a spiritual or anagogic meaning on his seminal experiences disregards a fascinating, yet more original aspect of, e.g., the Spots of Time (to explain which I borrow an expression of Weiskel's without quite following his use of it): *their underdetermination of meaning.*[25] What we can say they mean, however ingenious our "reading," never does justice to their extraordinary negative power, their visionary dreariness with its emphasis on the bare, the naked, and the blank suggesting the revelatory immanence of insignificance.[26] Even though bombast and inflated writing in general, favorite targets of Shakespeare ("This was lofty!"), had always been pretty meaningless, no one writing before Wordsworth had ever tried not to mean.

It is again Wordsworth himself who is most helpful, once we adjust to the way he hints without declaring: "the range of poetic feeling is far wider than is ordinarily supposed, and the furnishing new proofs of this fact is the only *incontestible* demonstration of genuine poetic genius" (*CL* 3, 178). A Bakhtinian way of reading this pronouncement would emphasize the "novelization" of poetry whereby new words, themes, and objects make their way into verse (as in Pushkin, Heine, and Byron) in rivalry with the new and more capacious forms of prose narrative. But merely to emphasize the way in which "humble subjects" made their way into Wordsworth's poems, Mayo having long ago shown how belated he was in this respect, would reduce him to a footnote in the history of changing literary decorum—talking about Macassar Oil in *Don Juan* being merely in this respect a much more signal accomplishment. Although the vulgarity issue was the chief complaint of critics like Jeffrey, we cannot suppose Wordsworth for all his defensiveness about it to think his rustic subject matter a sole proof of genius. Would he have supposed Milton to have made new *subjects*, humble or otherwise, poetical? The question remains, what does it mean to confer "poetic feeling" on the "thousand thoughts" the poet holds "in common with other Men" (ibid.)? Not all such thoughts are humble, and we have noted already that the specialized thoughts of the expert are not primarily at issue either, even though the example of Erasmus Darwin had encouraged Wordsworth to predict the future versification of science in the 1800 "Preface." What *is* poetic feeling?

Wordsworth's reflections in the "Essay, Supplementary" on what Hans Robert Jauss would call "horizon change" in literary history come close to an answer: "Genius is the introduction of a new element into the intellectual universe: or, if that be not allowed, it is the application of powers to objects on which they had not been before exercized.... What is all this but an advance, or conquest, made by the soul of the poet?" (*Criticism,* 212).[27] The retrenchment here ("if that be not allowed") returns us to the letter to Gillies quoted above, but the daring first formulation brings us face to face with our question: what new element of thought has he introduced? He was, again, neither an original nor a systematic philosopher. He is not to be consulted for new meanings or, when at his best, for any kind of meaning at all. And in any case, surely "poetic feeling" is not a meaning but an aura of cosmicity. The new element then must be, in Wordsworth's case, the exhilarated feeling of unity inspired by the indifference, the lack of meaning, in all registers of nonhuman being.

## Sole on Ice

The Skating episode in *The Prelude,* Book I (1805, 452–89), begins with an ignored announcement of dinnertime (the cottage lights are on, the village clock tolls six) that is the first of several less and less exclusively human perceptual frameworks. But these successive backdrops are neither eclipsed nor suppressed; they are simply held at bay, a composite foil to the pared-down state of awareness that is finally reached. Eventually the boy will go to his cottage, later in Book I to be the site of its own "poetic feeling" but not an "application of powers to a new object," as the pastiche of open debts to Pope, Cowper, and Burns is perhaps meant to indicate — until, that is, the structure of Skating is inverted by the audition of splitting ice in the background (ll. 566–70: in Skating the split is foregrounded, visual — "cut across the image of a star" — and, as we shall see, crucial). The child moves out into the nonhuman, "like an untired horse, / That cares not for its home." The movement proceeds in small stages, as one social group is chosen instead of another, each *less* social — that is, less socialized — than the last. Postponing the atavistic security of domestic shelter, a group of "[c]onfederate" children in experimental independence practices grown-up roles, as observed by child psychologists from Aristotle to Piaget, and just as in the role-playing strophe (7) of the Intimations Ode — the games here again inverting the foreground and background, inside and outside, of the parlor games to come: "All shod with steel [properly for a horse as well as a boy], / We hissed along the polished ice in games / Confederate, imitative ['as though his whole vocation / Were endless imitation'] of the chace." The hiss and polish of the moment, plus the choice of an upper-class practice to imitate, shows how little removed from the serpentine veneers of more elegant adult parlors the mimetic phase of childhood actually is, this being the lament also of the Intimations Ode.

And yet, as though in resistance to such polish, the child has become equine, and seems to play the part of hound and hare as well. Miniaturizing what I take to be an essential paradox in Wordsworth, as he becomes less human the child becomes more human. The "din" these little savages create in "the darkness and the cold," so that "every icy crag / Tinkled like iron" (an oddly implausible simile that seems to keep the acculturation of nature in the form of horseshoes before us), is a noise that once again anticipates the splitting ice of the later hearth scene, with its "dismal yellings, like the noise of wolves." But in all this there is still too much social confederacy for a "spot" revelation.[28] For the memorable disclosure to occur, suspending all determination of difference, the boy must obliterate the very principle of observation itself, first detaching himself from the specularity of human otherness ("leaving the tumultuous throng"), and then severing reflection as such: "To cut across the image [1850: "reflex"] of a star." He can then cease to move, like Lucy in "A Slumber Did My Spirit Seal," and merge, as a still point, with the minerality of the planet, referring all things seen to an unseen, nonhuman yet still personified force — "yet still the solitary cliffs / Wheeled by me — even as if the earth had rolled / With visible motion her diurnal round." — a perfect emblem of the nonhuman in the human.[29]

At this moment, as in "Tintern Abbey" when we are laid asleep in body (and, yes, do also in the Empsonian muddle become a living soul), human consciousness is virtually eclipsed in a liberatory enfeeblement projected likewise onto others:

> Behind me did they stretch in solemn train,
> Feebler and feebler, and I stood and watched
> Till all was tranquil as a dreamless sleep.

The nonhuman in the human, the thinghood human being has in common with all being ("She seemed a thing that could not feel" even when she was alive) is the somatic zero-degree where life and death intersect. The emptying-out of the social and the cultural in the first verse paragraph of "Tintern Abbey," with its "one green hue," and "hedge-rows, hardly hedgerows" (seemingly a picturesque scene but really a solid green canvas) is neither political apostasy nor political amnesia. It is the kind of site in which Wordsworth's anthropology, in "repose," in the "dark," in view of "plots," can disclose "Thoughts of more deep seclusion" from the human in the human, "where I no more can hear / Thy voice." The oft-maligned Wordsworthian solitude is sought for being alone, not just to be alone.[30]

# Wordsworth in the Rime

*He singeth loud his godly hymns*
*That he makes in the wood.*
— *The Rime of the Ancient Mariner*

The purpose of this chapter is to indicate that from the beginning of the friendship and collaboration between Wordsworth and Coleridge, Coleridge correctly and disapprovingly diagnosed Wordsworth's preoccupations as I have introduced them in Chapter 1: his vocationally empowering realization that the ontological unity of human and nonhuman things appears in the moment when the differential significance we confer on things is bracketed by the underdetermination of significance in lyric utterance. As I shall eventually enumerate them, Coleridge in the dialogue that was *Lyrical Ballads* levels six charges against Wordsworth, all implicit in *The Rime of the Ancient Mariner*. The obliquity with which I shall approach this conclusion is justified in part, I hope, as affording an opportunity to clarify Coleridge's own views and to underline the considerable gulf separating them from Wordsworth's; and also as a sustained reading of the *Rime* that allows an understanding of Wordsworth's response to Coleridge's charges in lyrical ballads of his own. I attach importance to this chapter and to the two that follow because I think there is a great deal to learn from the earliest responses to an author. While there may be much that we understand better than Wordsworth's first readers, and even than Wordsworth himself, there are also matters that were quite clear to them, novelties of which his readers typically disapproved, that we have lost sight of owing to the very complexity of the lengthening interpretation history through which we read him.

There is an immense amount of intellectually engaging commentary on the relationship between Wordsworth and Coleridge. Although this literature has frequently been biographical, not just in the fine standard lives of each poet but also in many of the studies pairing them, quite a bit of work has been done, at the other extreme, on the interchange of verbal allusion, most notably in books by Paul Magnuson, Lucy Newlyn, and — rendering allusion finally a matter of ventriloquism — Susan Eilenberg. In addition, there have been studies somewhere in between that are best characterized as dialogues in intellectual history.[1] Of course it oversimplifies to divide the field in this way, if only because all three choices of emphasis have the same end in view: How did Coleridge and Wordsworth resemble one another and how — and when — did they differ? To study a human relationship is always to perform an exercise in reader-response criticism, and that is what I propose to do in my turn, like my predecessors. However, following only Magnuson and Eilenberg in this respect, I shall use *The Rime of the Ancient Mariner* as a special point of intersection, where the two poets — I shall claim — can be found reading each other.

Let me say right away what I hope to accomplish that is new, and why I find the *Rime* a good text for the purpose. First, I think the *Rime* shows that in late 1797 Wordsworth and Coleridge were already conscious, mutually conscious, of the disagreements that most commentators consider to have surfaced only amid the circumstances surrounding the publication of *Lyrical Ballads* a year later, disagreements that then led, all agree (frequently using the ensuing history of the *Rime* as evidence), to a series of well-documented moments of deepening estrangement: Wordsworth's unforgivably cavalier treatment — and Coleridge's uneasy revisions — of the *Rime* in 1800, linked to disagreements about the role of the supernatural (entailing a number of weighty metaphysical and literary questions); the tense, rhetorically generous conversations about "the great philosophical poem"; the poetic dialogue of 1802 enacted between the drafts of "Dejection" and the first four strophes of the Intimations Ode, with glances back to "Tintern Abbey" by both writers; Wordsworth's pseudo-Coleridgean "Preface" of 1815; and Coleridge's long-harbored critique of Wordsworth in the *Biographia Literaria* of 1817 — together with all the equally well-known interpersonal frictions of the same period. These lines of disagreement are already drawn, I shall claim, in the *Rime* itself; and I shall claim further that once one sees them there they show that even the later intellectual divergence between the two is greater than is commonly believed.

My evidence will be of various sorts, but will hinge most crucially on a perhaps somewhat bold choice among the "reader-response" options. I shall infer the presence of an in itself not unfamiliar dialogue between the poets in text-specific terms, but I shall draw more from subsequent evidence than from past evidence. In contrast with Magnuson, for example, who is able to establish interesting links among the *Rime,* the already-existing "Adventures on Salisbury Plain," and Wordsworth's evidently direct response in "The Discharged Soldier" (composed before the *Rime* was finished), I shall make the riskier decision to refer a tissue of allusions to the *Rime* in Wordsworth's 1798 poems prepared for *Lyrical Ballads* back into the text of the *Rime,* as though Wordsworth were saying, "This is what Coleridge evidently thinks I would say, and to some extent he is right, but he misunderstands why I would say it, and I am now going to set him straight." Having elsewhere written in comparable terms linking *The Idiot Boy* and *Christabel* in what might be called a mutual reading,[2] I shall be especially interested here in the mutual reading that takes place between the *Rime* and a great many Wordsworth poems — including *The Idiot Boy* — written over the next two years.[3] This mutual reading in turn points toward the question that rests uneasily between the poets for the next decade, the question of what "spousal verse" is, how it should be written, and who should write it.

There is one asymmetry that should be stressed at the outset, however. I don't think there is any evidence that Coleridge for his part is saying, at any point, "This is what Wordsworth thinks I would say, but he misunderstands why I would say it, and I am now going to set him straight." The reasons for this are no doubt in part psychological. Only those who believe that all was perfect amity and agreement during those first walks across the Quantocks believe that there was as yet no trace of insecurity, hence no compulsive deference to his friend, on Coleridge's part. But I think it also has to do with the differing nature of the two poets' minds and ideas.

For one thing, Coleridge runs less risk of being misunderstood. He is in obvious ways the more "difficult" of the two, yet at the same time he leaves relatively little doubt in the competent reader's mind: one needs a good deal of philosophy and theology, together with a taste for discursive convolution and a knowledge of his highly conscious changes of opinion, to be fairly certain of what Coleridge is saying; and readers in possession of these prerequisites have in fact formed a broad consensus about his main ideas and local meanings that has remained in place since his own time. The *Rime* itself is only an apparent exception: the wildly divergent readings of this poem, with Robert Penn Warren and E. E. Bostetter stationed at the Christian and nihilistic extremes, and the fact that it lends itself to so many different reading methods, leave an impression at last that is wonderfully composite, building a cumulative understanding of a poem that we all continue to recognize in its self-identity. In the case of Wordsworth, on the other hand, there are relatively few superficial impediments to understanding, yet intelligent readers have always sharply disagreed, and continue to disagree, about the meaning, the purport, even the very *raison d'être,* of his poetry. If Coleridge's expression is sometimes obscure, Wordsworth's premises are nearly always obscure (so overdrawn or understated that they explain everything but the poetry), and thus it is Wordsworth who is always the prime candidate to be misunderstood. Compare the conflicting readings of, say, "A Slumber Did My Spirit Seal" in their cumulative effect with what I have said above about the conflicting readings of the *Rime.*

And Wordsworth is misunderstood not least, I shall want to say, by Coleridge, at least in Wordsworth's own opinion. One can read the rest of the 1798 volume, culminating in "Tintern Abbey" with its comment both on the *Rime* and on "Frost at Midnight," as Wordsworth's way of saying, "That is not what I meant. That is not what I meant at all." "Not what I meant," certainly, in "Adventures on Salisbury Plain" and "The Discharged Soldier" and *The Borderers* (with the problematic of the expatriate returned from the sea giving the *Rime* its narrative base in all three instances), but also and just as interestingly in those moments of the *Rime* when Wordsworth thinks he hears himself saying things that he wouldn't have said, or would have said for different reasons.

Wordsworth's reading of the *Rime* I shall actually take up here, again, as a kind of afterthought, as it is the main business of this and the next two chapters to show in a variety of ways how Wordsworth's "originality," as identified in Chapter 1, has been historically and recently misunderstood — or, where it has been understood, has been winced away from in disapproval. Thus I shall mainly consider the *Rime* as a reading of Wordsworth — both of his *oeuvre* to date and also of what Coleridge must have deduced from his conversation, especially in view of Coleridge's opinion, expressed in 1796, that Wordsworth was "at least a *Semi*-atheist."[4] Admittedly it is not easy to know just what Coleridge meant by this epithet. Persons holding agnostic views and sometimes even Deists and pantheists were then called atheists. We may plausibly infer that in Coleridge's view Wordsworth's tentatively formulated pantheism (influenced most notably by the odd, "sympathetic" behavior of natural objects reported in Erasmus Darwin's *Zoönomia*) was just too vague and too frankly subjective to harbor any definite transcendental principle. During that same year Coleridge struggled with this issue himself in "The Eolian Harp" (in ll. 44–49, not the Schelling-influenced ll. 26–33, added 1817), but for him the appeal of pantheism was short-lived. Between the profession of faith in natural religion and the expression of sympathy with the beings of the natural world there is no reliable distinction, Coleridge seems to have felt; and his feeling in turn seems confirmed when Wordsworth in "Tintern Abbey" calls himself "a worshipper of nature" — a phrase that Wordsworth himself, grown more conventionally pious, later regretted.

Suppose, then, that the *Rime* were to be considered a commentary on Wordsworth's alleged version of natural religion. We can learn that Coleridge had this point of dispute much on his mind by looking no farther than two of his three other contributions to the 1798 *Lyrical Ballads* (here setting aside "Lewti: The Indian Love Chant," which appears in the withdrawn print run of some fifty copies). "The Foster-Mother's Tale" (excerpted from a tragedy, then called *Osorio,* which Coleridge had recently composed) describes the educational growth of a boy subject only to the influences of nature, like Wordsworth's Boy of Winander in the 1798 poem, later part of *Prelude* 5, the draft for which was prefaced by a brief attack on pedantic schooling: "most unteachable," Coleridge's boy "knew the names of birds, and mock'd their notes, / And whistled, as he were a bird himself." He planted wildflowers "on the stumps of trees," and was raised by "A Friar, who gathered simples in the wood," presenting thereby a composite image of the Hermit in the *Rime* and the mossy stump that serves him as an altar. This boy becomes an amoral young man, in this resembling the youth in Wordsworth whose childhood education is pointedly never mentioned, but who has lived among American savages and abandons Ruth in the poem of that name (late 1798). The fragment called "The Dungeon" (also from *Osorio*) returns in a seemingly more positive spirit to the Wordsworthian theme of education by the great outdoors, but sees this education as the chastening of an already-existing criminality that is merely superior to the supposed chastisement afforded by prison: "With other ministrations thou, O Nature! / Healest thy wandering and distemper'd child." For the Christian Coleridge, "nature" even at her most appealingly Wordsworthian can do no more than homeopathically cure the original sin with which she herself has infected her "child."[5]

Here I must pause to avoid another sort of misunderstanding. Many important critics, from Bostetter and Empson on through to Jerome McGann and Richard Matlak, have read the *Rime* as an ironic attack on the trinitarian mysteries to which the Unitarian Coleridge was not yet converted — an approach that has been especially devastating to the "sacramental" emphasis of Warren's reading.[6] On this view, the narrative, which concerns events in themselves perfectly natural, is filtered through the superstitious delusions of a pre-Reformation fanatic and has to be understood as a critique, not just of Catholic and — by extension — High Church pieties but also, more broadly, of the belief that any form of received religion can successfully navigate the unsheltered soul though its encounter with the cruelty and immensity of the universe. In arguing that the issue raised by the poem is a religious one, and more particularly a critique of Wordsworth's nature-worship, I intend no open or implied disagreement with the main thrust of these readings, which are in fact very close, as I shall show, to what appears to be Wordsworth's reading. What all such readings overlook, however, in sharing what Hans-Georg Gadamer calls the Enlightenment's "superstition against superstition," is that the issue between Coleridge and Wordsworth as *Lyrical Ballads* began to take shape, the issue that divided their tasks and made their collaboration on the *Rime* impossible, was precisely the role of superstition itself in the poet's journey toward understanding. It is nearly always for some reason assumed by readers of the *Biographia* account that the two poets divided up the work arbitrarily, as if by drawing straws. But it was Coleridge and Coleridge alone who was interested in the "delusion" of "supernatural agency" because he believed, and wanted to prove to Wordsworth, that "dramatic truth" could be arrived at only through the conduit of this delusion.[7] That form of delusion in which poetry allows us to suspend our disbelief is for Coleridge, as for Hegel, the anthropocentric concretization of the metaphysical, but nothing other than this delusion can reveal the necessary presence of the metaphysical behind the Hartleyan illusion (a form of disbelief within the theocentric history of thought) that empiricism is a self-sufficient basis, not just for epistemology but for theology.[8]

At the beginning of the *Rime,* the Mariner comes upon a world that from his point of view requires an infusion of sobriety. Its "merry din" is founded on the idea that marriage, with its lusty, Burnsian flowering ("Red as a rose") and bold harmony (the loud bassoon rising above the merry minstrelsy), is an adequate rite of communion. The Wedding Guest is the one singled out among three companions because even though the others too appear to be guests he in particular is the "next of kin" — is closest in belief and kind, that is, to the erroneous faith in natural communion that inspires the marriage.[9] The Mariner is not averse to society, but he finds it "sweeter" to go to church with a goodly company, he says, than to "the marriage-feast"; and the Wedding Guest, whose selection as listener has sometimes perplexed readers, is an obvious choice to be "Turned from the bridegroom's door" and sent home a more soberly reflective and "wiser man": "That moment that his face I see, / I know the man that must hear me" (1817).

One of the two passages we are told that Wordsworth contributed during the walk from Nether Stowey to Dulverton (or, as Wordsworth would have it, via Kilve to Watchet, returning though Dulverton), concerns the Wedding

Guest duly mesmerized and listening "like a three-years' child." This is pure Wordsworth, we say at once, with our heads full of "Three years she grew," "two-years' child," "six-years' darling," and so forth; and with this in mind we are likely to add that Wordsworth is slipping in his bit of what William Empson in *Some Versions of Pastoral* called "child cult" — the nineteenth-century sentimentalism, from Wordsworth to Lewis Carroll, that we have observed Coleridge subtly repudiating as it were in advance in the two published fragments from *Osorio*. In a way, though, Wordsworth's contributed expression suspends the issue of delusion between the two poets: the listener in a state approaching the *tabula rasa* of infancy is buttonholed by a dotard speaker (who will help to inspire Wordsworth's many evocations of the senile and the decrepit in the coming months) and joins that speaker in a condition outside of, and apparently more limited than, the ordinary sphere of human intercourse. That was the common project of Wordsworth and Coleridge: to see the ordinary, and rethink the nature of the ordinary, from the standpoint of the marginal — but always with opposite ends in view.

The Mariner immediately accomplishes this movement beyond and beneath the ordinary, but in proleptic fashion, as the movement goes as "merrily" as the wedding-feast itself. He gets his ship "below the kirk" (evoking low-church Presbyterian pieties that the medieval Mariner does not seem to share, any more than he belongs in the world of the seventeenth-century "bassoon" or "lighthouse"); "[b]elow the hill" (natural home of the Wordsworthian shepherd, who is a landlocked alternative to the Mariner, as *The Brothers* makes clear); and "[b]elow the lighthouse top," which is allegorically identifiable as the Enlightenment materialization of light sources — the sun, moon, and stars that will soon irradiate the poem — that can be assimilated to ideas of transcendence more easily where earthbound illumination is not present. The top of a lighthouse is as high as you can go on land; but if you get "below" it, or below the height of a hill, or below a steeple, you can go higher.

The coming of wind (l. 45) Coleridge had trouble with even in 1798. "Listen, Stranger!" is too insistent, making the Mariner's hypnotic powers seem less than perfect. He changed the line unsatisfactorily in the 1800 text (introducing a senseless comparative, "more fierce": yes, there has been a breeze, as the 1817 Gloss points out, but it was not even a little fierce), having proposed yet another line to Biggs and Cottle in a letter of that year,[10] and settling finally in 1817 on "And now the STORM-BLAST came." We know how important the sequence of wind and calm is for Coleridge, notably when the apathetic calm of "Dejection" is dispersed by a gust of stormy imagination. For him the relation is dialectical, with states of death-in-life overtaking sometimes destructive but always exhilarating tempests of thought, and vice versa. The capitalization of 1817 encourages personification ("and he / Was tyrannous and strong") and points toward the opposite and even more Miltonic personification of "LIFE-IN-DEATH" at l. 193. Here we find Coleridge in 1817 responding to Wordsworth's 1800 response to him, "A Whirl-blast from Behind the Hill" ("The wind sent from behind the hill" in a 1798 MS.),[11] which is a complex co-presencing, rather than sequencing, of a hailstorm together with the persisting calm of the sheltered bower it passes over. Wordsworth's version of *Stille in Bewegung* is a Lockeian emblem of the mind's self-sufficiency, with the calmly receptive surface of the sensorium and the active imaginative principle operative together within the single faculty of understanding, shaped and fully naturalized as the spherical surface of a hillside bower. Coleridge, whose Mariner has long since dropped "below the hill," would simply see the calm of such a bower as the "dead calm" of mind (the expression is from the 1798 "Frost at Midnight," and is later revised to the more Wordsworthian "deep calm"). Such a calm may indicate either landlocked normalcy or the calm of a windless ocean, and Coleridge views it as an unalterable state unless it is invigorated by a strong wind "sent" (as Wordsworth himself had first written) from without, from some originary source outside the mind's immediate sphere and setting.

Driven helplessly southward, the Mariner is henceforth in a position to say that the compass afforded by Wordsworthian tranquility is useless. It scarcely makes sense to say whether one navigates or is simply driven forward in such a state. Wordsworth in "Tintern Abbey" scrupulously attributes this confusion to a past condition, both a moment in his own life and a moment of pseudo-gothic in eighteenth-century nature poetry, when nature "[t]o me was all in all" — lacking as yet the ethical overtone of humanity's still sad music — and when he was "more like a man / Flying from something that he dreads, than one / Who sought the thing he loved." But Coleridge in 1817, lingering in revision over the storm-blast passage, replies sternly to Wordsworth that any orientation confining itself solely to the laws of the natural world must remain subject to this confusion between drivenness and agency: "As who pursued with yell and blow / Still treads the shadow of his foe, / And forward bends his head" (1817, ll. 46–48). Naturalism, in a word, is necessitarianism, and to get beyond that condition is to enact, with the Mariner, an unprecedented revolution in human consciousness: "We were the first that ever burst / Into that silent sea" (1817, ll. 105–06).

Without the compass of some external determinant, it is futile to interpret the signs of nature, or the signs clung to by natural man hungry for meaning. The Mariner has shot the albatross: who knows why, or what it may portend? (Perhaps it was for food, as Empson suggests, the "biscuit-worms" of 1798 having spoiled the provisions.[12] The explanation is as good as any.) The Mariner himself is tempted by sacramental readings, and circumstance sways the crew to believe this or that yet more primitive omen. To this provocation Wordsworth responds at great length, seemingly in this case the more superstitious of the two, in "Nutting" and in the narratives of childhood trespass in the Two-Part *Prelude,* which include two offenses against birds. In these narratives he insists that nature's chastisement of man's environmental violations is unmistakable and infallible: "There is a Spirit in the woods." Once again, however, Wordsworth qualifies a clearly vulnerable argument by stressing that it pertains, like the confused submission of youth to natural law, only to an early phase of human development, a phase in which benevolence and superstition are mutually supportive instincts. He would agree that in natural "breathings" and the like there is a strong affinity with the more openly gothic and horrific visions of "Salisbury Plain" or of the moldering gibbet-mast in the Hanged Man episode of the Two-Part *Prelude.* Coleridge for his part never wavers, however, concerning any phase of human growth, from the theme that links "The Foster-Mother's Tale," "The Dungeon," and the *Rime* together: there is only one state of nature, benign but amoral and lacking in freedom, and curative to a relative degree of the wounds for which it is responsible.

The attack on Wordsworthian calm persists throughout the second, third, and fourth parts of the *Rime.* When the idiot Johnny affirms the ontic identity of the sun and the moon ("The sun did shine so cold") at the end of *The Idiot Boy,* Wordsworth is responding directly to the terrifying state of in-difference that prevails, from the Mariner's viewpoint, in a becalmed world:

> All in a hot and copper sky
> The bloody sun at noon,
> Right up above the mast did stand,
> No bigger than the moon.

Wordsworth finding spiritual enlightenment in the unity of all things, *qua* things, can favor such a state, telling Coleridge in the 1805 *Prelude,* with what must be heavy irony:

> Thou art no slave
> Of that false secondary power by which
> In weakness we create distinctions, then
> Deem that our puny boundaries are things
> Which we perceive, and not which we have made.

So far indeed does Coleridge believe in and value such a faculty (each accuses the other throughout this covertly fierce dialogue of being a slave) that I believe he is thinking rather bitterly of this passage when in the famous discussion of the imagination in the *Biographia* (chapter 13), itself a masterpiece of distinctions made or perceived, he assigns the discriminatory power of writing poetry to "the secondary imagination," confining the primary imagination, to which Wordsworth supposes himself devoted, to the joyous but inarticulate *participation mystique* in the *fiat* of divine creation.[13]

Ordinarily for Coleridge, the moment of Wordsworthian indiscrimination is a horrific nightmare. Without wind or current, nature rots, a mixture of primordial slime and parched aridity. Speech, *pace* Wordsworth, becomes impossible. Or rather, when it comes, aided by an act of auto-vampirism aptly corresponding to the grotesque person of the approaching female specter, speech gets blurted out as Coleridge's own textbook example of the feeblest of all rhetorical devices, the synecdoche, or part taken for a whole: "A sail! A sail!"[14] Indeed a repetition in the finite mind, this synecdochic speech (which serves no useful purpose, as many commentators have remarked) stands in deliberate contrast to what Coleridge always meant by the symbol.[15] Far from being a "translucence of the special in the individual, or of the general in the special," and so on,[16] synecdoche is an inorganic, dry transparency or false reflection, like the desiccated, barred sails of the death-ship itself. The sun has to "peer" through rigging that is like a "dungeon grate" — and also, of course, like the ribs of an emaciated person, corpselike though alive. Synecdoche is the dungeon of perception, language as prison-house.

Here one confronts what seems the most overdetermined figural recurrence in the poem: the skeletal ribs of persons or sea sands, bars or grates (with the barred clouds of "Dejection" and the fireplace grate of "Frost at Midnight" corresponding in important ways) through which nothing organically healthy can see or be seen, the veins of leaves along the Hermit's brook, and the rigging of ultra-thin sails that are either slack or blown upon by supernatural agents. In the realm of natural symbol, poetry for Coleridge is language fanned by a current or wind: an eolian harp, a ship under sail. But there is always the risk — the Wordsworthian risk — that this sort of imagery will lend itself to the disinspirited naturalism that is represented allegorically in the 1817 *Rime* as LIFE-IN-DEATH, the opposite of the STORM-BLAST. Allegory, synecdoche, a sail without its ship — that is all poetry is if it lacks what Wordsworth had so derisively called "the false secondary power." Hence a certain remystification is needed: in "Frost at Midnight," the "*stranger*" on the "bars" of the grate, seeming to survive even the last embers, burns like an *ignis fatuus* without a visible fuel source, and the creative frost itself, most memorably, is "[u]n-helped by any wind." This is why it is no accident, as Arden Reed has shown most fully, that after his Antarctic adventure the grizzled Mariner produces "rime," or hoarfrost.[17]

From the Mariner's point of view, however, at least at this point in the poem, the most frightening thing about the approach of the ghost ship is that it comes — like the ship that brings plague to Bremen in the later Dracula story — "without a breeze." But the Mariner is himself, as nearly all readers agree, at most but the vessel of understanding. It is one of the most extraordinary effects of Romanticism that Wordsworth and Coleridge together could transform the classical figures of the wise and virtuous *senex* and cunning but impotent *senex* into a single *vieillard* and yet imbue that diminished figure, together with the child, the outcast, and the idiot, with the capacity to stumble "unawares" into the presence of radical truth. Here again the stream of Wordsworth and Coleridge runs in a common bed, but with a different source and destination; and it is at this point that one can observe the most complex and interesting interchange of opinion that takes place in the *Rime*. It is possible to show, following the figural matrix here emphasized, that whereas Wordsworth subversively and mischievously associates the Coleridgean dungeon of perception with the Mariner, Coleridge in turn links this blindered state to the other *senex* of the poem, the Hermit, and furthermore brilliantly identifies the Hermit with Wordsworth.

The first part of this claim is easily established. The second documented verbal contribution of Wordsworth to the poem (who reports that he also suggested parts of the plot, including the shooting of the albatross) is the frightened outburst of the Wedding Guest, who thinks the Mariner a ghost and is made by Wordsworth to recall the sails of the ghost ship: "And thou art long and lank and brown / As is the ribb'd Sea-sand."[18] Wordsworth, who seems even on the first walk to have been subtly out of humor with the poem ("We found that our styles would not assimilate"), might well identify with his other contribution, the Wedding Guest, who has also resembled "a three-years' child." A member of the wedding, Wordsworth recoils from the living dead and stands for the minstrelsy or spousal verse of mind in the natural world, while retaining that saving naïveté and directness that characterizes both Wordsworth's typical *dramatis personae* and his then-developing theory of poetic diction, featuring the "real language" of men rooted in rural life and its "best objects." From this dissenting standpoint, at least insofar as Wordsworth is thus able to subvert the mesmerism that dispels it, the Mariner is lost at sea without a sextant, all dried up, possibly not even alive.

Coleridge's comeback is reserved for the moment when the Mariner returns to the everyday, shoreline world of Wordsworth (both poets are then living near the broad Bristol Channel) and is greeted by — Wordsworth himself in the person of the Hermit:

> THIS Hermit good lives in that wood
> Which slopes down to the Sea.
> How loudly his sweet voice he rears!
> He loves to talk with marineres
> That come from a far contrée.

(Here especially the returned sailor in "Adventures on Salisbury Plain" and "The Discharged Soldier" is relevant. *The Brothers,* a "pastoral" conversation between a country parson and a returned sailor who would rather have remained a shepherd, will be one of Wordsworth's responses to these lines.)

> He kneels at morn and noon and eve —
> He hath a cushion plump:
> It is the moss that wholly hides
> The rotted old oak-stump.

Coleridge gently discredits the piety of the Hermit as the comfortably provincial repose of a person too close to the soil, soil whose very element is organic decay, the "rot" from which the Mariner had at first felt such revulsion.[19] The Hermit literally worships at the altar of nature. Coleridge then ascribes to the Hermit a reaction to the Mariner's ship, linking it to the ghost ship, that resembles the reaction to the Mariner assigned by Wordsworth to the Wedding Guest, adapting the same cluster of images to a sylvan setting. The Hermit's revulsion from the appearance of death cannot now be considered life-affirming, as was the alarm ascribed by Wordsworth to the Wedding Guest, so much as it is simply narrow, a landlocked form of superstition (in contrast with the Mariner's solitary and oceanic form) differing little in kind from that of the Pilot's Boy:

> "The planks look warp'd! and see those sails
> "How thin they are and sere!
> "I never saw aught like to them
> "Unless perchance it were
>
> "The skeletons of leaves that lag
> "My forest-brook along:

— and here Coleridge adds an obviously gratuitous touch of horror-gothic from the eighteenth-century models that both he and Wordsworth saw themselves as having advanced beyond, suggesting once again that Wordsworth cannot be allowed his belief that superstitious anthropomorphism is an adolescent phase through which the nature poet passes en route to a soberer account of universal sympathy. If you are going to worship nature, in short, you'll never outgrow the fascinations of the charnel-house:

> "When the ivy-tod is heavy with snow,
> "And the owlet whoops to the wolf below
> "That eats the she-wolf's young.

It is easily overlooked that when the Hermit asks "What manner of man art thou?" (a question Wordsworth may still be thinking about when he asks the Leech Gatherer, "How is it that you live? What is it that you do?"), he becomes the first person to whom the Mariner feels compelled to tell his tale; and this, together with the fact that he is also one of three ("I saw a third"), shows him to need the same sort of education that the Wedding Guest needs.[20] In "Tintern Abbey," Wordsworth will snatch this hermit back, bestowing upon him, invisible in the depths of the woods, a solitude as profound as the Mariner's.

Coleridge's point is not at all, obviously, that spiritual man needs to be weaned away from the love of nature: the albatross, the sea creatures, and above all the "moral" (adequate to its occasion or not) would scarcely make any sense in that case. His point is, rather, that human engagement with the natural world needs to be a dialectical process if it is not finally to extinguish the spark of mind in the dank moss of organicity. In order to recognize our autonomy, we need to betray nature. The more seemingly without meaning the gesture is, the better: tear off a hazel bough, rob a nest, shoot an albatross. But if we superstitiously accept the imagined forgiveness of an admonishing environment (in Coleridge's view, the crew in good weather saying it must have been a good thing to shoot the bird would be like Wordsworth in *The Prelude* saying, oh well, at least stealing a rowboat taught me something), then the necessarily radical alienation from all forms of life and perhaps even from God that is initiated by our trespass cannot take hold and we can never orient ourselves toward nature except from within its fundamental state, the state of rotting decay against which our alienation causes us to feel revulsion. The redemptive part of the dialectic, in which an externally induced, aesthetically driven glimmer of redemption makes the Mariner find the sea creatures and the moving moon beautiful, is what Coleridge addresses in the fourth part of the poem. Falling into the sea like lead, the albatross, which is neither a Dove nor an invisible "Lavrock," has been a material cross to bear, a natural burden. When the ship goes down later, also like lead, one can say that the tenor no longer needs its vehicle, any more than frost, or a ship propelled by spirits, needs wind — or any more than corpses, our natural bodies, can man the ship without the aid of spirits, or than our human voices can tell the truth without "strange power of speech." Nature cannot resurrect nature, only transcendental consciousness can. Never mind the empiricist juggling act of what we half create and half perceive: "Ours is her wedding garment, ours her shroud." Even Wordsworth's trademark evocation of calm (most often this is *horror vacui* to Coleridge), as in the "Night Piece" of early 1798, is finally redeemed under the radiance of numinous agency:

> There was no breeze upon the bay,
> No wave against the shore.

> The rock shone bright, the kirk no less
> That stands above the rock:
> The moonlight steep'd in silentness
> The steady weathercock. (1798, 511–16)

The cost is steep. The Mariner is crazed, obsessive, permanently alone — a descendant of the Wandering Jew and an obvious precursor of Conrad's more sinister Kurtz. But the Mariner's solitude can be exaggerated. It is his business to talk to people, after all, and he has simply wanted to redefine the sort of company that it is best to go to church with, not to go there alone. His "woeful agony" can be ascribed in part to the pain of criticizing the attractive and beneficent natural religion of a friend. And as to the inadequacy of the "moral" ("Don't pull poor pussy's tail," wryly paraphrases Empson): well, the point Coleridge has been driving at all along, whatever his means of getting there, has been painfully simple, embarrassingly simple if even Anna Barbauld, who wrote didactic hymns for children, could feel that it was not a moral at all;[21] and he is speaking, he thinks, however much Coleridge may have revered Wordsworth from the beginning, to a three-years' child.

Insofar as one feels the need to choose sides in this debate, I incline to the side of Wordsworth, not Coleridge, for reasons elaborated throughout this book. I shall give Wordsworth the last word by examining those poems, written for the most part over the first six months of 1798, in which he seems to be essaying various sorts of response to the *Rime,* both to Coleridge directly and to the portrait of himself that he finds Coleridge to have smuggled into the poem. In choosing this emphasis, I am very far from denying that the *Rime* was a tremendous inspiration to Wordsworth — that something about it and about its having been written made possible the best, one is tempted to say the most characteristic, poetry he had yet produced. I think it probable, however, that it was in fending off and reconstituting what he took to be Coleridge's misrepresentation of his poetic project that Wordsworth for the first time fully realized what that project was; and if that is the case, then there is nothing inconsistent in my adversarial emphasis with the plain fact that Coleridge had inspired him. This supposition should also lend some credence to what may have raised a measure of suspicion about my procedure on the part of the attentive reader. Mine is largely a *post hoc* argument, as I have said. The criticism of Wordsworth that I have found in the *Rime* may seem too often to be directed at poetry that Wordsworth has not yet written. I have partly met this objection by supposing an anticipatory strain in Wordsworth's conversation of 1797, on analogy with the documentable fact that in intellectual outlook Keats's letters, for example, are a year or so ahead of his poetry. Thus if we find Coleridge in some degree inventing the Wordsworthian old man or indeed inventing the Wordsworthian idea that nature can be all in all, if only to have achieved a preemptive strike against the authenticity of such *topoi*, I think it nevertheless legitimate to infer that these and other such matters had been Wordsworth's topics all along.

In Coleridge's poem we have found the following six separate admonitions to Wordsworth:

1. A mariner is a more heroic figure than a shepherd, as exploration is worthier than dwelling in place.
2. A merely natural calm is life-in-death, and mere passivity can have no merit apart from a transcendental doctrine of inspiration.
3. Dwelling too exclusively in natural process is a sign of dullness, even dotage, which is also a regression to the ignorance of childhood (exemplars being the Hermit, the three-years' child, and the Pilot's Boy).
4. Failure to differentiate properly among objects is a sign of the mind's immersion in the ontic sameness of the natural world.
5. Nature is to some extent a healer, but not a teacher.
6. Nature is not, because it cannot be, a self-sufficient and self-originating entity, either as mind or as world.

I shall now take up Wordsworth's responses to these dicta, drawing exclusively on poems published in the 1798 *Lyrical Ballads,* and concluding with remarks about the curious peace Coleridge made with all of his own objections in his last contribution to *Lyrical Ballads,* "The Nightingale."

"The Thorn," Wordsworth wrote in the 1800 edition, no doubt combating the critics' frequent assumption that the strain of fatuous garrulity in his poems is his own, is narrated by someone resembling

> a Captain of a small trading vessel . . . , Who being past the middle of life, had retired . . . to some country town of which he was not a native, or in which he had not been accustomed to live. Such men having little to do become credulous and talkative from indolence; and from the same cause, and other

predisposing causes by which it is probable that such men may have been affected, they are prone to superstition. (*Lyrical Ballads,* 350–51)

Here certainly is the Old Navigator (as it amused Coleridge himself to call him) in a diminished light, the "predisposing causes" that are left coyly un-enumerated by Wordsworth being perhaps the experiences narrated in the *Rime.* The issue of superstition is joined immediately, with the strong implication that it is not the gothic elements of the story (the face in the pool, and so on) that will capture the sensible interlocutor's attention (no Wedding Guest he), but the pathos surrounding the madness of an abandoned unwed mother.

The narrator being out of his element miscasts this lamentable but quotidian event and its aftermath as a kind of inland *Rime:* "There was a thorn," he begins, echoing the Mariner's first words, and then describes the destruction of an innocent being, followed by the effort of penance in its presence. But all the symbols undermine his intent for them: The thorn itself, gnarled and no higher than "a two years' child," is a candidate to become a natural cross, like the albatross, and possibly also a crown of thorns, but the gravitational force of the natural world, the mossy element of Coleridge's Hermit (thus child and *senex* are met, as vegetation, in the degree zero of their bodily existence), conspires to level the thorn with all other organic being: it has "no thorny points," it is overgrown with lichens "like a stone," and "heavy tufts of moss" conspire "[t]o bury this poor thorn for ever." This burial, subsiding into the organic mould, the thorn has in common with the equally moss-laden grave, which has all the phosphorescent-seeming colors of Coleridge's slimy sea (which "Burnt green and blue and white") — colors that this time from the beginning the retired captain, perhaps in spite of himself, finds to be "lovely": vermilion, olive-green, scarlet, and white.[22]

The pond, which is as small ("Two feet long and three feet wide") as the wide, wide sea was large, constitutes an element of destruction, drowning the child, rather than a medium of absolution that swallows up the albatross and ship only when they no longer serve as instruments of atonement. There is water, water everywhere in the *Rime,* but not a single instance of death by water. I remember thinking, as a youthful reader, how unlikely it was that the albatross would fall into the ship — and Gustave Doré's illustration made it seem even less likely. Wordsworth in plotting "The Thorn" seems to have felt this as well. However the speaker of "The Thorn" may strain to reconstruct the *Rime,* the visionary dreariness of the scene suggests rather that the truth of ontology is not oceanic but mineral. *Sta viator,* the admonition of a stone, is the occasion of many Wordsworth poems, beginning with the "Lines" left under a yew-tree; and this moment has been humanistically revised by Cole-

ridge as the Mariner's interception of the Wedding Guest: but the moun-
tainous domain of shepherds and travelers proves to reveal more about life
and death than the fluid element of Mariners precisely in revealing less — as the
narrator inadvertently admits:

> For one day with my telescope,
> To view the ocean wide and bright,
> When to this country first I came,
> Ere I had heard of Martha's name,
> I climbed the mountain's height:
> A storm came on, and I could see
> No object higher than my knee. (ll. 170–76)

Through the storm-blast — or whirl-blast on the hill — he thinks he sees a jut-
ting crag, but the crag is Martha *Ray,* "sitting on the ground," a beam of light
who is also clay.[23]

   Insofar as *The Idiot Boy* reflects the *Rime,* its hero is the moon, partly
because the moon's pale fire reflects the state of joyous indifference that Words-
worth associates with idiocy. "Who's yon," asks the narrator at the moment
when the idiot is found, "Beneath the moon, yet shining fair, / As careless as if
nothing were"? — syntactically distributing this carelessness equally between
moon and boy. If the sun to the becalmed and sweltering Mariner was no bigger
than the moon, Johnny himself, for whom the sun did shine so cold, is both son
and lunatic, object and focus of his almost equally imbecilic mother's faith
(Foy). The horse, which moves sometimes and stands still at others, according
to its gentle whim (unlike Johnny, "he is a horse that thinks!"), is Johnny's ship,
completely out of his control; it disappears with Johnny, cheered by Betty's
joyous face, beyond a lighthouse-like sign of the familiar: "He's at the guide-
post — he turns right, / She watches till he's out of sight." The awful monotony
of sameness Coleridge dreads at the point when the sun resembles the moon
("Water, water, every where") is for Wordsworth, with "the moon in heaven,"
the distribution throughout the landscape of the undifferentiated idiocy with
which he associates the truth of being, elusive only because it is the object of the
frantic Betty's quest rather than the revelation of quietude: " 'Twas Johnny,
Johnny, every where." When Johnny is finally in view, he seems as insubstantial,
as little himself, to Betty as the Mariner seemed to the Hermit and his compan-
ions: "Why stand you thus Good Betty Foy? / It is no goblin, 'tis no ghost."
Something similar has happened, but it is reported with amused forbearance in
a carefully inverted context. The disagreement concerns the ontology of the
poetic: whereas the Mariner in a state of undifferentiated calm is deprived of
speech except for a lone synecdoche, Johnny, whose burring all along has been

more authentically the language of nature even than "the real language of men," can finally speak, out of the undifferentiated element in which he moves, the language of radical metaphor: "The cocks did crow to-whoo, to-whoo, / And the sun did shine so cold."

"Anecdote for Fathers" and "We Are Seven" teach this same lesson to adult victims of the false secondary power. In asking a child to choose between locales, whether Kilve (evoking the walk that engendered the *Rime* as Wordsworth remembered it) or Liswyn farm, the "Anecdote" speaker forces him to discriminate meretriciously, and thereby teaches him what Plato called poetry and Wordsworth chooses for a subtitle, "The Art of Lying." That the boy both is and is not on the site of the Mariner's return (he is not on "Kilve by the green sea"), and at least claims to prefer another site, is proven by his repudiation of the "weathercock" by means of which Coleridge in the *Rime* had attempted to make his peace on his own terms with Wordsworthian states of numinous calm: "The moonlight steeped in silentness / The steady weathercock." "We Are Seven," the poem that called forth the note to Isabella Fenwick reminiscing about the composition of the *Rime,* dispels the gloom of what Coleridge calls "life-in-death" by refusing to distinguish between life and death. From the standpoint of a "simple child," none of the *Rime*'s scrupulous distinctions among modes of being alive, being dead, and being both at once can affect the simple animism of believing that there is only one state of being. Objects wherever they may be — here, there, above- or below-ground, but never partly here, partly "in heaven" — are unified indissolubly by their state of common existence, whether frolicking or lying still, in the churchyard of process.

Thus "We murder to dissect." It is understood that "Expostulation and Reply" and "The Tables Turned"[24] were written to admonish Hazlitt during his visit to Wordsworth and Coleridge. But why Hazlitt, or Hazlitt exclusively? I hope that my argument will have shown how precisely the lines are drawn, albeit as caricature in each case, between Wordsworth and Coleridge in these two poems. Wordsworth casts himself as the Hermit, on "an old grey stone," inveighing against the idea that the only teachers are "science" and "art," which are made to resemble the crew on the Mariner's ship: "the spirit breath'd / From dead men to their kind" — that is, perhaps, from dead men to dead men. These poems are Wordsworth's corrective to the notion that the Wedding Guest, who also "sat on a stone,"[25] must be "sadder and wiser." There is "more of wisdom" in the linnet's voice or that of the throstle ("no mean preacher") than in any iterable, booklike tale about the death of a bird. Anticipating Keats's critique of Coleridge and his "irritable reaching after fact" while also anticipating the concept of negative capability, Wordsworth sets forth his own doctrine of "wise passiveness."

Perhaps strangest of all, Coleridge seems to have taken all of Wordsworth's counter-assertions to heart, and accepted them, in the poem he composed last for *Lyrical Ballads*, "The Nightingale" (April 1798). In an opening setting of untroubled, beatific calm, a penseroso scene, there is "nothing melancholy" about the nightingale's song, which is, and seems sufficiently to be, the "merry ... love-chant" from which the Mariner had barred the Wedding Guest. There is a sardonic reflection on persons of sensibility whose idea of nature comes from books — "youths and maidens most poetical, / Who lose the deepening twilights of the spring / In ball-rooms and hot theatres," and "Full of meek sympathy must heave their sighs / O'er Philomela's pity-pleading strains." But Wordsworth and Dorothy and Coleridge together, he is at pains to say, "have learnt / A different lore," the teachings of nature that he is now eager to share with his "dear babe," whose restlessness, like the Idiot Boy's, is soothed by the moon. The concession seems total, and while it is possible to point to passages that, on various grounds, only Coleridge could have written, they do not materially alter the poem's theme and motive, which appear to be a peace-offering. The only difference in this moment, a difference however which amounts to a guarantee that the rift must reopen, is Coleridge's strange compulsion (visible also in the "Friends, whom I never more may meet again" of "This Lime-Tree Bower My Prison") to exile himself from paradise: "Once more, farewell, / Sweet nightingale! Once more, my friends! farewell." And perhaps, after all, looking forward to more visionary speech whatever loss of friendship may be entailed, the parting voice is still the Mariner's.

# 3

## *Jeffreyism, Byron's Wordsworth, and the Nonhuman in Nature*

In this chapter I wish to suggest a new way of understanding Jeffrey's attacks on Wordsworth, and to point out the degree to which these attacks, viewed in this way, influenced Byron's 1821 dispute with Bowles and the earlier Dedication and first Canto of *Don Juan*. I shall claim that Jeffrey balks at the ascription of ontological importance to the realm of the nonhuman. As an Enlightenment humanist, well versed in the writings of the Scottish successors to Hume and firmly opposed to idealism in philosophy, Jeffrey rejects any valuation of the natural world either for its own sake or for the sake of the allegedly pantheistic claims that hostile readers of Wordsworth and Coleridge always gleefully dismissed as unintelligible. This is not to say that Jeffrey was indifferent to nature, or even that he invariably denied the possibility of poetic interest arising from the investment of nonhuman beings with human feeling. He constantly assumes, however, that the sole purpose of describing the natural world in poetry is to illustrate human characteristics or thoughts, and to enliven metaphors for human feeling.

In 1808, the *Edinburgh Review* (but not Jeffrey himself: it was Henry Brougham, as Byron later learned) airily dismissed Byron's first reviewed volume of poems, *Hours of Idleness* (1807), for what they largely were, the adolescent aristocratic pastime indicated in the title. Deeply hurt, Byron took his revenge in *English Bards, and Scotch Reviewers.* To surround the Jeffrey assault (featuring a comparison with Jeffreys the Hanging Judge and the *soi-disant* duel with Thomas Moore), Byron padded his poem with mockery that he soon came in varying degrees to regret — attacks on his later allies Scott and Moore, and on Bowles (rather less regretted, and in any case the original lines were written by Hobhouse) — together with amusing broadsides on the Lake "School."[1] (Like Jeffrey, Byron was always hard put to find enough fish to fill this pond, or classroom.)[2] While Byron no doubt regretted his attack on Jeffrey, he had little or no occasion to be haunted by it. Despite encouraging a challenge from Jeffrey in the "Postscript" to the second edition of *English Bards,* he was not further provoked. Although the two appear never to have met (Byron implies as much in his first letter on Bowles), it came to be understood that they took a largely cordial view of each other: as gentlemen, as Liberals, and as partial sharers of a national identity.[3] For the next decade Jeffrey wrote several mixed reviews of Byron's publications, much in the tone of the times, praising his copiousness, imagination, and originality while censuring his licentiousness and morbidity. Byron never took offense.

Shortly after Byron returned to England in 1811, armed with the two cantos of travelogue *à clef* that made him famous overnight, Jeffrey published a review of Archibald Alison's *Essays on the Nature and Principles of Taste,* in which one can find, in abstract terms (although one suspects Jeffrey had Wordsworth in mind throughout, as so often), the only systematically intelligible basis for his dislike of Wordsworth's poetry.[4] The question whether Byron read this review, or took special note of it if he did, is perhaps not as important as this preamble would make it seem, because after all many aspects of Jeffrey's critique of Wordsworth were in the air. Wordsworth affected simplicity, he invested vulgar and banal subjects with false, necessarily bathetic feeling, he mistook personal whims and megrims for general truths — all of this everyone had been saying ever since the publication of *Lyrical Ballads* and its controversial "Preface." However, in the documents to which I shall be attending especially here, one finds in addition to the commonplaces, and indeed largely as an elaboration upon them, a particular line of attack, an original and coherent view that is not achieved by other reviewers — not even by Hazlitt, whose view of Wordsworth derives largely from his view of Rousseau and forcibly aligns both of them on the Milton side of his great organizing contrast between Milton and Shakespeare. Although Byron would recycle Jeffrey's general view of Wordsworth while participating in the quarrel of Thomas Campbell, Isaac Disraeli, and Octavius Gilchrist with Bowles's edition of Pope, the basis for his claims in the letter against Bowles is most clearly revealed in Jeffrey's discussion of beauty and taste in the Alison essay.

Jeffrey himself must have thought a good deal of this review, as he expanded it for an 1824 *Encyclopedia Britannica* article on "Beauty" and made the expanded version the opening piece in the massive 1843 collection of his own work in four volumes, *Contributions to the Edinburgh Review.*[5] In his interesting brief "Preface" to this collection, he is concerned chiefly to discuss his important decision to preserve the politically partisan flavor of the *Edinburgh* —a decision that had come to a crisis of sorts in 1808 when he decided to decline the Tory Walter Scott's offer to contribute with the proviso that the review henceforth cease to be partisan. The *"right leg"* of a review, Jeffrey recalls having told Scott in response, is politics, however certain it remains that the left leg is literature (*Contributions,* viii).[6] There is undoubtedly a "politics of" the issues with which I am here concerned, as the firmness of Jeffrey's belief that these branches of endeavor belong to a single body would imply; and although I am somewhat hesitant to say very firmly what such a politics might be (it is belied by exceptions of every kind), Byron does appear to endorse a comparable literary politics or politics of literature in first setting to work on *Don Juan;* and that is one reason why I think it important to conclude with that poem.

Jeffrey had corresponded with his friend Alison concerning the 1790 edition of the *Essays* (hence already had an aesthetic basis for his first attack on Wordsworth in 1802), and Alison had, one supposes, revised some passages accordingly for the new edition.[7] Jeffrey's review then appeared in due course, partly to publicize Alison and partly to elaborate his own version of the argument, which resolves all points of controversy under a single heading: objects have no inherent aesthetic qualities but appear beautiful or sublime only in association with remembered human feelings or traits of character. There are also hints of the thumbnail history of aesthetics that Jeffrey expanded for the encyclopedia article, but it is already clear that German developments from Baumgarten to Kant are to be disregarded altogether.[8] Modern readers for whom Kant provides the only real excitement in the history of aesthetics, however, should be aware that the great Continental doctrine of "multëity in unity," eventually domesticated by Coleridge, was already featured as a modestly empiricist idea in English works noticed in Jeffrey's encyclopedia version of the Alison review, especially Francis Hutcheson's *Inquiry Into the Original of Our Ideas of Beauty and Virtue* (1725). So much emphasis indeed was thrown on "variety" and "multiplicity" in the eighteenth century that it goes some way toward explaining the outcry against Wordsworth's "simplicity."

Two caveats are immediately in order, however. First, Jeffrey does not himself hold that complexity is an aesthetic property of objects any more than any other quality is or can be; nor indeed does he think that the human feelings (e.g., contentment) or qualities (e.g., innocence) with which objects are associated by taste are necessarily complex either. If this relativizing of baroque, rococo, and picturesque standards makes Jeffrey himself seem in some sense Wordsworthian, that is worth bearing in mind — if only to explain why Jeffrey was after all more sympathetic than many others to much of what we call the romantic turn — but it needs to be qualified by a second caveat of crucial importance. *It is a simple category mistake to suppose, despite unguarded encouragement from the poet himself, that Wordsworth's representation of the natural or the human world is governed primarily by aesthetic considerations of any kind.* Whatever he may say, it scarcely matters to him that "the permanent and beauteous forms" of nature be either "beauteous" or even "forms"; nor are the "best objects" best in any sense other than in simply constituting the approved rhythm of rural existence. The aesthetic aspect of nature scarcely matters to Wordsworth as a *poet*, that is, however much it may matter to him as a person, as an amateur landscape gardener, and as the author of the *Guide to the Lakes*.[9] As Arnold was still insisting, Mr. Wilkinson's spade is not beautiful. But then Wordsworth never thought it was.

All critics including Wordsworth himself agreed that the *medium* of representation must be judged aesthetically, because the purpose of poetry was to give what Coleridge called "immediate pleasure." Jeffrey, however, together with virtually all his contemporaries, confuses the medium with the object of representation even while trying, as he does in the review of Alison, to keep them separate. The fallacy arises from the argument whereby one dismisses the "Dutch School" of painting because of its "low" subject matter; accordingly, there appears in Jeffrey on Alison (Jeffrey is actually here quarreling with Richard Payne Knight) the usual scornful reference to a dunghill, together with the "filthy and tattered rags of a beggar" and "the richly fretted and variegated countenance of a pimpled drunkard" (see *Contributions*, 36, 24). As Jeffrey knew from painterly examples but wished to deny in principle, even a dunghill (like an idiot or a spade or a stunted thorn tree) could be rendered an aesthetic object by introducing such new categories as the ugly or the grotesque, or by expanding the domain of the picturesque.

In short, by subjecting the matter as well as the manner of representation to the standard of "taste" (the *Excursion* review speaks of "the errors of early taste"),[10] Jeffrey brings Wordsworth's poetry into focus in a way that cannot be rewarding. He sees that Wordsworth sometimes represents objects (even human beings) just *as* objects, and since he has foreordained that objects lack even the intrinsic qualities normally ascribed to them, this procedure will seem to him doubly absurd — indifference to normative canons of beauty being the less forgivable when their "social construction," as we say today, is unrecognized or ignored. Wordsworth in other words is not entitled to say that an object is beautiful (supposing that that is what he does say) unless he is willing to conform to the agreed-upon associations whereby taste comes to be widely shared. In the original Alison article, Jeffrey approvingly quotes "Tintern Abbey" from memory (*ER* 18 [May 1811]: 37: the passage on the feelings inspired by the "uncertain notice" of chimney smoke) in order to suggest that *even* Wordsworth sometimes shares the common taste of humanity.

Moreover, Jeffrey's insistence on the aesthetic neutrality of objects utterly precludes, no doubt unwittingly, any other sort of non-sensory human interest suitable for poetry (natural philosophy aside, that is) in the nonhuman world. Art criticism, again, supplies this prejudice. The tyranny of the commonplace strictures on the Dutch and Flemish, embargoing unpeopled landscapes, barnyard imagery, and the kitchen genres of *nature morte,* likewise prevented anyone's attending to the more profound — not merely counter-aesthetic — reflections of painters like Chardin on the sheer objecthood of objects, their self-identity and ontological unity. From this divergent standpoint, the fact identified in part by Jeffrey and fully entailed in the logic of his position — the fact that objects lack intrinsic attributes, whether aesthetic *or* semantic — is not what renders them irrelevant to human self-reflection. Rather, this lack is precisely what makes them interesting: objects make us realize with otherwise inaccessible clarity, through the experience of the nonhuman, what it is to be human. Much of Wordsworth's poetry, preeminently the structuring of the Spots of Time and the poetry representing human beings from infants to idiots to dotards in drastically reduced, zero-degree states of consciousness, deliberately underdetermines both the meaning and the appearance of external things in order to disclose, in the space left vacant by the refusal to explain, their being — and thereby our own being, laid bare through the suspension of thought and connoisseurship.

Here is Jeffrey's contrasting position: "We could almost venture . . . to lay it down as an axiom, that, except in the plain and palpable case of bodily pain or pleasure, we can never be interested in any thing but the fortunes of sentient beings; — and that every thing partaking of the nature of mental emotion, must have for its object the feelings, past, present, or possible, of something capable of sensation" (*ER* 18 [May 1811]: 8). He infers this axiom from his own comments on companion genre scenes, a beautiful English countryside and a sublime "Welsh or Highland" scene, respectively, which he has composed verbally in order to drive home his — and Alison's — conclusion. What moves us to appreciate the beauty of the English scene is "the picture of human happiness that is presented to imaginations and affections": "comfort, and cheerful and peaceful enjoyment," "industry," "piety," "simplicity," "health and temperance." The sublime scene evokes "primeval simplicity," "romantic ideas," "ancient traditions," and so on (*Contributions*, 24–25). All very Wordsworthian, one is actually tempted to say, given the enviable ease with which Jeffrey can pass from the aesthetic into the ethical, from the appeal of the scene to its social significance; until, that is, one is struck as always by Jeffrey's serene anthropocentrism:[11]

> It is man, and man alone, that we see in the beauties of the earth which he inhabits; — or, if a more sensitive and extended sympathy connect us with the lower families of animated nature, and make us rejoice with the lambs that bleat on the uplands, or the cattle that repose in the valley, or even with the living plants that drink the bright sun and the balmy air beside them, it is still the idea of enjoyment — of feelings that animate the existence of sentient beings — that calls forth all our emotions, and is the parent of all the beauty with which we proceed to invest the inanimate creation around us. (*ER* 18 [May 1811]: 14)[12]

This still arguably sounds like Wordsworth, composed perhaps with the Intimations Ode echoing in the background; and supposing that this were the case, it would certainly stand as Jeffrey's most subtle challenge to the poet who so persistently troubled his thoughts. Jeffrey here seems almost to identify the issue that, as we shall see, he can only dance around figuratively in his actual Wordsworth criticism. What he appears obscurely to have perceived in Wordsworth, and here to repudiate, is the priority Wordsworth accords to "the inanimate creation," "rocks and stone" being two-thirds of the mass that orbits with Lucy. What unifies and levels being in Wordsworth, its "ground," hence the true object of the imaginative faculty which exists to disclose unity, is the minerality of "inanimate creation" from which "sentient beings," all of whom are linked ontically to the world by their own inanimate (i.e., somatic) nature alone, are estranged by enlightenment anthropocentrism. In the Intimations Ode almost uniquely in the Wordsworth canon (it is perhaps his least characteristic poem), "the meanest flower that blows" is the lowest rung on the order of being, with insentient things — earth, ocean, cataracts, and hills — all powerfully humanized. It is possible that Jeffrey here preaches to Wordsworth with his own text, the very text he professed to find unintelligible at the end of his 1807 review.

In turning now to the series of reviews in which Jeffrey waged his campaign against Wordsworth, it is helpful to begin with Jonathan Wordsworth's excellent summary of the issues in his facsimile reprint of these reviews.[13] Emphasizing the actual inconsistency in Jeffrey's seemingly invariant themes (belying the claim that the standards of poetry are immutable with which Jeffrey launches his career in the Southey review of 1802), Jonathan Wordsworth stresses the already-anachronistic anti-Jacobin agenda of the covert attack on Wordsworth in 1802 (the evidence that this is Jeffrey's main point is perhaps disputable), giving way to the subsequent absurdity of talking in the later reviews about a school of poets being spoiled by "system" when so little of the work actually under review (Wordsworth poems added to *Lyrical Ballads* by 1807, *The Excursion, The White Doe of Rylstone,* three Coleridge poems) follows the presumed dictates of the offending "Preface."[14] This is all that common sense requires by way of commentary, and may admittedly be all that can be said; but it leaves Jeffrey seeming even more negligible than posterity has judged him to be. Perhaps he can seem more respectable when supposed to think philosophically as well as judicially.

The pretext of having Southey's *Thalaba* "before us," as the future Judge Jeffrey always puts it, is, of course, amazingly flimsy. The plaintiff is nearly invisible—though not quite *in absentia,* as we shall see. This in itself should give pause. Why should Jeffrey have been so eager to devote his first effort as a reviewer, in the first issue of the *Edinburgh,* to a sustained rebuke of Wordsworth's "Preface," "a kind of manifesto, that preceded one of their most flagrant acts of hostility" (*ER* 1 [1802]: 65)? Hostility to what? Why is hostility in the air? Jonathan Wordsworth ascribes it to politics and Jeffrey's xenophobia (Jeffrey marshals the names of Rousseau, Kotzebue, and the Schiller of *Die Räuber* among the leading malign influences), but passions can run high about literature as well. Yes, there is also the complaint about affected rusticity. Wordsworth should know better because he has been to college, educated language is self-evidently superior to that of "inferiors," etc.; but this is all just snide parry and thrust, soon to be the main weapon of the *Quarterly* arbiters but never the chief concern of Jeffrey and his more liberal stable—who made no such scruple about Burns.

In my view, the chief provocation arises from the ontology displaced as aesthetics which had preoccupied Alison and Jeffrey in recent years. If Wordsworth's "beauteous and permanent forms of nature" can be found valuable in themselves, then the fixed standards Jeffrey announces in the first sentence of his career are not standards of art but standards of nature—and not even human nature but the "inanimate creation" Wordsworth brings to the fore in deriving authentic passion from the rustic soil. That opinion must be laughed out of countenance because, if taken seriously, it would make the happy standards of civilized taste achieved by enlightenment consensus seem like the arbitrary and capricious hothouse growth Wordsworth says it is in the "Preface." Jeffrey's anthropocentric appeal to humanist standards is squarely at odds with Wordsworth's geocentric appeal to humanity, and there will of course be hostility when what is at stake is the very idea of the human itself. Are we "children of nature," like the school of Wordsworth (ibid., 68), or are we disciples of the "excellent" (ibid., 67), as Jeffrey wants us to be? Are we autochthonous, as Lévi-Strauss on the Oedipus myth would have it, or are we born of two human parents, the binary that fixes our place in an unbroken tradition of socially authorized sentience?[15]

*Thalaba* receives its more or less well-deserved dismissal, but on various grounds scarcely relevant, as all agree, to the opening salvo aimed at Wordsworth. There is, however, one flicker of relevance, cited from a footnote to Southey's poem over which Jeffrey tellingly pauses. "Mr Southey's partiality to the drawling vulgarity of some of our old English ditties" (*ER* 18 [May 1811]: 78) — the sort of thing that inspired, insofar as anything literary inspired, the *Lyrical Ballads* — is proven from his citation of a ballad in which "[t]he heroine is an old *mare* belonging to John Poulter." Jeffrey then quotes three stanzas quoted by Southey in which the mare is endowed with human consciousness and treated like one of the Wordsworthian downtrodden in *Lyrical Ballads*. Now, although this ballad indeed has something of the 1798 Wordsworth's tone, Wordsworth never wrote anything quite so straightforwardly Aesopian as this (excepting the moral parables in dialog like "The Oak and the Broom"), not even in *Peter Bell*, "Hart-Leap Well," or *The White Doe*, poems in which the degree of responsiveness to be imputed to animal consciousness is handled with subtle ambiguity. Nevertheless, Jeffrey has noticed something that will continue to irritate him, namely, the leveling of consciousness effected by the refusal to acknowledge a hierarchy of being, with its description of the human in its nonhuman, somatic registers, and its offsetting personification of the nonhuman: "the chattering of Harry Gill's teeth [the *teeth* chatter in nonsense syllables, not the person], . . . the one-eyed huntsman 'who had a cheek like a cherry'" (ibid., 68). Simon Lee sometimes "reeled, and was stone blind" (in just those moments the subject-object of a Spot of Time, both skater and blind beggar), but he was also, in the 1798 text but not later, one-eyed. This cyclopean feature is what Jeffrey notices, bestially estranging the senility of Wordsworth's anti-hero (not an old mare, but almost) as completely as possible from the civilized, binocular perspectives and complexities of enlightenment consciousness.

In 1807, Jeffrey is still exercised at the "alarming innovation" (*ER* 11 [Oct. 1807 — Jan. 1808]: 214) of *Lyrical Ballads* and its "Preface," and relieved to find his "public duty" in attacking it justified by the disappointing volumes "before" him (ibid., 215). He begins by distancing Wordsworth from the source of autochthonous strength he had earlier noticed, claiming that "the new poets are just as great borrowers as the old," drawing merely on "vulgar ballads and plebeian nurseries" rather than "their illustrious predecessors" (ibid., 218). Having thus shorn the poet's locks of a dangerous strength, Jeffrey turns to the risible subject matter, passing over Mr. Wilkinson's spade to begin with "To a Daisy" (one of the poems Wordsworth wrote with the express purpose of celebrating the being of the ordinary), of which he complains that the conclusion —

> Thou long the poet's praise shalt gain;
> Thou wilt be more beloved by men
> In times to come; thou not in vain
> Art Nature's favorite —

is an "unmeaning prophecy" (ibid., 219). Jeffrey sees that the "poet" is just this poet, that the daisy's future vogue will be owing to this poem, and that the proof of nature's affection is not qualitative but quantitative (nature produces a lot of daisies: "The scope of the piece is to say," Jeffrey rightly says, "that the flower is found every where" (ibid.); but he can scarcely approve the profuse egotism shared by poet and nature (for neither of whom is affection sanctioned by men of elegant taste) and calls the prophecy unmeaning because the outcome foreseen is not determined in the slightest by human reason or judgment. The poem just *will* make its way, who knows why, and nature in collusion just *will* make daisies popular for no good reason.

Jeffrey next bridles at the comparison of "Louisa" with a vigorous wild animal, and at the suggestion addressed to the robin, another commonplace object, that "All men who know thee call [thee] their brother" (ibid.). Continuing in this vein, he arrives at the conclusion of the "Ode to Duty," which he acknowledges to be in "the lofty vein," albeit a failure. This is an overdue concession that the general fault, the true subversiveness, of Wordsworth is after all neither his simplicity nor his banality. It is (and the main shaft, mentioned above, is reserved for the Intimations Ode) his unintelligibility, heralded by the "unmeaning" part of "To the Daisy." Clearly the trouble with Duty from Jeffrey's standpoint is that Wordsworth sees its prototype not in the historical progress of human character but in the rigorous devotion to order and comity reflected in the universe, the "inanimate creation": " 'Thou dost preserve the stars from wrong; / And the most ancient heavens through thee are fresh and strong' " (ibid., 221). The question of "The Godhead's most benignant grace" aside, what Wordsworth evokes here is a principle, ostensibly human-centered, that is manifested in and through all modes of being equally. (When he returns to this theme in *The Excursion*, it is the first passage that Jeffrey quotes against him [*ER* 24 (Nov. 1814): 10].) All of this the humanist attaching no intrinsic value to natural objects finds simply incomprehensible. The same sense of a naturalized covenant (the perdurable rainbow) linking all created things in "natural piety" pervades "My Heart Leaps Up," which Jeffrey quotes entire, witheringly without comment. "Resolution and Independence" is dismissed chiefly for its vulgar subject, but Jeffrey does scornfully notice the poet's failure to attend to the actual human speech of the Leech Gatherer, wincing away perhaps from this hint that it is not as a person but as a composite being (stone, sea-beast, and cloud) that the leech gatherer is finally restorative. Vulgarity remains the ostensible chief objection, but one can already see, even while Jeffrey still clings to the idea that the "system" is the problem, that "mysticism" (ibid., 3) is what threatens most.

Only good company, Jeffrey decides by 1814, can cure the malady (here Byron's version of the critique, inverted for *Childe Harold,* III, becomes noticeable):

> Solitary musings, amidst such scenes [of lacustrine seclusion], might no doubt be expected to nurse up the mind to the majesty of poetical conception, — (though it is remarkable, that all the greater poets lived, or had lived, in the full current of society) (ibid.)

This passage modulates into the central theme, derived ultimately from Hume, of taste by urbane consensus, "the few settled and permanent maxims, which form the canon of general taste in all large and polished societies" (ibid.), that concludes the Alison review. When Jeffrey professes not to be able to understand *The Excursion,* it is hard to understand him in turn, given his declaration that nine-tenths of the poem consists in homiletic bromides more prolix than the matter of "any ten volumes of sermons that we ever perused" (ibid., 5). Dull, perhaps, but unintelligible? Only in the last sentence preceding his summary of the poem do we find that the only real difficulty, as usual, concerns the "inanimate creation": "His effusions on what may be called the physiognomy of external nature, or its moral and theological expression, are eminently fantastic, obscure, and affected" (ibid., 6). He does seem honestly confused here, and it should be said that Wordsworth's treatment of nature in *The Excursion* does lend itself to confusion. For the first time in this poem since the early 1790s, and hereafter for the rest of his career, Wordsworth intermittently lapses back into the "book of nature topos" (as Curtius calls it)[16] that had dominated the Deism-inflected topographical poetry of the eighteenth century. Byron is fooled by, and imitates, the same regression in *Childe Harold,* III ("But let me quit man's works, again to read / His Maker's," st. 109). Neither Jeffrey nor Byron ever fully realized that for Wordsworth at his most original the natural world encountered without humanist or Deist preconceptions cannot be read at all. It should be remembered in extenuation, however, that "There was a Boy" was the only Spot of Time they ever had a chance to read — unless "The Discharged Soldier" be counted as one — and no doubt they, like most readers, would have leapt to the conclusion that that poem is about communicating with nature, not about the sudden silence of the owls breaking the illusory circuit of communication to anticipate the unknowingness of death.

A further proviso is in order, however: We must presume that both Jeffrey and Byron saw something more in Wordsworth than conventional nature allegory — which is always after all anthropocentric. Their very insistence (apart from Byron's Alpine aberration of 1816) on Wordsworth's unintelligibility and mysticism strongly suggests this. No one ever called Thomson or Beattie or Cowper — or Bowles — unintelligible, even though effusions about nature were in no shortage among them. Both Jeffrey and Byron must in some measure have realized that Nature and Wordsworth did *not* speak "[a] mutual language, clearer than the tome / Of his land's tongue" (*Childe Harold*, III, st. 13). It is in any case a different kind of voice that bothers Jeffrey the most:

> The Ninth and last [Book of *The Excursion*] is chiefly occupied with the mystical discourses of the Pedlar; who maintains, that the whole universe is animated by an active principle, the noblest seat of which is in the human soul; and moreover, that the final end of old age is to train and enable us
>
> 'To hear the mighty stream of *Tendency*
> Uttering, for elevation of our thought,
> A clear sonorous voice, inaudible
> To the vast multitude whose doom it is
> To run the giddy round of vain delight — ' (*ER* 24 [Nov. 1814]: 9)

Note that Wordsworth's Wanderer does not here say "*in* a clear sonorous voice." His unusual and interesting assertion is that "tendency" (the way things incline through time) utters a voice. It is not a voice that says something, just a voice uttering itself, recalling the "rapturous mystical ode to" the Cuckoo that so exasperated Jeffrey in 1807: " 'O Cuckoo! Shall I call thee bird, / Or but a wandering voice?' " (*ER* 11 [Oct. 1807–Jan. 1808]: 225) This, however, is one of those moments that almost inadvertently finds the Great Decade resurgent in Wordsworth; and elsewhere his no less "mystical" but more accessibly theistic belief in a signifying and significant nature apparently makes an easier target: "We should like extremely to know," harrumphs Jeffrey concerning the Pedlar's education by nature in Book 1, "what is meant by tracing an ebbing and flowing mind in the fixed lineaments of naked crags?" (*ER* 24 [Nov. 1814]: 12). But only apparently: as in *The Prelude*, Wordsworth's passage, written in 1798, is specifically about the primitive way in which a child experiences nature, the same child who thinks a looming mountain is minatory. For the most part, nonhuman voices in *The Excursion* (*even* in *The Excursion*) are surrounded by an "as if" that Jeffrey misses: " ' — "List!" — I heard, / From yon huge breast of rock, a solemn bleat; / Sent forth as if it were the Mountain's voice!' " (ibid., 16). Almost better, perhaps, if the mountain did have a voice (as it was revised to do in 1845),[17] a voice that speaks something other than its own being; it would be thus far subdued to Jeffrey's humanism. Among the passages he singles out for praise is the description of a river source, not yet speaking but soon to speak: "The Mountain Infant to the Sun comes forth / Like human life from darkness" (ibid., 28).

*The White Doe of Rylstone* unfortunately comes before Jeffrey in 1815, the ink of the *Excursion* review scarcely dry, as the sad case of a poet making a pother about a deer, recalling the old mare in the ballad quoted by Southey:[18]

> In consequence of all which, we are assured by Mr Wordsworth, that she [the doe] "is approved by Earth and Sky, in their benignity; and moreover, that the old Priory itself takes her for a daughter of the Eternal Prime — which we have no doubt is a very great compliment, though we have not the good luck to understand what it means" (*ER* 25 [June–Oct. 1815]: 363)

By now Jeffrey has a following, as the 1816 review of *The White Doe* by Josiah Conder in the *Eclectic* (quoted by the poem's Cornell editor, Kristine Dugas) would indicate:

> Let him delight to indue the nobler life of animal consciousness with reflex intelligence, and realize the fables of the Pythagoreans; the same propensity which led the grosser imaginations of the heathens to carry their uninformed sympathy with inferior and even inanimate nature into idolatry. Through all these changes, we may recognize the poet's power, but we cannot accompany him: and we would gladly, when the Proteus again becomes man, fix him in that shape forever.[19]

The review of Coleridge's *Christabel, Kubla Khan: A Vision, The Pains of Sleep* in 1816 is the most gratuitously vicious of the whole series. This may be because, as Duncan Wu argues, it was written at least in part by Hazlitt.[20] The Coleridge review need not detain us long, as there is very little in it that actually tars Coleridge with the Wordsworth brush (although the *White Doe* is singled out once again for special dispraise); but there is one moment, concerning *Christabel*, in which the glorification of the nonhuman resurfaces: "We now meet our old friend, the mastiff bitch, who is much too important a person to be slightly passed by" (*ER* 27 [Sept.–Dec. 1816]: 63) — as if to say, we never left the precincts of the *White Doe* after all.

It was Byron, the *Edinburgh* announces with great ironic to-do, who had the bad taste to recommend *Christabel* for publication. Perhaps, if Jeffrey is indeed the author, this suggests that matters still stood uneasily between them; but Byron in 1816 was hearing far worse things said about him while perhaps imagining worse yet, and in any case he usually tried to appear aristocratically unruffled in the face of merely bookish disagreements. In the 1820 Dedication to *Marino Faliero,* he told "Baron Goethe," who had been roughly handled in an 1816 *Edinburgh,* that "our critics . . . are at bottom good-natured fellows, considering their two professions — taking up the law in court, and laying it down out of it."[21] Perhaps in any case Byron accepted the announced verdict on *Christabel:* within a year or two, Coleridge was to join Southey, Wordsworth, and Castlereagh in the pantheon of scoundrels lurking throughout the Dedication and first Canto of *Don Juan* (and still present, until he deleted some stanzas at Murray's behest, in Canto 2 as well). The addition of Castlereagh to the mix will allow the argument of this chapter to gesture in the end, as promised, toward politics. Jumping ahead to 1821 in the meantime, I take up Byron's first "Letter to John Murray, Esqre, on the Rev. W. L. Bowles's Strictures on the Life and Writings of Pope" (a second, more personal and less pertinent letter on Bowles went unpublished until 1835) to illustrate the degree to which this politics, or literary politics, resembles Jeffrey's.

True, Byron had lately been in better humor with the *Quarterly* than with the *Edinburgh* because the *Quarterly* had defended Pope against Bowles while Jeffrey in the *Edinburgh* was praising Keats, author of the attack on heroic couplets in *Sleep and Poetry* that triggered Byron's volley of remarks on Keatsian onanism: "Nobody could be prouder of the praises of the *Edinburgh* than I was, or more alive to their censure. . . . At present *all the men* they have ever praised are degraded by that insane article" (*LBLJ* V, 121). This may illustrate in passing (only in part because Byron's allegiance to Pope was at least in some respects arguably anomalous)[22] the danger of boiling down any discussion of Regency literary politics to a contrast between the *Quarterly* and the *Edinburgh.* Byron's publisher Murray himself was the publisher of the *Quarterly* and at one time also a suitor, as Byron often reminds him, to become Wordsworth's publisher. However, the occasion of the letter to Murray was not Jeffrey's praise of Keats nor even the offending passage in Keats but Bowles's defense of his commentary on Pope in his 1806 edition of ten volumes. Bowles for his part had recently responded (under the amusingly Jeffreyan title *Invariable Principles of Poetry*) to comments by Thomas Campbell in his 1819 *Specimens of the British Poets,* and also, in *The Pamphleteer* for October 1820, to a *Quarterly* article by Isaac Disraeli, ostensibly on Spence's *Anecdotes* but really a defense of Campbell and Pope against Bowles (this is the article Byron admired), which Bowles mistakenly believed to have been written by a green-grocer and Pope scholar named Octavius Gilchrist.

Among many other points of controversy to be passed over here, Bowles in the *Invariable Principles* argued that Pope failed to value the natural objects of the external world except as a backdrop to the human scene and as a source of illustration for human transactions. Today this seems obviously true, and scarcely detracts from even the most fervent admiration of Pope. It is taken for granted by Johnson's Imlac in *Rasselas,* who enumerates among the ideal poet's impossibly polymath acquisitions the ability to study "all the appearances of nature," but only because "every idea is useful for the enforcement or decoration of moral or religious truth." Byron assails Bowles with the argument of Jeffrey's Alison review, intermittently alluding and referring to Wordsworth. The great works of art and architecture, he writes,

> are direct manifestations of mind, and *presuppose* poetry in its very conception; and have, moreover, as being such, a something of actual life, which cannot belong to any part of inanimate nature, unless we adopt the system of Spinosa, that the World is the Deity. . . . Take away Rome, and leave the Tybur and the seven Hills, in the Nature of Evander's time. Let Mr. Bowles or Mr. Wordsworth, or Mr. Southey, or any of the other "Naturals," make a poem upon them, and then see which is most poetical, — their production, or the commonest guide-book. . . . (*LBLJ* V, 548)

Contrast these eighteenth-century *données,* mediated by Alison and Jeffrey, with the following passage in Wordsworth's "Preface": having said that the poet's passions are associated with our "moral sentiments," Wordsworth then speaks in addition of "our animal sensations," and "the causes which excite" both. Human events and emotions are prominent on the list of causes, which also includes, however, "the operations of the elements and the appearances of the visible universe; . . . storm and sun-shine, . . . The revolutions of the seasons, . . . Cold and heat."[23] The lines are drawn. Bowles sides, albeit less reflectively, with Wordsworth (the questionable models he cites are Cowper and Thomson), while Alison, Jeffrey, and Byron seek philosophical reinforcement for what is after all a rearguard opinion. The movement from Johnson's pious rationalism (and Cowper's and Thomson's as well) to Jeffrey's and Byron's humanism is marked by the disappearance of religion from the latter authors' human-centeredness; and in this respect Johnson is actually closer to what Wordsworth *believed* himself to be saying (at least in retrospect, he considered the purpose of his poetry to be spiritual) than to Jeffrey. Even for Wordsworth, as the passage from the "Preface" shows, all things, things even in that ontic nakedness which neither Johnson nor Jeffrey and Byron would understand or appreciate, are to be referred to their role in human consciousness. The difference, by no means an absolute or polar opposition, is the difference between the reinforcement of human self-importance by nonhuman analogs and the disclosure to human reflection of the nonhuman unity, perhaps also the spiritual unity, of all somatic existence — including that of the human body itself.

Byron's attacks on Wordsworth and Southey in *English Bards* must certainly have been influenced by Jeffrey's repeated criticisms. (Jeffrey's review of *Poems, 1807* appeared just a few months before Brougham's review of *Hours of Idleness.*) Byron had already had his first innings with Wordsworth in an undistinguished, only partly negative review of *Poems, 1807* (*Monthly Literary Recreations,* July, 1807), but the final couplet of the lines on Wordsworth in *English Bards* ("And all who view the 'idiot in his Glory' / Conceive the Bard the hero of the story") is much closer to Jeffrey — and to the guiding theme of the Dedication and the first Canto of *Don Juan.* The only aberration from this viewpoint, again, had been *Childe Harold,* III, written during the period of "exile" in 1816 when Byron's near-paranoid misanthropy, together with Shelley's having force-fed him a diet of Wordsworth, encouraged the misreading of Wordsworth as a lover of legible nature that I have discussed above. Even here, however, Byron turns his back on humanity only to rediscover it in the human face of nature. The governing idea of *Don Juan,* at least up to the point of Juan's expulsion from Spain, is that only humanity is vital and reproductive, whereas all else — including abstracted, reified, and autocratic forms of consciousness — is impotent and dead. A dry Bob (Southey), a eunuch (Castlereagh), a pedantic hypocrite (Donna Inez), and three meta-physicians (Plato, Wordsworth, and Coleridge) all stand, or fail to stand, in opposition to the polyphiloprogenitive "lineal sons of Eve" (Jose, Juan, Donna Julia's grandmamma) who "begat" not only their mixed fate but also the reproductive momentum of the "*Juan* stanza" itself, digression and adultery suggesting themselves as parallel expressions of unregulated human energy.

I do not wish to linger too long on what should be the familiar ground of Byron's critique of Wordsworth in some of its more obvious — and by no means un-Jeffreyan — forms. Much of the Dedication and first canto are Byron's way of saying "This will never do" to *The Excursion,* and it is helpful to consider that "My poem's epic" is asserted in contrast with a poem that also makes epic claims, explicitly so in the "Prospectus" quoted by Wordsworth in his prose preface to that poem. (Wordsworth: "the mind of man" is my focus. Byron: "I want a hero," a more fully human focus, even if "want" in part means "continue to lack.") Byron's prose preface, unpublished until the twentieth century, begins with an attack on the prose preface to "The Thorn" in order facetiously to introduce his own fictitious narrator, equivalent to Wordsworth's retired sea captain;[24] but not far away lurks the Wanderer, who likewise consorts, for much of Wordsworth's poem, with "the Curate of the hamlet."[25] The most telling affinity between those antipodes, the *Juan* narrator and the Wanderer, is their lack of family ties, stressed by Wordsworth (as De Quincey noticed) in the Wanderer's solicitous yet unhelpful role in Margaret's tragedy, and his repeated serene chastisement of the married Poet's indulgence in vicarious grief. To this dramatically interesting feature of the poem Byron's narrator alludes as follows: "But if there's anything in which I shine, / 'Tis in arranging all my friends' affairs, / Not having, of my own, domestic cares" (*DJ* I, 23).

The contempt heaped on "The Thorn" (à la Jeffrey: "prosaic ravings" passing for poetry) will soon be directed toward the unintelligibility of *The Excursion,* which is linked in turn to that of Donna Inez: "Her thoughts were theorems, her words a problem, / As if she deem'd that mystery would ennoble 'em." Byron's quarry is in part the professional jargons ridiculed by his predecessors Smollett and Fielding: the lawyers' "talk's obscure and circumspect" (*DJ* I, 33), and, for Byron's plain country squire persona, writing itself, especially bluestocking writing (the link between Joanna Southcote and Wordsworth), is suspect: Julia's friendship with Inez is odd because "not a line had Julia ever penn'd" (*DJ* I, 66). But the vice of obscurity infects Juan and Julia themselves, or anyone in whose interest it is to mystify plain facts. Juan falling in love becomes a Laker; hence of the reason for his embarrassment in Julia's presence "he had no more notion / Than he who never saw the sea of ocean" (*DJ* I, 70; the Lakers need to see the world, Byron often says). This of course leads to the famous comic indictment of "Plato" ("You're a bore, / A charlatan, a coxcomb — and have been, / At best, no better than a go-between" [*DJ* I, 116]), but even in Byron's chosen terms of ridicule one detects the true object of the attack: Juan in love has become a nature lover, and this leads directly to echoes of the indictment of Wordsworth in Jeffrey's review of Alison — and of *The Excursion:*

> Young Juan wander'd by the glassy brooks,
> Thinking unutterable things; he threw
> Himself at length within the leafy nooks
> Where the wild branch of the cork forest grew;
> There poets find materials for their books,
> And every now and then we read them through,
> So that their plan and prosody are eligible,
> Unless, like Wordsworth, they prove unintelligible.
>
> He, Juan (not Wordsworth), so pursued
> His self-communion with his own high soul . . . (*DJ* I, 90–91)

Broadly with reference to *The Excursion* ("books," "read them through"), Juan here becomes the author of the "Prospectus to *The Recluse*," where somehow or other "the Mind of Man — / My haunt, and the main region of my song" (as Blake likewise complained) "to the external World / Is fitted," all to create "the spousal verse / Of this great consummation."[26]

From Byron's point of view, this "fitting and fitted," as Blake called it, is "not at all adapted to my rhymes" (*DJ* I, 3), or is at most soon be demystified as a perfect fit of a very different kind. "If *you* think 'twas philosophy that this did, / I can't help thinking puberty assisted" (*DJ* I, 93). It simply makes no sense, as the logic of Jeffrey's position finally dictates, to be a nature poet, as nature is nothing without a human face: "He thought about himself, and the whole earth, / . . . And of the many bars / To perfect knowledge of the boundless skies; — / And then he thought of Donna Julia's eyes" (*DJ* I, 92). *The Excursion* for Byron must remain Wordsworth's "new system to perplex the sages" (*DJ* Dedication, 4; Byron shows in this stanza that he has read the "Preface" with its Prospectus carefully), because of the way in which its scheme incorporates nonhuman things.

When the "intellectual eunuch Castlereagh" becomes a "thing," henceforth called "it" in the invective that ensues, there can be no more savage indictment, underlain as it is by the contempt of a humanist for the dehumanized object-world. And how much worse if the object "thinks," like the horse in *The Idiot Boy* (a poem full of Byron's *bêtes noirs*), which thus seems more human than the idiotic people. Dehumanization for Byron consists in the objectification of authentic human feeling by "system," and it is here that nature poetry and excessively calculating politics reveal, for him, their common Toryism. It is in this respect, but perhaps in no other, that Jeffrey and Byron can be said to share a Whig interpretation of Wordsworth. Byron may not know it, as in his view "the Edinburgh Review and Quarterly" alike "Treat a dissenting author very martyrly" (*DJ* I, 211), and as there is no doubt much to be said about the difference between moderate and Holland House Whigs; but in this one respect there is common ground.

An important book remains to be written on the "Regency voice" in English literature. It would account, not just for Jeffreyism, but the whole poetic pantheon that Byron in *Don Juan* (see *DJ* Dedication, 7) creates over against the pretensions of the Lakers: Scott (whose ballads are narrative, not "lyrical"), Rogers (whose Italy, like Byron's, hides nature under human monuments), Campbell (joined by Byron in attacking Bowles), Moore (who joined John Hookham Frere, William Stewart Rose, and the comic Byron in ennobling the genre of *vers de société* as a sure line of defense against nature poetry), and Crabbe (the rural anti-Wordsworth, as Jeffrey had shown in his 1808 review of Crabbe). An important contribution to this end has been Peter Graham's lively and thoughtful *"Don Juan" and Regency England* (Charlottesville, Va., 1990), the first chapter of which concentrates on Byron's critique of Wordsworth in the earliest stanzas of *Don Juan*.

In my view, however, such a book should in some measure come to terms with the issue raised in this chapter. Teetering in the balance is the question whether it means anything to be a thing — whether aesthetic or any other humanized value inheres in things. Wordsworth discovers the ontic unity of the human and the nonhuman in the sheer minerality of things. Coleridge shares this discovery but hates it, arguing that without the shaping spirit of imagination things in themselves are "fixed and dead." Shelley turns to advantage the conviction that the natural world is a charnel-house throughout his career. Keats writes "the poetry of earth." It is not the case, in fact, that Jeffrey, an exemplary Regency mind, disagrees with any of these views, although of course there is no trace in him of — for example — Shelley's consolatory immaterialism. Jeffrey's insistence that inanimate objects lack innate qualities is just what I have wanted to emphasize. For the whole Western world, whether it knew it or not, "things" had once for all been neutralized and alienated by Kant, who finished the job begun by the apocalyptic imagery of the Bible. But for Jeffrey this was neither a crisis nor a particular triumph, any more than it was for Beau Brummel's fat friend. It merely justified the secular anthropocentrism against which Wordsworth rebelled.

# 4

## Green to the Very Door?
## The Natural Wordsworth

There is dazzling and varied revisionism in the Wordsworth criticism of the past thirty years, yet all the most influential rereadings of every kind have but one refrain: Wordsworth was not a nature poet. The seventies commentaries stressing visionary apocalypse took their point of departure from the dialectic between the tyranny of the senses and the dark, unpleasant moments of "blank misgiving" in "the abyss of idealism," moments when as a child Wordsworth had to grasp a wall or a tree to be sure that such things existed.[1] The rhetorical analyses suspending anthropomorphic language rather than imagination over this abyss argue that Wordsworth is one of "the first modern writers to have put into question, in the language of poetry, the ontological priority of the sensory object."[2] And in the eighties return to the issue of social determinants theorized in its most sweeping form by Alan Liu, history manifested as ideology takes over the role hitherto played by language or imagination and reveals, through commentary, a parallel truth: "there is no nature except as it is constituted by acts of political definition made possible by particular forms of government."[3]

Infighting aside, all the criticism identifiable with these three positions — together with the feminist criticism that reflects either the psychoanalytic leaning of the first or the social historiography of the third — has continued to envision itself in collective reaction against a grand metanarrative about

Wordsworth that is purportedly so durable, so indifferent to changing reception horizons, that only Paul de Man's knowingly period-blind expression "Wordsworth and the Victorians" has a sufficiently focused energy of condescension to wrestle it into submission. In this view, there is enough of the old Leslie Stephen remaining in every successive Wordsworth scholar and critic to warrant the repetition, ever and anon, of the Matthew Arnold mantra, "poetry is the reality, philosophy the illusion"—but always with the proviso that Arnold was, as he finally admitted, no better than "a Wordsworthian" himself. According to this whole tradition—or stubborn prejudice—nature not only exists but it responds to human desire by communicating, among other things, ethical lessons ("philosophy"), and Wordsworth is the supreme poet of this communion.

Within the past forty years, a good many critics have continued to uphold this latter view in one form or another but in most cases have not attracted much attention because the determined simplicity of their argument and procedure, sometimes calculated, sometimes apparently innocent, has left little for more intricate thinking to attach itself to (better to dismiss "the Victorians" once more with a wave). And the more formidable critics who have come forward to champion the so-called "humanist" nature poet, preeminently M. H. Abrams and Jonathan Wordsworth, have seemed compromised, ironically enough, by signs of complicity with the positions they attack. Revisionary critics have always been too generously aware that they stand on Abrams's shoulders, many having drawn their apocalyptic bent from his teachings, to want to quarrel with him as vigorously as he himself might have wished. And Jonathan Wordsworth, despite his affiliation with the Cornell-Dove Cottage network of textual scholars who have little patience with amateurs lacking the ability to date holographs, nevertheless betrays too many symptoms: his deep engagement with the Spots of Time, his preference for the earliest possible *Prelude* manuscripts, and his intense dislike of the later Wordsworth make him an antinaturalist *malgré lui*.

In response to these tendencies, one point to be made in passing is that both sides of the "nature" controversy exchange positions more readily than they realize. It is worth at least sketching in the view, as I shall below, that within the traditional mainstream there have been plenty of blank misgivings about nature, while for the newer mainstreams the abyssal elements in Wordsworth are themselves, in their most uncompromising forms, the very prior sensory objects that were supposed to have been put into question. But these imputations are not meant to seem surprising or controversial; far from appearing as the glamorous result of antithetical critique, they arise merely from the almost inevitable confusion anyone is likely to feel when trying to say what nature *is*.

(It is not surprising that so many distinguished minds have taken refuge in saying, in a certain sense correctly, that it is nothing.) A glance or two therefore at the historians of ideas who took an interest in Wordsworth's "nature" will resolve very little, undoubtedly, such is the hermeneutic circularity that undoes all such projects, but at least it will provide a kind of multiple definition to appeal to as need arises.

And need will indeed arise, if anything comes of the prognostication by Jonathan Bate, in *Romantic Ecology: Wordsworth and the Environmental Tradition,* that a "green" criticism of the future — supplanting the "red" criticism of the eighties — will make Wordsworth a nature poet once again.[4] I too think that Wordsworth is a nature poet, and realize now that I thought so even when I was most deeply influenced in manner, tone, and selectivity of perception by the visionary wing of the "Yale School."[5] But I still prefer to emphasize the *via naturaliter negativa* that I learned to recognize from that school (differing from Hartman — and from Hegel — only in doubting that this road points, or is meant to point, beyond itself), and I am inclined to criticize the notion of nature as "environment," as organic-systemic totality rather than ontological unity, that governs the polemic of Jonathan Bate. It is by way of interaction with Bate's interesting book in particular, then, that I shall try to bring some measure of discrimination to bear on the difficult plight of not being very green yet still wanting to claim that Wordsworth is a nature poet.

In what follows, I attempt first to reconsider and relocate the nature *topos* in the diverse traditions of Wordsworth commentary; to participate in the return to nature heralded by Bate as much as possible on my own terms (with remarks in passing on *Home at Grasmere*); and to show how and where nature remains even and especially in Wordsworth texts privileged by the commentaries of the past thirty years — and in the commentaries themselves.

By Wordsworth's time, "nature" was a "technical" term (the expression is C. B. Tinker's), rather like our "physics," referring to the laws and operations of the physical world. Being "closely connected to the brutal and anti-Christian views of nature in the minds of Helvétius and Holbach," this sense of the term, which can be traced back through Locke, tended to be used by those who were hostile or condescending toward poetry.[6] Part of Wordsworth's novelty consisted then simply in reinvesting the scientific of the term with poetic aura — "the breath and finer spirit of all knowledge," as he called such mediations of science in the 1800 "Preface." He owned the 1781 edition of Holbach's *Système de la Nature* and criticized it sharply in 1809, but not without having absorbed its physics.[7] All he needed was a metaphysics, and that, we generally assume, was the "*active* universe" of the "Blest the Infant Babe" passage (1805 *Prelude:* II, 266). As

Basil Willey summarizes: "his 'creative sensibility' had taught him that he was not alone with an 'inanimate cold world,' but with an 'active universe.' "[8] H. W. Piper, the historian of ideas who has done most with this concept, perhaps overextends its pantheistic implications and its influence on the Unitarian thinking to which Coleridge especially was exposed in the 1790s, but he is able to argue authoritatively, citing Priestley, Erasmus Darwin, Hutton, and Cabanis, that "the belief that inanimate objects were in a literal sense alive came nearest to establishing itself as a scientific orthodoxy during the years of Wordsworth's most active poetic life."[9] It is to such an "external World," Wordsworth writes to the disgust of Blake in 1800, that the "individual Mind" is "fitted," and vice versa, authenticating the imagination's "spousal verse" with nature.[10]

This is the basic information that has stood behind the debate about nature in Wordsworth — and did so implicitly even before it was set down in order by the historians of ideas. It would be obstinate to deny that there are many passages in Wordsworth, passages indeed reflecting something like an overall conscious design, that conform to this general outline, leaving traditional critics to disagree about questions of metaphysics: more or less pantheism, more or less mechanism (active or reactive), more or less of the insistent transcendence one finds in the Pisgah view from Snowdon or in the assertion that the Spots of Time make us feel that "the mind / Is lord and master." For all such critics, no matter how much they stress transcendence, Wordsworth is a nature poet.

But scientific and metaphysical ideas about nature do not exhaust the subject. There is also the ontology of nature: its mode of being, its status as beings or as a being, its relation to human being, and the being of its being. These are the issues, both in Wordsworth himself and in the history of his reception, that begin to confuse the way he has been and can be read. The results of this confusion can seem unproductive, empty of meaning (it is in its ontological register that nature in the critic's hands gets lost in a chaos of referents); but for all who feel that the most characteristically brilliant verse of Wordsworth is always in some way an evocation of being as such, the subversion of meaning itself becomes a technique for making nature appear. It is with respect to the ontology of nature that I wish now to reconsider certain strains that can be heard, albeit faintly, in the criticism preceding that of the past thirty years.

Although de Man calls it a "temptation" to condescend to Victorian Wordsworth criticism, he himself perpetuates the notion that the nineteenth-century reading of Wordsworth was "moral and religious" (*Rhetoric of Romanticism*, 85). Yet Pater, for example, stresses "the quiet, habitual observation of inanimate, or imperfectly animate, existence." He speaks, to be sure, of the "sense of a life in natural objects," but he notes the "sensuousness" with which this sense is perceived (playing, in anticipation of Empson, on the senses of "sense" in Wordsworth); and he places the "active universe" theme in the service of an onto-phenomenological intuition that I am inclined to call *a leveling of being:* "By raising nature to the level of human thought [Wordsworth] gives it power and expression: he subdues man to the level of nature, and gives him thereby a certain breadth and coolness and solemnity."[11] Wordsworth's observation is trained, in other words, on the point of intersection between human and nonhuman being in order to reveal something about the "widest commonalty" of being. Hazlitt had written repeatedly (in *Lectures on the English Poets* and again in *The Spirit of the Age*) of this "leveling" in socio-political terms, and from this standpoint he noticed how many of Wordsworth's characters ("female vagrants, . . . idiot boys and mad mothers" — joined, he might have added, by the very young and the very old) are only marginally possessed of normative human consciousness.[12] The ontic common denominator sought by Wordsworth is what makes his "philosophy" seem illusory to Matthew Arnold, in his turn, precisely because it is undifferentiated, a universal diffusion, in widest commonalty *spread,* of "joy." To say, then, with Arnold, that Wordsworth "has no style" is also to say that, having successfully resisted the "false secondary power, by which, / In weakness, we create distinctions" (1805 *Prelude,* II, 221–22), Wordsworth also has no meaning — or, more precisely, that he underdetermines the signifier.[13] According to the lines from Arnold's 1850 "Memorial Verses" that seem most to have influenced the language and purport of Pater's assessment, Wordsworth "laid us as we lay at birth / On the cool flowery lap of earth."

This way of looking at Wordsworth did not disappear in the first half of the twentieth century. Agreeing that philosophy in Wordsworth is the illusion, F. R. Leavis remarks that the poetry of *The Prelude* looks like a "paraphrasable" argument but in fact is not.[14] Here again is the "muddle" ascribed to "Tintern Abbey" in William Empson's *Seven Types of Ambiguity,* pointing toward Empson's analysis of the *Prelude*'s "unintelligible" confusion of sensation and imagination in *The Structure of Complex Words* — readings that de Man considered to be the sole flickerings of truth in antediluvian Wordsworth criticism.[15] Leavis too finds no coherent argument, and imputes the "wisdom" of Wordsworth's very incoherence to "his sense of communion with the nonhuman universe" ("Revaluations," 250). By the time Basil Willey wrote his "Background" books, what he called the "mergence with the inanimate" in Wordsworth was commonplace.[16] It had already inspired the clearsighted invective of Irving Babbitt against Wordsworth's "primitivism."[17] Quoting Emile Legouis at length on the prevalence of children, crazed and idiotic persons, animals, and plants in Wordsworth (Legouis, as we have seen, was following Hazlitt), all of them beings "whose senses, not yet distorted by analysis, yield them immediate perception of the world," and citing with approval Byron's joke in *English Bards* ("the Bard himself" is the hero of *The Idiot Boy*), Babbitt expresses the fervent wish that Wordsworth had rehabilitated his "secondary power," misguidedly called "false."

"It is no longer necessary to protect the Romantic poets from the charge of neoprimitivism," wrote Geoffrey Hartman in 1968.[18] Hartman aligns Wordsworth's "nature in its childhood or sensuous radiance" with Blake's Beulah, arguing that "from Francis Jeffrey to Irving Babbitt," Wordsworth's *"labor of the negative* (Hegel) was mistaken for . . . a crude nature worship." In emphasizing dark transcendence in Wordsworth, Hartman, Harold Bloom, and their disciples have always scrupulously acknowledged an antecedent tradition: Pater on "the abstract expression of desolation in the long white road" ("Wordsworth," 129) inspiring A. C. Bradley's memorable pages in the *Oxford Lectures* on "the sublime" as "visionary power" in Wordsworth, followed by G. Wilson Knight on "the hidden eternity-music in the inanimate," and D. G. James (appropriating Bradley for Christian purposes) on "visionary dreariness."[19] But even in this tradition there are moments of naturalism, signaled by Knight's mystical disclosure of the eternal in the mineral—the stone carried by the Arab in the dream of *Prelude* 5. For James, the Beulah state revealed through Wordsworth's struggle for "unity of prehension" is the *only* state that can be known without the aid of Christian revelation, and he sees Wordsworth as the prophet of his own belief that the imagination's meretricious way of achieving unity is necessarily linked to skepticism (*Scepticism and Poetry*, 115). In this he resembles John Jones, another precursor acknowledged by Hartman, who attacks the notion that Wordsworth is a unitarian poet, yet speaks of "the relational and monistic coherence" of *The Prelude*.[20]

Just so, naturalism in the criticism of the past thirty years persists as a moment to be overcome dialectically. Hartman's dismissal of the primitivist view reflects his powerfully articulated belief that Wordsworth is an Enlightenment thinker—which is to say, a strong and knotty thinker.[21] And yet, Hartman would agree, Wordsworth's intellectualized version of anti-self-consciousness, his chief gesture as Schillerian Sentimental Poet, is precisely to think the primitive, to make the primitive an object of phenomenological reflection: "the desire of the Romantics is perhaps for what Blake calls 'organized innocence,' but never for a mere return to the state of nature" (*Beyond Formalism*, 300–301). Still more problematic for the sublation of nature is the monism Hartman concedes in Wordsworth, in common with James and Jones: "there are no sharp breaks or ritual passings between one state of mind and another: vision is always continuous with sensation. Even such licensed rapture as Keats's 'Already with thee!' is avoided" (*The Unremarkable Words-worth*, 11). For Hartman here, as for all commentators at such moments, questions pile up (showing, I have said, that the issue being skirted does not concern physics or metaphysics but touches rather on the being of being) — questions like: "Vision" of what? "Sensation" of what?

Vision of nature, sensation of spirit: whatever it is, it is what remains when the owls fall silent, suspending the Boy of Winander's belief that there is a natural channel of communication ("responsive to his call"), a fit, between human beliefs about nature and nature itself. As the pathetic fallacy hangs in the balance, a new vision of the "visible scene" possesses the boy. The most influential modern critics agree that this is a vision not of any life within us and abroad but of a silent being in nature which, somatically signaled, is also a being toward his own imminent death. As he once hung in life, so the site of his burial hangs now, suspended in permanent estrangement above that social scene of instruction ("the Village School") where nature continues to seem significant, as typically it does in those "Books" on which Book V remains an ambivalent critical meditation. If this account of the Boy of Winander, intro-duced as it is by Wordsworth's trademark reduction of the loco-descriptive to sheer ostension ("There was"), appears merely to be a paraphrase of de Man's account in "Wordsworth and Hölderlin," a comparison can prove useful. Here is de Man:

> the sudden silence of nature was an anticipatory announcement of his death, a movement of his consciousness passing beyond the deceptive constancy of a world of correspondences into a world in which our mind knows itself to be in an endlessly precarious state of suspension: above an earth, the stability of which it cannot participate in, and beneath a heaven that has rejected it. (*The Rhetoric of Romanticism*, 54)

What I for my part am not saying, though, is that "the mediation of poetic language" (ibid.) puts into question the priority of the sensory object. Poetic language is in "books"; it is what makes the owls hoot like people. The absurd-ity of Coleridge's having reproved Milton in "The Nightingale" for anthropo-centrically calling nightingales melancholy and then having called them cheer-ful drunkards himself cannot have been lost on Wordsworth. This is what happens when you talk about the "jocund din" of birds; you are always "al-ready with" them by unlicensed means.

But with poetic language one can think the primitive, again, without being the primitive. Lionel Trilling relates the children sporting upon the shore in the Intimations Ode to the passage in *Civilization and Its Discontents* in which Freud describes the "primary ego-feeling" as "oceanic."[22] But it is the dark interpreters of Wordsworth themselves who have altered our taste in Freud—and Wordsworth—and refer us now to *Beyond the Pleasure Principle:* "The aim of all life is death." Where it was, there shall poetic language be. What the Boy of Winander realized is that "inanimate things came before animate ones," putting into question the priority of language to the being of death disclosed in the sensory object. In response to Alan Liu's recent version of the modern critics' revolt against nature—"nature is the name under which we use the nonhuman to validate the human" (*Wordsworth: The Sense of History,* 38)—the reader who still thinks Wordsworth is a nature poet might want to say that nature is our own nonhuman existence, forgotten once named.

Jonathan Bate rightly attributes Liu's insistence on the construction of nature by "particular forms of government" to the recent "interest in questions of landownership" among Romanticists inspired by the work of John Barrell (*Romantic Ecology,* 15). In response to such questions, Bate wants to say that environmental peril transcends—and has outlived—political peril: it is as true now as it was before the fall of the Iron Curtain that for every Three Mile Island there is a Chernobyl.[23] Well, yes, the issue of ownership is long overdue for a rest; and Bate's repeated quotation of Edward Thomas's "lord of that he does not possess," together with his reminder that John Clare could write of dwelling itself as possession despite never having owned any property (see ibid., 100–101), make for a welcome change of tune. Not that these very citations could not easily be demystified as exceptions proving the hegemonic rule of proprietary figurations of home: the point is, despite this available rejoinder, that feelings which are unquestionably in some sense proprietary (and not just the communist nationalism of "This land is my land" but the transitory sojourner's "This is my kind of place" are involved here) run deepest at the very moments when one is most conscious of exemption from the burdens of ownership. That is why people feel proprietary about public parks, "historic districts," and the like. When "man" (the word is Hölderlin's) dwells poetically, he is on someone else's property, even and most especially in those poems on country seats written by guests and beneficiaries of patronage that have been laid bare in successive critiques of pastoral from Raymond Williams to Tom Stoppard. To further complications of this issue I shall return in commenting on Wordsworth's *Home at Grasmere.*

Bate's position, then, is the environmentalist position (its rallying-cry, as every first-grader knows, is the non-proprietary possessive "*our* planet"), and he wants to say that that is Wordsworth's position too—that for Wordsworth the only important thing about owning a cottage, in *Home at Grasmere,* is that it surrounds one with a "deep vale," a "concave" mirror image of the whole earth that can become a regional "haunt" in "the mind of man" (92, 40, 102). This position is certainly congenial to the much older author of *The Guide to the Lakes,* featured in Bate's second chapter, and congenial also to the tradition of British Wordsworth readers passing from the Ruskin of *Fors Clavigera* through William Morris to Edward Thomas and to Seamus Heaney (the name of John Berger might well be added), which Bate identifies as a genuinely left-leaning genealogy of literary Greens. (I think his patriotism justified, by the way. In most other countries environmentalism has been most typically a plank of rightist platforms and has served, not always by design, the interests of privileged classes, as is well documented in Anna Bramwell's *Ecology in the 20th Century: A History,* an extremely intelligent book that appears in most respects to shape Bate's understanding of the complex relation between environmentalism and politics.)[24] But Bate's position remains — to revert to my earlier distinction — a metaphysical view of nature, and fails to take into account how an ontological view might differ from it. "Wordsworth," in other words, is still at stake.

To make my point as clear as possible, let me juxtapose two descriptions of a nuclear power plant against the backdrop of a seacoast. The first is Bate's, to the tune of "Wordsworth, thou should'st be with us at this hour":

> If we ascend Coniston Old Man, the mountain beneath which Ruskin lived in the years when he was writing *Fors,* the most prominent sight on the coast is the Sellafield nuclear reprocessing plant, with its abysmal record for dumping contaminated waste. "Still glides the Stream, and shall for ever glide," wrote Wordsworth of the Duddon in his concluding sonnet; but now it is not only water that glides inexorably into the sea off Wordsworth's coast. (61)

American readers can no doubt put hands on comparable descriptions of Seabrook on the coast of New Hampshire, juxtaposed perhaps with evocations of Thoreau on the Merrimack. The real plangency of Bate's sentiment, expressed over against the odds Wordsworth wagered upon in the Duddon sonnet (unlike the late Ruskin, Wordsworth was evidently untroubled by environmental panic), consists in Bate's distress at knowing that *things don't stay the same.* Thoughtless human beings tamper with the metaphysics, the Aristotelian "natural form," of nature's essence. Nature was not "meant," one says, to have a power plant in it. The hanging in independent suspense of this "meant" is what shows us still to believe that "nature," with Wordsworth its prophet, is in fact intrinsically meaningful, at once the subject and the object of human agency. But the amazingly *un*-ecological, anthropocentric hubris of thinking human threats to planetary health too powerful for the earth understood simply as earth to pass through and beyond, just as it has passed through catastrophes in which humans have played no part (not only the massive ones that changed the course of living forms but also such threats to species as rabies, elm blight, and hemlock disease)—this hubris can perhaps be humbled, and our burden lightened, by a more truly Wordsworthian kind of nature description.

In the ontological view, things *qua* things do stay the same; they just may not be the same things. Ontic sameness, not this or that visible form, stays the same. Here is a passage from a recent detective novel by P. D. James. Having detailed a panorama that includes a ruined abbey, a village, and a church as surveyed by her detective, Dalgleish, James continues:

> to the north the view was dominated by the huge bulk of the power station, the low-roofed administration block with, behind it, the reactor building and the great steel, aluminum-clad building of the turbine house. Four hundred metres out to sea were rigs and platforms of the intake structures through which the cooling sea water passed to the pump house. . . . Directly to his left the flint walls of Martyr's Cottage glistened . . . less than half a mile to the north, set back among the Californian pines which fringed that part of the coast, was the dull cottage . . . , a neatly proportional suburban villa incongruously set down on this bleak headland and facing inland as if resolutely ignoring the sea. Farther inland . . . was the Old Rectory, set like a Victorian dolls' house.[25]

History is welcome here, as is geography, each period and place jumbled together with its inharmonious characteristics, yet from flint to aluminum, it is implied, walls remain walls. Modes of dwelling, as of power (God, witchcraft, cozy imperial culture, nuclear energy) recirculate like coolant through a pump. The author revels in the mastery of detail (I have left out a lot), and while the passage is not without value judgments (the specific "nature" of objects as well as the mutuality derived from their very distinctness of being is emphasized), its overwhelming purpose is simply to place the discrete parts of the scene before the eye in their indiscriminate vividness. The nuclear power plant figures importantly in James's plot, just as it does in this panorama, but in both cases she carefully avoids aligning its role with either its messianic or its diabolical public images. Like Mont Blanc, it is a soulless image on the eye but no less for that reason a power source, timeless *as* power despite being a latecomer in the scenery. This is a "bleak headland," says James; it has the visionary dreariness of Wordsworth: a gibbet, a naked beacon, a girl with a pitcher making her way against the wind, all just unforgettably there together. That they are what they are is interesting, and suggestive, but strictly for the purpose of furnishing the ontological shock that makes them a spot of time, they could have been anything else: a road, a blasted crag, a tree, and a sheep, for example — anything, that is, in which an aestheticized symbolism of spiritual shelter and nurture, the hostelry of meaningfulness, has been effaced or carefully neutralized.

Judging from the example of Bate, an environmentalist criticism is prone to conclude that description is valuable because the things it describes *are those things,* and somehow in fact depends for this value on their continued (and, for that matter, their past) real existence. Thus Bate on reading Keats's "To Autumn" once global warming has increased the severity of winds in northern Europe: "the swallow has the greatest difficulty in coping with wind. . . . The poem will look very different if there is soon an autumn when 'gathering swallows twitter in the skies' for the last time." In addition to the shaky ornithology entailed here in Bate's having forgotten that swallows don't just twitter when preparing for autumn migration but also twitter every evening, when returning to their barns and chimneys, from late spring until autumn (these are not idle facts but serve to complicate Keats's already complex conclusion in important ways) — in addition to this there is also a deeper issue, touching on a matter that may be said to contradict even the bird-lore I have just culled from observation. *Will* the poem look very different in the sad aftermath of global warming? I think that, supposing there is then anyone around to read it, the poem will in fact look much the same, or perhaps even better. The identity of the swallows is not comprised in their real present existence, and certainly not in an exact description of their habits (though it is fostered by the impression of exactitude), but in their having been realized, as fictitious birds might be, as a species that exists at present; and this form of identity if anything would gain in poignancy, I am sorry to say, in ways foreseen by the poem itself, from the imposition of pastness by extinction. (Why does Bate speak of "the certainty of the following spring's return"? Isn't Shelley, insofar as even he is certain, writing about the need for a violent wind during that same autumn?) Just so, on the awful day when all the trees are gone and we shall finally be entitled to say, *pace* Liu, "There is no nature" (*Sense of History,* 56), just then and not before, if some of us survive, we will realize, concerning what de Man called "the ontology of the poetic" in a passage cited by Bate (104), that poetry is an epitaph, not a landscape. Taking his turn with the Boy of Winander episode, Bate writes: "Let us not forget that it is . . . about a boy alone by a lake at dusk blowing mimic hootings to unseen owls. Which are there to answer him" (115). And then to stop.[26]

I should like once more to compare the position I have been taking with that of de Man on Wordsworth in order to show where I differ:

The miracle of Wordsworth's figural diction is that, by stating its own pre-
cariousness so to speak face to face, without aesthetic evasion, it recovers the
totality of the phenomenal world of sky and earth and thus, in a deeper sense
than any color or melody could achieve, recovers the aesthetic in the process
of its refusal. (*The Rhetoric of Romanticism*, 87)

"Aesthetic" is a difficult, evermore important word in de Man's later work that
I shall not attempt to unravel. Here, though, clearly enough, it is aligned with
"totality," the Kantian "purposive, not purposeful" manifold which criticism
has learned to call an "evasion" because it suspends historical engagement.
The "refusal" de Man speaks of is Wordsworth's insistence that all phenome-
nality without exception is in fact purpose*ful*, while the return of the aesthetic
is the all-inclusiveness of this very insistence, making the realized phenomenal
world a world-picture or song of the earth after all. It seems to me that de
Man's sense of a Wordsworthian aesthetic is after all very close to an ecology,
and results in a view of Wordsworth that surprisingly resembles Bate's. It
turns, I believe, on the failure to distinguish between *totality* — the comprehen-
sive manifold or "multëity in unity" dear to Coleridge of which, in my view,
there is very little in Wordsworth — and *unity*, unity to which the presence or
absence of multëity is immaterial, which I take to be Wordsworth's essential
subject.

Undoubtedly this is a fine point of distinction on which all too much may
depend. Where, for example, does this eloquent passage in Alfred North
Whitehead, so impressively evocative of Wordsworth, fall between totality
and unity?

Of course he recognizes, what no one doubts, that in some sense living things
are different from lifeless things. But that is not his main point. It is the
brooding presence in the hills which haunts him. His theme is nature *insolido*,
that is to say, he dwells on that mysterious presence of surrounding things,
which imposes itself on any separate element that we set up as an individual
for its own sake.[27]

It falls, I would say, on the side of unity, the mysterious presence obtruding itself
on the poet as the being of beings. Karl Kroeber, in a 1974 article called " 'Home
at Grasmere': Ecological Holiness" (*PMLA* 89), acknowledged by Bate as his
forerunner in the field, offers comparable conflations of terms that I am less
confident of enlisting in my cause. Kroeber sees Wordsworth's indifference to
environmental prettiness (the "natural beauty" that apparently makes some
ecosystems worthier than others) placed in the service of an all-embracing
"ecological unity," or, again, of "wholeness," and that sounds like the return of

the aesthetic in the form of totality; but in saying that Wordsworth makes "the finest poetry out of the commonest and most everyday *beingness,* merely 'what we are,'" Kroeber, with his Native American–influenced perspective on dwelling in the presence of the inanimate, decidedly does not look forward to a "green" criticism. Indeed, perhaps it is finally a question whether the nature poetry of Wordsworth is green or *gray;* and critical insight should perhaps be commended in proportion as it serves to remind us that "rocks and stones" make up two-thirds of the Wordsworthian cosmos, the other third being Lucy — "thing" that she once seemed and now is — and the trees.[28]

An offensive, in some ways authentically Thoreauvian article in the *Harvard Alumni Magazine* shows very clearly what happens when environmentalism becomes selective.[29] The author contrasts a beach that is difficult of access, hence frequented by gracefully rugged people (a "kayak elite" in no-nonsense clothes carrying a minimum of gear), with a nearby public beach frequented by ordinary, unattuned people with all their obtrusive equipment ("apparatus of happiness," Jane Austen called it in *Emma,* satirically yet not without fondness). The author implies that his "kayak elite" is classless, as though the outdoorsy shabby gentility he evokes for his already-converted audience were not the very essence of patrician, quiet-money New England. Of course outsiders can join this class, just as outsiders can rise or sink to any other American class; but the snobbery and exclusiveness of each and every class (the public beach crowd with its gas barbecues and jet-skis knows how to sneer back at the narrow Yankee soul) remains always the key sign of the false secondary power whereby we multiply distinctions.

Hence although there have certainly been plenty of occasions on which what Bate calls the "red" criticism of the eighties has been simply malapropos, a breach of scale, there is one purpose for which red criticism is evidently still needed, and that is the demystification of green criticism. Consider this startling distinction without a difference in Bate:

> Wordsworth's concern for the preservation of the Lakes has often been put down to a selfish desire to keep away artisan day trippers from Manchester. But in his 1844 letters to the *Morning Post* concerning the projected Kendal and Windermere Railway, Wordsworth's principal objection was to large-scale organized Sunday outings. . . . It is precisely this problem of *mass* tourism that threatens the Lake District today. (*Romantic Ecology,* 50)

Indeed, by the 1840s, Wordsworth *was* an Environmentalist "considering," as Bate says, "the evolving and increasingly disruptive influence of man on his environment" (ibid., 45) and more and more concerned to select his human and nonhuman company during the successive editions of the *Guide to the Lakes* that Bate documents. "Is then no nook of English ground secure / From rash assault?" he enquires in the sonnet published with his 1844 letters against the Kendal and Windermere Railway, ranging the "pausing traveller" of his early poems and the small yeoman landowner with his "paternal fields" over against "the false utilitarian lure" of mechanized mass tourism — including, needless to say, the artisan day trippers. Keep "nature" hard to reach, and only the right people will make themselves at home in it, leaving everyone else stranded in environmental limbo.

By contrast, in *Home at Grasmere,* which is one of the relatively few early poems that Bate has or can have much to say about, Wordsworth writes that it takes all kinds: "I came not dreaming of unruffled life, / Untainted manners" (MS. B, 428–29). This more forgiving view points to inclusive unity rather than any subtly exclusive totalization ("aesthetization") of the natural. "Bleak season was it" when the poet and his entourage arrived (218); he and Dorothy identify with a pair of swans that chose arbitrarily to live in Grasmere Vale despite lacking roots there and may have been shot — hard pastoral indeed! — by a thoughtless shepherd (cf. 322–56); the un-self-consciousness of "sensation" and natural want among "untutored shepherds" is not "unhallowed" (cf. 665–72); and the spirit of leveling first noticed by Hazlitt here as elsewhere promotes ontic equality:

> I begin
> Already to inscribe upon my heart
> A liking for the small grey Horse that bears
> The paralytic Man; I know the ass
> On which the Cripple in the Quarry maimed
> Rides to and fro (723–28).

This is not the author of the *Guide to the Lakes* but the earlier poet moved by intimations of somatism, attending to the human creatures Alan Bewell has called "marginals,"[30] discovering and delineating the human by feeling tentatively around the edges of humanity in that moment of faint sentience, never far from bedrock, where death and life graze each other.

That is the moment within which Wordsworth imagines himself to be embraced in the much-contested first verse paragraph of "Tintern Abbey," and indeed in the whole poem ("If I should be where I no more can hear / Thy voice"). This moment calls, in my view, for a criticism that is neither red nor green but gray, not dull gray but gleaming at times the way rocks, depending how you look at them, gleam at times. The "soft inland murmur," the thought of "more deep seclusion," the poet's "repose" under a dark tree from which he can view other "plots" — these are indications that the speaker is on the extreme verge of life, which is also of course to say (and here red criticism pounces) of social existence. All social forms, including the notoriously "repressed" village charcoal burners and homeless persons in the Abbey a few miles distant, are reduced, leveled, to that mode of being in which the aestheticized features of their distinctness — pastoral farms, beauteous forms — vanish. Orchards hard to distinguish from groves and copses, hedge-rows hardly hedge-rows: all specificity of cultivation and habitation is obscured by the ubiquitous monotony of green to the point of being, at most, an "uncertain notice."[31] It is here that, "the breath of this corporeal frame / And even the motion of our human blood / Almost suspended, we are laid asleep / In body." The burthen of the mystery is *not explained,* Wordsworth never says that it was or is; he only says that it is "lightened," meaning that in the ontic moment it no longer seems to matter that the world is "unintelligible." Or so the "philosophic calm" of Wordsworth's nature poetry appears, in any case, from the standpoint of a stone-colored criticism.[32]

# 5

## The Novelty of Wordsworth's Earliest Poems

Wordsworth scholarship has not ignored his earliest poems, which it is not improper to call juvenilia. The long poems especially have always been read with interest, *The Vale of Esthwaite* (1787) and *An Evening Walk* (1787–89) as decent if belated contributions to the stroll or *Spaziergang* tradition stretching from Thomson to Cowper with a dollop stirred in of equally retrograde horror-gothic, and *Descriptive Sketches* (1793) as a rehearsal for *Prelude* 6. The *Vale* too anticipates a Spot of Time, "Waiting for Horses," while *An Evening Walk* gains biographical and even literary interest as a first address to Dorothy. Yet there appears to have been a kind of quiet consensus that even if we consider these poems apprentice efforts there is not much point in looking in them—as one looks in Keats's *Endymion*—for anticipations of later work, at least apart from the interest in rural and mountainous scenery that was by then traditional. Writing to Anne Taylor in 1801, Wordsworth appears to share this judgment. Although "they contain many new images, and vigorous lines," "they would perhaps interest you, by showing how very widely different my former opinions must have been from those which I hold at present."[1] And so we have come to view these poems much as Wordsworth himself appears to have viewed them—as documents necessary to preserve if the record is to be complete; and because to this end Wordsworth meticulously and repeatedly revised them, we have benefited greatly from the editorial labors of James Averill and Eric Birdsall.[2] It goes almost without saying that the one critic who has read these poems as faint anticipations of important things to come is Geoffrey Hartman, who discerns even in the fragmentary plot of the *Vale*, and in the other very early poems, an exploration of "the Mind of the Poet" in its mood swings.[3]

I follow Hartman, then, in arguing that Wordsworth's originality already surfaces in these poems, while admitting willingly enough that it is at most a flickering presence. It is hard to think of any eighteenth-century literary conventions — including fictional conventions — that cannot be found in the poems written by Wordsworth between 1787 and 1793. Surely there's no libertinism, one supposes; yet in the *Descriptive Sketches* the prurience of Wordsworth's interest in the girls along the way is scarcely furtive. The Annette Vallon with whom Wordsworth played a character out of Fielding or Laclos has not yet conveniently disappeared into the story of Vaudracour and Julia. I shall return in a moment to note the interest of Wordsworth's early eroticism; but apart from an eventual nod to *The Vicar of Wakefield*, my interest here is not in those conventions that one might call novelistic but is confined to the loco-descriptive conventions of topographical poetry and of the whole Wartonian canon — the gothic and penseroso effects one finds everywhere from Thomson and Lyttelton to Beattie and Charlotte Smith. I want to argue that even at a time when Wordsworth retains most of the manner and vocabulary of his predecessors, he is already experimenting with a strikingly new way of thinking about nature.

In a word, he appears from his first poetic efforts to have felt that nature becomes even more astonishing if you give up the belief that you can read it like a book. This is easy to demonstrate in the poetry of Wordsworth's so-called Great Decade — the Arab in the Dream of *Prelude* 5 is a maniac resembling Don Quixote precisely because he thinks a stone and a shell are books — but it is rather less easy to show in seemingly rearguard efforts like *The Vale of Esthwaite, An Evening Walk, Descriptive Sketches*, and even *Salisbury Plain*, where moralizing emblems and anthropocentric landscape moods continue to appear. Yet it is worth the effort, because discovering what is new in these poems can help to show why it is so important to Wordsworth, at the period of their composition, that he become a poet. That is to say: If he kept plugging away at verse-writing — and the effort just to keep going is sometimes even more visibly painful than it is in Keats's four thousand lines — it was not just to avoid getting a job. Even the biographers seem half inclined to this last reduction, influenced by the equivocal, duty-haunted letters to his sister during the walking tour with Jones, and of course by the sheepish "hope, that prudence could not then approve, / That clung to nature with a truant's love" in *Descrip-*

*tive Sketches* (43–44). This self-censure appears late, but in *The Prelude* the jaunt is called "an open slight / Of College cares and study" (VI, 342–43).

Recent, skeptically historicist work on Wordsworth's "profession" as poet by Thomas Pfau, Clifford Siskin, and others in effect discredits the notion that Wordsworth's vocation was spontaneous, finding instead various ways of arguing that poetry *was* a job, and that Wordsworth was one of those responsible for making it one.[4] Perhaps one might have it both ways. After all, even though we can never know whether Wordsworth actually had a "morning of election" ("one particular hour"), there is something about the very imprecision with which that incident is explained in *The Prelude* that makes it credible — one of the beauties of pure fiction by contrast being that incidents are typically chosen because they have intelligible causes. A look at the episode in Book IV may help us toward the business of the present chapter. It took place, Wordsworth indicates, shortly before *An Evening Walk* was composed. The memory of it "rises up," like the huge cliff, the drowned man, the imagination in Book VI — in short like nearly every obstacle that constitutes a "Spot of Time." During his first summer home from college, feeling a slightly guilty condescension toward his boyhood surroundings and acquaintances, Wordsworth goes to a local dance and dances all night. The eroticism that for some reason most readers — notably excepting F. W. Bateson and Kenneth Johnston[5] — prefer to ignore in Wordsworth, even after Beth Darlington's publication of the correspondence with his wife, is here in full view, with its "[s]light shocks of young love-liking interspersed / That mounted up like joy into the head, / And tingled through the veins" (1805, IV, 325–27). What follows is well known: the walk home during a glorious sunrise, moving Wordsworth to realize that he was "a dedicated spirit." The conjunction of the eroticized dance with the conversion experience is what places Wordsworth's confessional autobiography most squarely in the company of Augustine's (from priapism to the *tolle lege*), Rousseau's (*Maman*'s spanking or Marion's ribbon inspiring introspection, the desire "to tell everything"), and Proust's (his mother's kiss and the *madeleine*), and makes him seem proto-Freudian: vocation is sublimation.

But vocation for what? Erotic sensation, not a directed passion but a simple symptom of adolescence which indiscriminately "tingled through the veins" and proceeded — in a prolepsis of the moment of sublimation — "up like joy into the head" — erotic sensation here translates itself during the homeward walk into an indiscriminate sense of joy abroad in the natural world, at least in the 1805 version:

The sea was laughing at a distance; all
The solid mountains were as bright as clouds —

with "all the sweetness of a common dawn" that "[w]as" in the foreground (333–37). "Was," "were": these verbs, objects of attack in modern writing manuals, just proclaim existence; they neither locate nor distinguish among the things that exist. This indiscriminateness is what is captured so brilliantly by William Empson in his 1940 radio talk emphasizing the difference between the 1805 and 1850 versions of the morning's "memorable pomp" (everything Empson says about the 1850 changes he disapproves of, most of them complex, stationing verbs, is to the point, but I must excerpt):

> In the new [1850] lines Wordsworth is painting a picture . . . he is giving a clear account of it. You see how cold this makes him; he is an expert on views of mountains. . . . The idea that pushing in more facts *about the view* makes the lines more interesting is simply an error. . . . [In 1850,] what *came up* was the sun, and the change puts your attention onto the sun. Possibly it was only the sun, not the morning in general, who was a ruler and *magnificent*. At any rate the sea *lay* laughing; it was flat on its back. It had no authority against the sun. . . . And then the mountains *shone*; they gave out light. So it is clear that they gave back light from the first rays of the sun. . . . They were not bright in themselves. They were only giving back light from the sun. So the old shock of surprise in *solid* and *bright* is quite gone. There is no secret about the morning. It was the *sun* that was making things bright. This is quite clear now that Wordsworth has given us all the details.[6]

This wonderful reading, which puts Strunk and White's *Manual of Style* in its place better than any other argument I know, out-Derridas Derrida while explaining why Wordsworth at his best in 1805 is *not* guilty of recycling the successive god-terms of Western metaphysics: Empson shows that the 1850 revisions turn a site of indiscriminate joy into an intelligible symbol, a heliocentric reflection of enlightened despotism or human reason. The 1850 passage is still splendid, but it loses track of the smooth sublimation (corresponding in adolescence to that of the blest infant babe at his mother's breast) from indiscriminate eroticism to indiscriminate *Naturgefühl*: by 1850 the vocation of a poet has become the vocation of a philosopher, humanist, or theologian.

I want to consider a few passages and texts in which I think I can detect Wordsworth subverting the book of nature *topos* from within, bolstering my claim at times by pointing toward comparable but more overt subversive moments in the later work, and concluding with some remarks on "Lines Left upon a Seat in a Yew-Tree," a poem of 1797 that was begun in 1787. It may be helpful to say in advance that I don't think one finds a comparable doubt about nature's legibility in Coleridge. In "The Eolian Harp," for example, Coleridge is not quite content with the moralizing epithets of the opening lines ("Meet emblems they of innocence and love!" "such should wisdom be"), and risks the disapproval of his new wife by stretching toward a daring organicist pantheism ("What if all of animated nature / Be but organic harps diversely fram'd?"). There is novelty in this, to be sure, but Coleridge's speculation does not abandon the idea — rather it develops it — that the natural world is intelligibly meaningful. This is the point of W. K. Wimsatt's great essay on the structure of the romantic nature image. By contrasting a sonnet of Bowles with a sonnet of Coleridge, Wimsatt shows how the affinity between nature and the imagination ceases to be emblematic and becomes organic in the Coleridgean strain of romanticism (with clear implications for the atomization of ideas about genre), but he does not go on to show that something different happens in Wordsworth.[7]

I think it does, and in trying to get at what it is I shall single out three conventions, reserving the question of moral emblems and personifications for my conclusion. These conventions are: the landscape of horror-gothic, the charmed space, and the crepuscular moment. But first one may ask why the youthful Wordsworth clings to all these conventions if he evinces a discernible skepticism about them. A good part of it is that he is still insecure about the reader's expectations. Whatever his personal understanding of nature, he does not yet believe that the rural scene is auratic enough to hold the reader's attention without the introduction of human or supernatural incident. Whereas later, in "Simon Lee," he will warn the reader that although a story may be conventionally expected "there is no tale" to be attached to the bare circumstances of this lyrical ballad, confirming in this the revolutionary pronouncement in his "Preface" that feeling gives importance to action and situation, not the other way around — whereas, that is, Wordsworth's hostility to colorful narrative is fully declared by 1798, the fragmentary poem of 1787 called *The Vale of Esthwaite* requires such narrative and says as much. Hoping in adulthood to fix his "feeble gaze" on "Nature's page" "As on a Book," he recalls that

> . . . while I wandered round the vale
> [From] every rock would 'hang a tale.' (493, 496, 505–06)

And indeed the poem is full of tales, especially those related in the Collins manner to the "forms of Fear" (557) by way of Helen Maria Williams (*Irregular Fragments*) — all vying with the "Invocation. To Horror" written by Anna Matilda in the same year.

Horror-gothic, to start then with that, has an unusual destiny in Wordsworth. We make much, and rightly so, of the "visionary dreariness," as he calls it, that characterizes the Spots of Time and other landscapes in *The Prelude*. Starting with A. C. Bradley, a succession of commentators has noticed in Wordsworth a phenomenology of blankness, an emptying out of natural plenitude featuring the bare, the bleak, the stark, the naked, the singleness and solitude of things. Marmaduke even when racked with guilt remains fascinated by "the Ordeal / Of the bleak Waste" (Act V, 2235–36) — as though it were the dark night through one passed en route to an oracle or to spiritual enlightenment — to which he has consigned Herbert in *The Borderers*. In the argument of the present book I myself associate this minimalist recourse of the imagination with what I call the "mineral" or bedrock basis of ontology in Wordsworth, the pervasiveness of the nonhuman even in the human that precludes any and all imputation of anthropomorphic significance to the object-world. Yet it goes unmentioned in the Bradleyan tradition, to which the "Yale School" commentators on Wordsworth belong, that this denuded landscape has its origin in horror-gothic. Take this fragment from MS. A of *The Vale of Esthwaite*:

> Hig[h] from a sable Steep I saw
> A dark and dreary vale below,
> And through it a river [something or other]
> In sleepy horror heav'd along.

We are moving from one mode to another, and sure enough, within a line or two all hell breaks loose:

> And on each sable rock was seen
> A form of wild terrific mien.
> Ha! That is hell-born Murder nigh
> With haggard, half-reverted eye
>
> .  .  .  .  .  .  .  .  .  .
>
> And Suicide with savage glance, [etc.]

In *The Prelude*, a landscape like this brings the child face to face with a moldering gibbet that stands proxy not for Murder but for a murderer; yet plainly there the connection between bedrock and death is generalized as a form of retrospective ontic awareness. I would suggest that the sable Steep and the dreary vale just cited, evoking the situation of Gray's "The Bard," are already candidates for this depersonifying form of perception, dragged back to overheated particularity by fear of the literary unknown. Just so, nature's obscure admonitions to the erring child, featured in the series of Spots in *Prelude* 1, taking the form of "breathings," "giant forms," and the like, still bear traces of the horror-gothic machinery one finds in passages like this one:

> Now hollow sounding all around I hear
> Deep murmurings creep upon my ear;
> No more the wild shrieks of the storm
> Drive to its cell the startling worm. (232–35)

Just so, the enigmatic "waiting for horses" Spot of *Prelude* 11, where the child in a dreary landscape later feels obscurely that his father's ensuing death has punished him for having been too eager to go home, is anticipated in some detail by these quite spirited lines from *The Vale of Esthwaite*:

> One Evening when the wintry blast
> Through the sharp Hawthorn whistling passed
> And the poor flocks, all pinched with cold
> Sad-drooping sought the mountain fold
> Long, long, upon yon steepy rock
> Alone, I bore the bitter shock;
> Long, long, my swimming eyes did roam
> For little Horse to bear me home,
> To bear me — what avails my tear?
> To sorrow o'er a father's bier. (427–36)

Once again, the connection between landscape and result is not a necessary or obvious one. As a final case in point, consider these stanzas of the 1795 *Adventures on Salisbury Plain*, when in the vicinity of Stonehenge, after much mood building about druid sacrifice, the returned conscript guilty of manslaughter "saw upon a gibbet high / A human body that in irons swang." All familiar enough, but by the next stanza the vagrant's fantasy has taken a strange turn that once again can only be rationalized as part of an overarching reflection on the mineral basis of existence, which in itself remains horrifying as long as it accompanies the shock of recognition: "The stones, as if to sweep him from the day, / Roll'd at his back along the living plain." The mineral world here still appears threatening, an Ordeal of the bleak Waste, but it points toward the time when it will be the cornerstone of Wordsworth's ontology. Something of these rolling rocks remains in the rocks and stones and trees that are rolled round with Lucy in earth's diurnal course, and likewise in the giddy moment that closes the Skating episode of *Prelude* 1, when "the solitary cliffs / Wheeled by me — even as if the earth had rolled / With visible motion her diurnal round!" (1805, I, 484–86).

The second transformed convention on which I wish to focus, using the wheeling about in such passages as a bridge, is the disenchantment even by the early Wordsworth of the charmed clearings or other spaces, themselves descended from the bowers of romance, in the Wartonian ode. The most memorable of these is in Akenside's "Ode to the Evening Star." The distraught speaker, having lost his Olympia, stumbles through a long walk, guided now by the nightingale, now by the evening star, until he comes to a clearing — "See the green space!" — which has the vaguely epiphanic quality of a nativity scene: "The stars shine out: the forest bends: / The wakeful heifers gaze."[8] This remarkable moment has already to some extent escaped the confines of convention, but Wordsworth makes its provenance even more enigmatic in a sonnet of perhaps as early as 1788 (the title, "Written in Very Early Youth," would seem thus to exaggerate, but not by a great deal):

> Calm is all nature as a resting wheel,
> The kine are couched upon the dewy grass;
> The horse alone, seen dimly as I pass,
> Is cropping audibly his later meal;
> Dark is the ground; a slumber seems to steal
> O'er vale, and mountain, and the starless sky.
> Now, in this blank of things, a harmony,
> Home-felt, and home-created, comes to heal
> That grief for which the senses still supply
> Fresh food; for only then, when memory
> Is hushed, am I at rest. My Friends! Restrain
> Those busy cares that would allay my pain;
> Oh! Leave me to myself, nor let me feel
> The officious touch that makes me droop again.

In the first line, which is not in the 1788 MS. D11 but was arguably composed as early as 1791,[9] the resting wheel suspends earth's diurnal course even as it calls our attention to it. It is like the still point of the turning world in Eliot's "Burnt Norton," even as it looks back to the sacred space suspending time in Akenside's clearing. The kine are couched, as in Akenside, but they don't gaze at anything, as no nativity is shadowed forth. The thoughtlessly chewing horse comes from Lady Winchelsea's "Nocturnal Rêverie," but more closely anticipates the torturer's horse scratching his innocent behind against a tree in Auden: although the human world may be fraught with emotion, the horse heals suffering not because it is a redemptive symbol of any kind (it can scarcely even be seen) but because it is just a horse, as in Randall Jarrell's "[t]he mare he rides crops herbs beside a skull." This is the mood both of a Lucy poem — "a slumber seems to steal" — and of *The Prelude*, where "this blank of things" (again, probably 1791) is all the significance that the semantically underdetermined Spots of Time can finally convey. Nature is reduced to blankness, both in the slumber of consciousness and in the world, and fixed as a spot of time by "[n]ow," the stationing convention (*iam . . . iam*) that the whole loco-descriptive tradition, especially the evening or serenade poem, derives from Latin examples.[10] We find Keats still using this convention to wonderful effect in "To Autumn," but Wordsworth would soon set it aside as "poetic diction."

The work done by this "now" is no less for that the work of a spot of time.

Here, however, insignificance is not just insignificance; it is the kind of blankness, rather, which happily corresponds to and induces a wished-for psychological state, obliviousness, when "memory / Is hushed." Hence the very absence of pathetic fallacy in the creatures and objects that make up the scene is itself a pathetic fallacy, creating a suitable setting, more poetical than a bottle of whisky but no less purposeful, for the amnesia into which the speaker hopes to escape from his troubles. The conventionally elegiac grief to which the sestet is devoted (perhaps the speaker too has lost his Olympia!) is still a necessary foil for what Wordsworth has encountered that is of interest in this scene; but a further attenuation of Akenside's already unusual fragility of meaning has been accomplished, and what was epiphanic now becomes, at most, ontophanic. That is what Wordsworth wants to say, and would say if this or a similar moment were evoked as a *Prelude* Spot; it is already what interests him most in nature, but he has not yet found a vehicle for his interest, hence writes the kind of nature walk sonnet written by Bowles, Smith, or Williams, in which anything notable in the natural world has its objective correlative in human thought or feeling — the kind of nature poetry, in short, with which a Jeffrey can be at peace. What is new in Wordsworth at this early point is the *prominence* given to "this blank of things" and its effect on consciousness. He seems to feel the awkwardness of the conventional tie-in, and in fact tries to avert it by adding an interesting subtlety in the chiastic contrast between the horse's stupefying "later meal" and the awakening "fresh food" of memory, showing thereby how hard it is after all to achieve a blank state of mind, and thus broadening rather than narrowing the gap between animal and human consciousness in accordance with Enlightenment thought.

I turn now to a third convention, already present in the evening scene of the sonnet, which I shall call the crepuscular. This is the moment in which the chiaroscuro of a picturesque scene darkens to obscurity, as at the beginning of Gray's Elegy, where the ploughman toiling o'er the lea "leaves the world to darkness and to me," and "[n]ow fades the glimmering landscape on the sight." Again, as with Akenside, arguably the genius of Gray here anticipates Wordsworth: the space for meditation cleared by the disappearance of difference in the natural world is itself the space in which the suspension of differential consciousness is most naturally confronted. But consider what Wordsworth does with the crepuscular convention in the following 1794 *Evening Walk* passage:

> How pleasant, as the sun declines, to view
> The total landscape change in form and hue!
> Here, vanish, as in mist before a flood

Of bright obscurity, hill, lawn, and wood;
These objects, by the searching [beams] betrayed,
Come forth, and here retire in purple shade;
Even the white birches' stems, the cottage white,
Soften the glare [before the mellow light;
The skiffs, at anchor where with umbrage wide
Yon chestnuts half the latticed boathouse hide,]
Shed from their sides, that face the sun's slant beam,
Strong flakes of radiance on the tremulous stream:
Raised by yon traveling flock, a dusty cloud
Mounts from the road, and spreads its moving shroud;
The shepherd, all-involved in wreaths of fire,
Now shows a shadowy speck, and now is lost intire. (155–70)

Observe that there are just too many painterly light effects in this notional ekphrasis, with its conventional "here . . . there" spatializations corresponding to the "now . . . now" of the landscape in time. The painting one thinks one sees is somewhere between the homely detail of genre scenes from Rubens to Gainsborough or Ruisdael and the more surface-oriented white flecks of future Constables; yet no painter could keep all of it in view, and it would surely be a challenge to see the boathouse peeping through the shade. No wonder the scene lapses into sound and the dust that seems like the smoke of a fire — which last will appear in "Tintern Abbey" as an "uncertain notice." It is this excess of detail that Wordsworth edits out in his revision of 1820. By that time, interestingly, with Beaumont's more or less approving approbation he would probably have seen some of Constable's Stour Valley six-footers. These strikingly resemble the 1793 lines in both subject matter and handling, yet Wordsworth in view of his simplifying revisions would seem not to have wanted anyone to notice the similarity.

Again, as with horror-gothic, a conventional motive masks an emerging preoccupation. In this case, Wordsworth's interest in the picturesque, which peaked, he tells us, during his period of disillusionment after the Terror, and which lingered as a prosaic concern in his landscaping projects and in the *Guide to the Lakes*, half-conceals his growing ontological interest in indistinctness. Much of value has been written about Wordsworth and the picturesque, as about his resemblance to Constable,[11] but I feel that as an emphasis or explanatory key these topics can become misleading. We know Constable to have been influenced by the picturesque sketches and theory of William Gilpin and others in his youth, as was the Wordsworth who had Gilpin's Tour of the Wye in his pocket as late as 1798 when visiting Tintern Abbey. Yet when Constable realizes his own style, say around 1812 or 1813, it is his business to retain the subject matter and techniques of the picturesque while transforming them. During the eighteenth century, the visual cant of the picturesque per-vaded influences as diverse as those of Rubens and Claude, but it was par-ticularly associated with the "Dutch" and their alleged preoccupation with boors and boorish subject matter. In English genre paintings the picturesque lent itself to the idealization of peasant life without ceasing to seem Dutch. All this Constable takes over, with Gainsborough's idealizing agenda intact, at least according to the school of John Barrell, but Barrell himself is brought up short by something: Constable's peasants, bargemen, and lock-keepers, with a notable ploughman of 1814, seem utterly absorbed in their work (Barrell complains that they lack the independence of will to wish for a rest or a visit to the pub), and they are expressionless, almost without faces.[12] The scenes of rural labor in which they move are as detailed as any older "barnyard scene" could be, yet there is in them, and in the figures, a preoccupation with the brushed surface that looks forward to Courbet, who boasted that he could paint a woodpile without knowing what it was, rather than back to Gains-borough or the Dutch. The picturesque is still visible ("View of Dedham" has a "Dutch" dung-heap in the foreground), but it now means "painterly" rather than being, say, arranged in a picture for the sake of demographic voyeurism or moral sentiment. Such is the novelty of Constable.

This is not to deny that Constable's depicted environs are nostalgic vehicles for social conservatism. Certainly they are, as he knew and said; and thus far of course one is safe to say the same about Wordsworth's *Excursion* of the same period, however one may disagree about the social investment of his earlier work. Nonetheless, Wordsworth and Constable resemble each other most in *having* transformed the picturesque, not in any similarity between their transformations. It is not just that they are drawn to a different body of imagery, although that is part of it: Constable was left cold by the lack of human cultivation in the Lake District—where his dutiful early sketches were indeed uninspired—and his art is as georgic as Wordsworth's is pastoral. What still needs emphasis, rather, is that by the mid-1790s Wordsworth took a minimalist approach to imagery of any kind. He is a nature poet, yes, but not a botanizing nature poet like Coleridge or a stroller with a Claude glass like the Thomson of *Spring*. Almost any natural description by Coleridge writing blank verse is richer in closely observed detail, more "organic," than what one usually finds in Wordsworth's blank verse. Not that Wordsworth is incapable of writing this way—there are Coleridgean moments in, for example, the "Poems on the Naming of Places"—but his habit of notation is typically indexical rather than descriptive. "There is a tree, of many, one" may seem unfair to single out, but what poet is there whose most memorable passages are likely to begin with "there was" or "is"? We both know what it looks like; he says to the reader, I just want to tell you that it is there.

To return then to Wordsworth's earliest work, once again we find a convention masking a novel attitude. The picturesque is there in plenty, and Wordsworth is quite excited about giving his descriptive powers free reign, pointing out decades later to Isabella Fenwick that the swan passage in *An Evening Walk* — "He swells his lifted chest, and backward flings / His bridling neck between his tow'ring wings" (1793, 201–02) — was based on "daily opportunities I had of observing their habits."[13] But as we have seen, and as many other passages could illustrate, his characteristic method as a scene painter is to provide a copious imagery which he then covers up, either by overburdening the mind's eye or with mist, dust, smoke, glare, or encroaching darkness. The loco-descriptive juvenilia are full of such compromises between the picturesque and the indistinct, all still continuously indebted to the opening and vocabulary of Gray's Elegy:

> hills o'er hills in gradual pride
> That swelled along the upland's side
> From the blunt baffled Vision pass
> And melt into one gloomy mass. (*Vale*, 113–16)

> Now o'er the eastern hill, where Darkness broods
> O'er all its vanished dells, and lawns, and woods;
> Where but a mass of shade the sight can trace,
> [The moon] lifts in silence up her lovely face.
> (*Evening Walk*, 1793, 399–402)

In "Tintern Abbey," with its "thoughts of more deep seclusion" and repose in a dark place surrounded by "plots," the painting that overlies the picturesque scene is solid green, not a dazzle of light effects. Everything you think you can see is "clad in one green hue," a green Malevitch or Ad Reinhardt. The orchard-tufts are un-orchard-like because their unripe fruits are green, hence they "lose themselves / 'Mid groves and copses." The hedge-rows are hardly hedge-rows, but just more sportive wood run wild, and the pastoral farms, which you think you can see, are likewise "green to the very door." And like Gray's ploughman or the shepherd of *Evening Walk*, there may or may not be a vagrant dweller — strange liminalizing oxymoron — buried under the green. As pastoral disappears with difference itself, the world is left to darkness and to the speaker until he belatedly and as it were posthumously discovers his interlocutor — Dorothy, to whom *Evening Walk* is also addressed. In the 1820 revision of the *Evening Walk* passage quoted above (ll. 155–70), perhaps with the influence of that verse paragraph intervening, the dwindling sunset is reinforced by mist and by the shroud of a dusty cloud, effacing "hill, lawn, and wood," until the shepherd, like Gray's ploughman, "now is lost entire." A scene is depicted in vivid detail for the purpose of showing that it is invisible, as if to say, underlying the glory of difference there remains the sameness of being.

I have suggested that even in his apprentice work Wordsworth modifies loco-descriptive conventions until they become a critique of difference, of that "false secondary power," as he calls it in *The Prelude*, "by which / In weakness we create distinctions, then / Deem that our puny boundaries are things / Which we perceive, and not which we have made." In particular what will soon cease to be legible in the book of nature is the chief stock in trade of traditional loco-description, the *moralisation* of the *paysage*. But this rationale for description is something without which at first Wordsworth would most feel the nakedness of his vocation. He wants to talk about nature: how can he justify this if nature is not, as his loco-descriptive predecessors appeared to believe, a repository of moral emblems? Still, in 1793 he is closer to his characteristic outlook than in the 1836 edition, when he dutifully moralizes the swan passage just cited above, "The eye that marks the gliding creature sees / How graceful, pride can be, and how majestic, ease" (219–20). Even then he quickly returns, as though in some private embarrassment, to the close observation of the swans' habits of movement, amplified further by the Fenwick note. In 1787, though, moralizing is reinforced by the still more egregious artifice of personification: "Pity, Autumn of the heart," summer, "[t]he laughing landscape of the breast," and "the long Winter of the poor" give us a brief but nicely varied tour through Thomson in a passage from *The Vale of Esthwaite* (140, 146, 152).

*Descriptive Sketches*, the poem on the first Continental walking tour with Robert Jones composed 1791–93 and oft-revised, is not necessarily more readable than the earlier long poems, but it is more polished, and while it is still far from recognizably "Wordsworthian," the conventions I have been discussing in this chapter are handled in a more subtle way than hitherto. Much of the eighteenth century breathes through it, of course (the rhymed couplets thud against the ear despite frequent enjambments), especially when the hard pastoral Liberty *topoi* surrounding the Happy Swiss are passed in review. But this sort of poem was far from obsolete in its time, and compares more closely with later poems like Rogers's *Italy* or Byron's *Childe Harold's Pilgrimage* than with earlier poems of continental travel—which are in any case not numerous, the philosophical and epistolary modes in prose favored by Montesquieu, Gray, and Wollstonecraft having been considered more congenial for travel writing. Indeed, Wordsworth's letters to his sister during this same tour in some ways resemble Gray's letters written in the same regions. "The wild, romantic scenes of Switzerland have not yet been celebrated by an English poet," writes *The Critical Review* of 1793 in announcing Wordsworth's poem, but then pronounces it a failure.[14] The choice of verse for writing of this kind is not easy, and anyone who reads the whole of *Prelude* 6 attentively (not rushing forward, that is, to the Simplon sequence) will find that for all the superiority of its blank verse the more selective travelogue of 1804–05 still passes through genre-imposed *longueurs* like those of *Descriptive Sketches*.

In a travelogue, whether in verse or prose, one did not typically moralize the landscape itself but paused from description here and there to reflect on historical associations, local habits, or national characters (perhaps stressing either the compatibility or the incompatibility of inhabitants with their setting), and sometimes on the human condition in general, at which point personification was likely to play a role. All of these generic requirements are met by Wordsworth in *Descriptive Sketches*. Readers of *Childe Harold* will find the following passage familiar (in the ensuing discussion I quote from the 1793 text unless otherwise noted):

> Say, who, by thinking on Canadian hills,
> Or wild Aosta lulled by Alpine rills,
> On Zutphen's plain; or where the softened gaze
> The old grey stones the plaided chief surveys,
> Can guess the high resolve, the cherished pain
> Of him whom passion rivets to the plain,
> Where breathed the gale that caught Wolfe's happiest sigh,
> And the last sun-beam fell on Bayard's eye,
> Where bleeding Sydney from the cup retir'd,
> And glad Dundee in "faint huzza's" expired. (308–17)

Yet even here, amid the litany of four heroic death scenes that made their four settings forever memorable, there peeps through the trademark expression of what I call the mineral basis of Wordsworth's ontology: "The old grey stones." To die, in each case, to be riveted to the plain, is to merge with the ground of being.

The conventions that his earliest work revisits do remain — although the horror-gothic still prominent in the Salisbury Plain poems appears here only in awed moments like the one just cited. Here for example is an instance of picturesque indistinctness: "Here half a village shines, in gold arrayed / Bright as the moon, half hides itself in shade" (106–07). There are also rather deftly handled emblematic and personified landscape features, as when he commands the sunrise to appear: "Gay lark of hope thy silent song resume! / Fair

smiling lights the purpled hills illume!"[15] (632–33; note the movement in two
lines from a compressed traditional figure to a much more characteristic pa-
thetic fallacy resembling "The sea was laughing"). For the most part, though,
setting aside the still up-to-date constraints of the travel poem genre itself,
together with the connective tissue of schoolboy declamation ("Is there who
'mid these awful wilds," etc. [418]), Wordsworth seems increasingly aware
that for him landscape description has an unprecedented purpose. Notable is
the moment in which he anticipates a privileged moment that occurred not in
the Alps but on the later walking tour with Jones (around the time this poem
was being written): the view from atop Mount Snowdon in Wales which is the
high point of *Prelude* 13:

> A mighty waste of mist the valley fills,
> A solemn sea! Whose vales and mountains round
> Stand motionless, to awful silence bound.
> A gulf of gloomy blue, that opens wide
> And bottomless, divides the midway tide.
> Like leaning masts of stranded ships appear
> The pines that near the coast their summits rear;
>
> . . . . . . . . . . . . . . . .
>
> Loud through that midway gulf ascending, sound
> Unnumbered streams with hollow roar profound. (495–505)

Here Wordsworth's future way of evoking natural sublimity announces itself:
indistinctness and concealment, the pleasing illusion that one visual setting
simulates another (pines in mist like masts on the sea, pointing toward the hills
like leviathans at sea breaching the mist in Snowdon), and finally the impres-
sion left by sound that is seemingly without a source, here making the ocean as
it were oceanic.

Wordsworth seems least imitative and for that reason most "obscure," most
fully caught up in reflections that have no definite point, when the painterly
sight of the landscape recedes and the scene is composed rather as consecrated
sound ("sound / Unnumbered"), a medley of audible elements that seem like
silence, featuring the transvaluation of idleness as creative reverie that will
predominate at least until the "Ode to Duty." These sounds culminate in
"savage joy," which points in turn to the young child as "naked savage" swim-
ming in *Prelude* 1:

> How still! No irreligious sound or sight
> Rouzes the soul from her severe delight.
> An idle voice the Sabbath region fills
> Of Deep that calls to Deep across the hills,
> Broke only by the melancholy [1820: soothing] sound

Of drowsy bells for ever tinkling round;
Faint wail of eagle melting into blue
Beneath the cliffs, and pine-woods steady sugh;
The solitary heifer's deepened low;
Or rumbling heard remote of fallen snow.
Save that, the stranger seen below, the boy
Shouts from the echoing hills with savage joy. (430–41)

Some of this is awkward, but the mood to come is in place, broken only by "melancholy," the fashionable Miltonism from "Il Penseroso" that Wordsworth later discards as a vestige of loco-descriptive anthropocentrism.

Wordsworth's new way of thinking about nature consists in saying that if we read the landscape like a book — and perhaps it is irresistible to do so at times — we must nonetheless recognize that reading it is what *we* do, not a practice dictated by nature itself. I conclude, then, by calling attention to the subtle handling of this theme, indeed Wordsworth's farewell to it, in the "Lines Left upon a Seat in a Yew-Tree." The poem is set in a landscape of absence. No dwelling is nearby, there is no river and no bee. There is a lake, but that serves only to "lull thy mind / By one soft impulse saved from vacancy." The entire scene is like a gravestone, with its *sta viator* embedded in its opening words: "Nay, Traveller! Rest." We are to learn from this site as from an epitaph, but what is the lesson? A moral is certainly attached, a warning against pride, but it is not grounded in the scene, or at least appears at first not to be. The youth who retired to haunt this spot, spurned by the city that ignored him just as it had once ignored the prodigal son in *The Vicar of Wakefield*, was attracted to the bleakness of the scene and built up the sod-covered stone seat to anticipate his own grave-mound. He made the scene like a gravestone, in other words. No doubt an exorcized self, proud and bitter like Milton fall'n on evil days 'mid evil tongues or the Wordsworth of "Tintern Abbey" recoiling from "the sneers of selfish men," the youth of this poem is the victim of a mistake about his relationship with the world around him which in fact has everything to do with his exaggerated self-importance:

And on these barren rocks, with fern and heath,
And juniper, and thistle, sprinkled o'er,
Fixing his downcast eye, he many an hour
A morbid pleasure nourished, tracing here
An emblem of his own unfruitful life.

The youth has failed to learn from human indifference the salutary lesson of nature's equal indifference. Just so, in making his embittered young man a seeker of emblems, a cultivator of loco-descriptive conventions, Wordsworth dismisses the eighteenth-century poet in himself.

# 6

## Hoof After Hoof, Metric Time

*She listens, but she cannot hear*
*The foot of horse, the voice of man.*
*— "The Idiot Boy"*

There is a widely accepted way of thinking about time both in and out of the romantic tradition that does undoubtedly cover a great deal of the territory. Poems according to this view are, in the expression of Harold Bloom, "lie[s] against time."[1] Which is to say, poems strive to resist time. In Sharon Cameron's *Lyric Time,* a formidable, now classic work chiefly devoted to Emily Dickinson, one finds Cameron saying things like: "Dickinson's poems fight temporality with a vengeance," and "the lyric is to substitute a more satisfying order for the dreaded temporality."[2] There are three premises that make remarks of this kind plausible and in some measure justified. First, to lie against time is to reject, to defy, the pathos of human loss together with the fear and indignity of death, of deathwardness, and of death-in-life. Falls are fortunate, and death shall have no dominion. Second, the promotion of such defiance to a matter of paramount importance that becomes the motive force for the production of lyric takes place against the backdrop of Christian eschatology, and part of this second premise is that the double perspective on time afforded by the Christian framework is inescapable in the Western lyric tradition. Third — and this is what folds secular or relatively secular lyric back into the formula — there exists a profane consolation in defiance of time that can be placed with varying degrees of confidence alongside the Christian promise: namely, the preservative strength of poetic form. Here the hatred of time that persists in Wyndham Lewis, T. E. Hulme, and other high modernists is characteristic, and leads to the literary techniques that Joseph Frank called "spatial form." Anglo-American formalism battens on this idea, speaking of the poem as a discrete ontological object not subject to decay.

In my opinion, however, "lyric" (by which term I do not mean "the lyric poem" as a formal entity) is not exclusively a machine for containing time. In its simple forward flow, poetry is chronometric, not chronophobic. It evokes and simulates time rather than containing, conquering, or repressing it. It records time, thematizing dailiness and the ontic continuity of things to the tune of its own time, meter. This is preeminently the case in the poetry of Wordsworth, often side by side with the poet's deference to Christian eschatology. But before turning to Wordsworth's recurrent figuring of feet as hoofs, his thematization of meter in relation to the marginal consciousness that lives in time without resisting it, let me begin by focusing once more on marginal consciousness itself, in this instance as it understands the being of human and nonhuman things in relation to time.

"We Are Seven" is one of those poems in which by example or precept the very young, the very old, or the very stupid teach those who are more sophisticated that the best way to think about objects of perception is not always analytic. Like "Anecdote for Fathers" (subtitled "showing how the practice of lying may be taught"), "We Are Seven" is a Lyrical Ballad concerning the perils of making false distinctions. It criticizes grown-up lies against time. One must concede right away, setting aside the first stanza for the moment (the first four lines of which were perhaps composed by Coleridge), that Wordsworth himself seems not to agree with this view in the 1802 "Preface" to *Lyrical Ballads* when he says that the poem is about "the perplexity and obscurity which in childhood attend our notion of death, or rather our utter inability to admit that notion."[3] Nevertheless, quite apart from the fact that both in this poem and in "Anecdote for Fathers" the grown-ups lose their temper, making us question their wisdom — nevertheless it is hard to see what this little girl fails to understand about death. What she evidently does not *believe*, which is another matter, is that there is a compensatory life elsewhere, to be experienced outside of time.

Wordsworth says that in composing the poem he began with the last stanza, in which it is hard not to notice that the adult speaker has become exasperated and rude:

"But they are dead; those two are dead!
Their spirits are in heaven!"
'Twas throwing words away; for still
The little Maid would have her will,
And said, "Nay, we are seven."[4]

Looking as hard as we can for the girl's alleged disqualifications as a judge of these matters, we find first that she is not at all perplexed or confused by difference as such. Throughout the poem there is a striking precision about numbers (numerous verse indeed!) with which she is quite at ease.[5] She states her age, eight, and accurately numbers her siblings, with whom she is absolutely at one even before the issue of the living versus the dead arises; a sworn foe of subjective distance, she never says *I have* six brothers and sisters. The refrain "We are seven" itself predicts her view not only of death but of separation in general; and in the seventh stanza the speaker, realizing this, seems to be as concerned about the fallacy of asserting existential unity with the four who are absent as he is later about the inclusion of the dead among the siblings. But the little girl's declaration of at-oneness can scarcely be confused with confusion about difference: she knows perfectly well that two siblings are elsewhere above-ground, two are at sea, and two are dead. She knows further that the absence of the dead is different in kind from the absence of the other four because, unlike many of us, this "little cottage girl" with nowhere to be but at the bedside has almost certainly witnessed the difference to her sorrow. Jane was "[t]he first that died," without euphemism, and the girl's description of Jane's painful dying and death is direct and unflinching. When the girl and her similarly fated brother John play where Jane is buried, they know they are playing "round her grave." They are not pretending to drink tea with Jane or any silliness of that sort any more than the girl is pretending to be dining tête-à-tête later when she eats her supper by the graves at twilight.

The composer of the poem (not the speaker) is careful to preserve this unembellished awareness: the girl takes her porringer to the twin graves earlier in her narrative yet later in narrated time than the period when she and John played by the grave of Jane, yet obviously this temporal chiasmus is not a containment device. It is an indication, rather, that neither in the girl's order of narration nor in the time of her life does chronology matter, because for her there is no *telos* at stake. Time is just continuous in either direction. So what does she not understand? One thing, and one thing only: the concept of "spirits . . . in heaven," which not the poet but the speaker of this poem frantically proclaims as his lie against time. The little girl knows that her buried siblings are bodies in the ground, just as she is a body, just as her four absent siblings are bodies localized in space and time, and in having realized this common denominator — the perdurability of things in time *mutatis mutandis* — she has made them all inseparable despite the pain of separation. The first stanza can now be read perhaps in two voices; by "death" ("What should it know of death?"), the unpleasant speaker of the last stanza can be understood to have meant "the afterlife," that strange state in which duration will no longer be experienced as breath, circulation, and pulse. But a second voice, more attuned to that of the child, may declare that to be "[a] simple child" consists in knowing only that bodies in whatever state are still bodies. Wordsworth's most cryptic and perfect expression of this view is "A Slumber Did My Spirit Seal," which appears to turn on the contrast invited by the gap of death between the two stanzas but actually repeats the same ontological condition in two different registers and time frames. My spirit *was* sealed, hence in my nonhuman sentience I knew nothing of death, just as Lucy, being a "thing," was oblivious to the deathwardness of "earthly years." Now Lucy is actually dead, like the little girl's two siblings, sadly without motion or force, but she circulates through time, as always before, with all the nonhuman objects in the world.

Poems of the kind here described, poems that release the poet from the obligation to contain time even though they refuse to wince away from the reality of death, actually open the way for encountering the pleasures of temporality. (I allude, I think appropriately, to an eighteenth-century theme category: the pleasures of imagination, memory, hope, etc.) These pleasures range from what Matthew Arnold rightly singled out as Wordsworth's most characteristic grace-note, "joy in widest commonalty spread," as on the happy morning of "Resolution and Independence," to the more tranquil sorts of contentment that Wordsworth calls, in the "Prospectus to *The Recluse*," "A simple produce of the common day" concerning "nothing more than what we are." These quieter pleasures, Wallace Stevens's "pleasure of merely circulating," are closely connected with the politics of custom that hostile critics of Wordsworth confine to the reactionary notions of agrarian hierarchy that in the long run he did openly espouse.[6] Yet in a certain sense, the exact relation of which to the political must be worked out with care — and in ontological terms — the pleasure of unredeemed time, of the continuities of existence, is egalitarian. The poems of 1802 in particular, celebrating pointedly ordinary flowers like the daisy and the celandine, pointedly ordinary birds like the cuckoo and the green linnet, evoking the way in which they exist oblivious to hierarchy in their own time and time span — all this generalizes Wordsworth's nostalgic village theme into an orientation toward temporal existence, toward historicity as distinct from historical being.

As the material or embodied ground of Wordsworth's poetics of lyric, this orientation can be called metrical time. As many theories of versification have indicated, metrical time can be understood in relation to breathing or the heartbeat. When it is connected with the sensation of the whole circulatory system, I have elsewhere called it "the hum of being," but let us here consider its more metronomic aspect, which leads likewise to the hypnosis that cancels difference, as in one of the — rather rough-hewn — fragments from DC MS. 15:

> Oh 'tis a joy divine in summer days
> When not a breeze is stirring, not a cloud,
> To sit within some solitary wood,
> Far in some lonely wood, and hear no so[und]
> Which the heart does not make or else so fit[s]
> To its own temper that in external things
> No longer seem internal difference:
> All melts away, and things that are without
> Live in our minds as in their native homes.[7]

Compare this with an observation by Geoffrey Hartman concerning the rhythm of "Strange Fits of Passion":

> The hypnotic ride lasts from the second stanza to the fifth, in which the lines:
>
> > My horse moved on; hoof after hoof
> > He raised, and never stopped,
>
> Suggest a monotone and supernatural slowing, motion approaching yet never quite attaining its end, and the horse advancing, as it were, apart from the rider, who is somewhere else.[8]

Meter does its work while the discourse of the poem does other things, or in any case seems to do other things.

Wordsworth offers a very strange argument about meter in the 1800 "Preface" — strange, that is, if we cannot appeal to the broad context I hope to develop in this chapter.[9] We know the general argument of the "Preface," which at least with respect to conventional norms is aggressively anti-formalist: a poet is a man speaking to men, with no special creative faculty to draw on (not differing in kind but only in degree), who uses the language really used by men; there is, in short, no essential difference between verse and prose. This would appear to leave little scope for any aspect of versification, prompting the question he asks: "Why, professing these opinions, have I written in verse?" (*Wordsworth's Literary Criticism*, 83). This carries him toward the discussion of meter, with some preliminary ambivalence: "a very small part of the pleasure given by Poetry depends upon the metre" (ibid.); and yet, a few sentences on,

"In answer to those who . . . greatly underestimate the power of metre in itself" (ibid.), one may point to long-enduring poems written in an even "more naked and simple style" (ibid., 84) than these lyrical ballads. What at least arguably he wants to say, overriding this apparent contradiction, is that meter works best when it is not accompanied by "other artificial distinctions of style" (ibid., 83) — i.e., when it is not heroic couplets accompanied by Poetic Diction. As he says in the second "Essay upon Epitaphs" (ibid., 146), a good writer should not "avail himself of the liberty given by metre to adopt phrases of fancy."

He then warms to the subject, soon arriving at a more definite and consistent account of the role of meter that is quite astonishing. Meter, he argues in effect, is a *pleasure thermostat*. If the subject-matter of a poem is too exciting, inducing hard-to-govern transports of joy, terror, or grief,

> the co-presence of something regular, something to which the mind has been accustomed in various moods and in a less excited state, cannot but have great efficacy in tempering and restraining the passion by an intertexture of ordinary feeling, and of feeling not strictly connected with the passion. (Ibid., 84)

As Hartman says of the moonlit ride in "Strange Fits," the rider is somewhere else; but, unlike Saul, for example, he does stay on the horse. Emotions otherwise difficult to bear or fathom are soothed by an under-girding monotony. This is of course impossible to prove, and a wonderfully Freudian compulsion moves Wordsworth to adduce in proof the claim that the reader finds *Clarissa* and Edward Moore's *The Gamester* unbearable because they are written in prose, whereas the tragedies of Shakespeare give pleasure because they are in verse. Well and good, but any and all of his readers would recall that Dr. Johnson, from whose precepts and whose very prose style the "Preface" struggles repeatedly to disentangle itself, read *Clarissa* with pleasure and approval, while announcing in the notes to his Shakespeare edition that he "could not bear the revisal" of the fifth acts of *King Lear* and *Othello*. Yet the very symmetry with which Wordsworth's compulsive slip points to the refutation of his claim does lend clarity to his attitude toward meter. Meter adds nothing to sense, it partakes not at all in what the formalist calls imitative form (the point of Pope's famous lines on swift Camilla and the slow snake in *Essay on Criticism*, for example, or Coleridge's three poems exemplifying meter), but serves rather to turn down the heat of emotion.

Or, as a thermostat, to turn it up:

> On the other hand (what it must be allowed will much more frequently happen) if the Poet's words should be incommensurate with the passion, and inadequate to raise the Reader to a height of desirable excitement, then, (unless the Poet's choice of his metre has been grossly injudicious) in the feelings of pleasure which the Reader has been accustomed to connect with

metre in general, and in the feeling, whether cheerful or melancholy, which he has been accustomed to connect with that particular movement of metre, there will be found something which will greatly contribute to impart passion to the words, and to effect the complex end which the Poet proposes to himself. (Ibid., 85)

It is the role of the "rapid" meter of "The Thorn," for example (ibid., 97), to offset the necessarily slow thought processes of the poem's garrulous old speaker. Meter, then, is the visible sign that Wordsworth believes what today is being discredited in every quarter, from neurophysiology and cognitive science to the most popular self-help magazines: he believes that there is a sharp distinction between thought and feeling. This is not to say that he denies the existence and function of what we rehabilitate today as "emotive reasoning." Emotive reasoning is just what he has in mind in many contexts, especially in his poetry itself, when he speaks of "feeling," or "the feeling mind." In fact he argues in this same "Preface" that thoughts when often repeated actually become feelings, in which form they furnish the materials of poetry. No, what his discussion of meter makes clear is that there is an activity of mind which may or may not entail feeling through association with the long-familiar (the "regular," on the one hand, the enlivening on the other), but which is *not in the slightest degree cognitive*. The role of this activity is to keep time. The more marginal the state of consciousness represented, the more dominant this activity becomes, and in the series of poems now to be considered Wordsworth invests the unreflecting time-keeping of consciousness in the regular movements of hoofed animals.

Wordsworth is literature's most famous walker. Why then is the speaker riding in "Strange Fits of Passion"? There are in fact many opportunities for horses to make their presence felt in his poetry that Wordsworth ignores. Although he never wrote the sort of heroic poem that in the first Book of *The Prelude* he records having considered writing, there are many sonnets and odes on military and patriotic subjects, written in a traditional lofty style, where you would expect to find coursers, gallant steeds, noble mounts, and the like appearing at least from time to time. But having gone through these poems in quest of such quadrupeds, I was surprised to find virtually none of them. Their absence is felt: how are the armies and squadrons of the Spanish Campaign sonnets related to the Cintra pamphlet supposed to get anywhere? And when horses *are* mentioned in a martial context, as in *The White Doe of Rylstone*, almost immediately something peculiar happens: the renegade northern patriarch Richard Norton dismounts on the eve of battle and wants nothing further to do with horses:

No steed will he
Henceforth bestride; — triumphantly,
He stands upon the grassy sod,
Trusting himself to the earth, and God.[10]

We shall return to this Antaeus-like decision, armed perhaps by that time with an explanation, but in the meantime clearly it reinforces the fact that horses are conspicuously omitted, spurned, in such poems, the more strangely because where Wordsworth does pay attention to horses and other ungulates (like the doe in *White Doe*), their presence is persistent beyond need or expectation.

Wordsworth himself was a rider of only middling skill. The few long trips he took on horseback — to Cambridge, for example — he got through without mishap but clearly with no ensuing wish to make a habit of it. He did no better when walking beside or riding behind horses, as the misadventures of the "Cart" shared with his sister and Coleridge at the start of the 1803 Scottish "walking tour" will attest: Every time the horse came to stream, it refused to cross it, and the three travelers inexpertly pushed and pulled to little effect. The Wordsworth household kept a pony in Grasmere, but mainly for labor and only for emergency riding; and Dorothy with a clear sense of estrangement from it touches upon the nuisance of maintaining this unnamed "Horse" in her letters. One may indeed suspect that while a horse is a decent enough picturesque ruminant ("The horse alone, seen dimly as I pass, / Is cropping audibly his later meal"; see Ch. 5), the awkward relationship Wordsworth had with horses accounts for their absence from the poems on elevated subjects, poems that in the sister art of History Painting would furnish steeds aplenty. Why then are they and other hoofed animals suddenly featured figures in the poems I wish to study now? With nods in other directions, I shall attend mainly to "The Idiot Boy," *Benjamin the Waggoner*, "Peter Bell," "Hart-Leap Well," and *The White Doe of Rylstone*.[11] There are horses in *The Prelude*, too, and a dromedary with which the dreaming poet tries to "keep pace," but with one exception (the races in Book 2) in fact they are just like the steed abandoned by Norton in *The White Doe*: left behind, together with Honest James, in Hanged Man, and yet to appear in Waiting for Horses — these being the Book 11 Spots in which it is claimed that the mind is lord and master. To this too we can circle back.

Horses have had an important provenance in thinking about being human, and more specifically about being human in relation to poetry, ever since antiquity. The proem to Sidney's *Apologie for Poetry* recounts the author's apprenticeship to an Italian master of horsemanship whose praises of that art were so fulsome that finally, Sidney unexpectedly concludes — as Phil-hippus — "I had almost wished myself a horse." *Allegorice,* Pegasus is somewhere nearby — or better, the wise centaur Chiron. If the horseman is man's "erected wit," in Sidney's terms, the horse is his "infected will" or animal nature, and the fusion or disciplined conjunction of these features of the human is human poetry (i.e., not divinely inspired hymnody). Swift's inversion of these same features as the high equine and the low human continues this theme in satire. Much of this fascinated humanization of the noble steed — Bucephalus, the weeping horses of Patroclus, the heroes' horses of medieval romance on which Don Quixote tries to model Rozinante — both belongs to and in a sense constitutes what is known in German culture as the *Ritter* tradition. The knight is iconically evoked as "rider" (*Ritter*), even when in Dürer's etching he encounters death and the devil.

This tradition reaches Wordsworth by way of the popular ballad, most particularly of course Bürger's *Der wilde Jäger,* and survives in an oblique and complex way in "Hart-Leap Well," as we shall see. The typical relation of a "lyrical ballad" to this tradition, however, is the creation of a calculated distance from it, as in the opening of "Simon Lee, the Huntsman." The distant baronial seat, Ivor-Hall, stands empty in its exotic Welsh setting, and all its surviving inhabitants — "men, dogs, and horses" — have departed from its feudal ethos to live on enclosed parcels of land dividing a present-day village green. Even when Simon in his prime was in residence at Ivor-Hall, however, he was *not* a rider but "a running huntsman merry," famous for his ability to "leave both man and horse behind." In other words, Wordsworth's trick of getting down and away from the horse is already at work, as it is again in a rather "Strange Fits"–like poem of 1802:

> While riding near her home one stormy night
> A single glow-worm did I chance to espy;
> I gave a fervent welcome to the sight,
> And from my horse I leapt; great joy had I.
> ("Among all lovely things my Love had been")

Although he proceeds to the house of "Lucy" (as she is called), goes into the orchard, and returns to the spot with her the following evening to observe the glow-worm, there is no further mention of the horse.

For the horse to matter in Wordsworth, it needs to be dissociated altogether from the *Ritter* tradition in which, as in Sidney, horse and man are a symbiotic emblem of horse-man-ship, of the mastery of a noble calling, the gallop or canter of a poem reined in by judgment. The "ship" too Wordsworth repudiates as a verse-vessel (most notably in disembarking from the flying boat of the Prologue to *Peter Bell,* a substitute for Pegasus ridiculed yet appropriated by Shelley and his generation), unless it becomes, as I explain in Chapter 8, a rowboat. The beast as an agent of human movement becomes welcome only where there is a human lack, where it is not a question of the bridle and the curb but simply of enabling, as in *Home at Grasmere:*

> I begin
> To inscribe upon my heart
> A liking for the small grey Horse that bears
> The paralytic Man; I know the ass
> On which the Cripple in the Quarry maimed
> Rides to and fro.

Like meter, such beasts supply whatever we lack. They teach those of us whose locomotor skills are all too kinetic what it might be like just to move steadily, yet with equal ease they themselves are the locomotion of the immobilized. In either case they move steadily and unreflectively through time, enabling human aims without themselves being purposeful or humanized.

Hartman notes of such free rides, however, as in "Strange Fits," that there is a "monotone and supernatural slowing" about them. This brings us to the Idiot Boy and his horse. Of all the Lyrical Ballads ridiculed by Wordsworth's anthropocentric Enlightenment critics, led by Jeffrey, the one called "The Idiot Boy" aroused the most contemptuous mirth, the joke turning for the most part on the entirely correct perception that even the speaker of the poem has more than a little of the yokel in him. As Byron put it most memorably: "all who view the Idiot in his glory / Perceive the Bard the hero of the story." But the horse has a claim as well, and the poem needs to be read with this claim in mind. Until the last lines of the poem, the idiot Johnny utters no articulate word, making only the excited sound transliterated by Wordsworth as "Burr, burr," blowing through his closed lips like a horse, and leaves us wondering whether he can do anything but neigh. The question is not settled by "his words were not a few, / which [his mother] Betty well could understand," as Betty speaks Johnny's language perhaps more readily than she speaks ours. But at the very end, having been repeatedly asked by Betty how he spent the night, Johnny suddenly makes the articulate observation that was in fact, as Wordsworth later told Isabella Fenwick, the germ of the poem: " 'The cocks did crow, tu-whoo, tu-whoo, / And the sun did shine so cold.' "[12] Johnny never dismounts from his horse, he has all four hoofs on the ground (unlike the Antaeus-like Norton), and his critique of analytic difference — the owls are roosters, night is day — and reflection — the moon is the sun — is issued with all the aplomb of the great tutorial centaur who is his ancestor: "Thus answered Johnny in his glory, / And that was all his travel's story." Eliding distinctions is the chief maxim of ungulate consciousness in Wordsworth, marking in this respect a sharp programmatic change from the educational agenda of the centaur. If the bestial energy of Chiron is needed to ensure that Achilles will become a hero, Johnny and his horse show by contrast that the ends of agency — in this case the cure of Susan Gale — are best accomplished by those who repudiate agency in favor of ontology. After all, what have Betty, Johnny, the horse, or the doctor *done* to accomplish the mysterious restoration of Susan's health?

Let us look more closely at the horse, which I take to be the heart of the mystery. The poem introduces Johnny by asking his mother what his connection is with the equine world: "why on horseback have you set / Him whom you love, your Idiot boy? / . . . what has he to do / With stirrup, saddle, or with rein?" One answer is, nothing: "the like was never heard of yet." Johnny is not a horseman, he is a horse-man. "His lips with joy they burr at you." And who is this "you"? The reader in part, but really just the you addressed in expressions like "you wouldn't know": you who are to be educated, if possible. Then we meet the horse, whose main, indeed only characteristic is that it is always the same, whether at work or leisure: "Her Pony, that is mild and good; / Whether he be in joy or pain, / Feeding at will along the lane, / Or bringing fagots from the wood." Once mounted, Johnny becomes a Green Man or spirit of the forest. "There is no need of whip or wand; / For Johnny has his holly-bough," and "shakes the green bough in his hand." The suggestion appears to be that although the horse does not need spurring, the actual lack of need is Johnny's own — to accommodate which self-sufficiency of happiness the horse obliges by nature.

When the horse starts to move, Johnny is no longer able to move:

> But when the Pony moved his legs,
> Oh! then for the poor Idiot Boy!
> For joy he cannot hold the bridle,
> For joy his head and heels are idle,
> He's idle all for very joy.

Here the symbiosis is complete, as the experience of moving without exercising the will deprives the boy of the will to move, and the joy of automated mobility discloses a new mode of being-human. The horse's movement too is unmotivated, no one has urged it to move and it has no evident wish to move, it just moves. In coming to be attached to the back of this horse, Johnny has an experience of consciousness that can described as unwilled percipient motion, not vegetable or mineral but animal, thanks to the horse alone:

> And while the Pony moves his legs,
> In Johnny's left hand you may see
> The green bough motionless and dead:
> The moon that shines above his head
> Is not more still and mute than he.

Neither vegetation rite nor celebration of lunar influence, this tableau links something like the privilege of epiphany to the intensity of stillness, and fills Johnny's mother with pride, as though Johnny were marked with special powers: "The silence of her Idiot Boy, / What hopes it sends to Betty's heart!" When he does make noise again, it is as though from the depth of insight he utters the sound of universal being, a sound common to all the objects and beings in the scene, a sound that any of them might make, together with the owlets in the next stanza:

> Burr, burr — now Johnny's lips they burr,
> As loud as any mill, or near it;
> Meek as a lamb the Pony moves,
> And Johnny makes the noise he loves,
> And Betty listens, glad to hear it.

Wordsworth, who later wrote defensively about the quasi-sacred status of idiots in many cultures and regions, has made Johnny the guru of nonhuman in-difference.[13] This noise is like the first song sung by the infant Luke in *Michael*. Blest the infant babe, says the doting father in that poem:

> "Never to living ear came sweeter sounds
> Than when I heard thee by our fire-side
> First uttering, without words, a natural tune;
> While thou, a feeding babe, didst in thy joy
> Sing at thy mother's breast."

But can this hum, triumphantly disclosing the unity of disarticulated being before the Mirror Stage, truly be called consciousness in the absence of a willing principle? This is the question "The Idiot Boy" next raises, with its usual good-natured irony. We know that the horse will embody the value of unchangingness even if or precisely in the event that he loses all the faculties of discrimination, in this case eyes and ears:

> His steed and he right well agree;
> For of this Pony there's a rumour,
> That, should he lose his eyes and ears,
> And should he live a thousand years,
> He never will be out of humour.

It remains, though, to wonder what happens to the locomotor apparatus in the intensity of this steadfastness. In Johnny, motion was suspended immediately, and we soon realize, at the word "thinks," with all its anti-Enlightenment irony, that the horse is no more capable of unmoved movement than the rider: "But then he thinks! / And when he thinks, his pace is slack." It is properly at this moment that the paradox of knowing without the power of distinction, awareness without seeing, without having eyes in the back of the head, is insisted upon: "now, though he knows poor Johnny well, / Yet, for his life, he cannot tell / What he has got upon his back." On automatic pilot, the centaur has now reached the state of undifferentiating enlightenment, or lunar suffusion, in which Johnny's climactic, triumphant conflation of night and day — as of man and beast — will be possible. During the happy reunion, Johnny never gets off the pony (and he never has done so, despite Betty's nocturnal fear that, like Norton, "Johnny perhaps his horse forsook"), so that Betty while dancing around for joy keeps patting various parts of the pony, not the boy. This is followed by a homeward journey with the recovered Susan Gale, who is sufficiently outside the charmed circle, like the rest of us, to pay no attention to the horse. Not so the poet, whose saving idiocy is never clearer than in expressions like "our *four* travelers homeward wend."

*The Waggoner* (or *Benjamin the Waggoner*)[14] features a different sort of marginal human figure, the alcoholic, viewed by Wordsworth with almost equal affection, despite a personal distaste for that form of irrationality bred in part by what he knew of Coleridge's life. Whence then the affection for the waggoner? The deterioration that had led to Coleridge's sojourn abroad was much on Wordsworth's mind in early 1806 because he and his family were now anxiously awaiting news of their difficult friend's return. The poem is dedicated to Charles Lamb, another friend with convivial habits, although (like Benjamin) he was more cheerful than Coleridge in pursuit of them, despite his private misfortune. "Methinks there is a kind of shadowy affinity between the subject of the narrative and the subject of the dedication," Lamb wrote to Wordsworth.[15] Lamb writes prose, Coleridge writes prose and verse, but the verse appears to have fallen silent. Benjamin the Waggoner does not ride his horses; unlike the idiot Johnny, he walks alongside them, yet his skill in driving them without recourse to the whip, and their eagerness to please him, is what is most appealing about him:

> He was patient, they were strong,
> And now they smoothly glide along,
> Recovering breath, and pleased to win
> The praises of mild Benjamin.

He controls their movement with his voice — " 'a word from me was like a charm' " — and it may be noted that their smooth gliding resembles the canter of verse: " 'Your huge burden, safe from harm' " — continues Benjamin — "Moved like a vessel in the wind!' " Foreseeing that Benjamin will take the blame from his merchant employer (publisher?) for being late, as Coleridge always was with everything he promised, the horses commiserate in just the language and tone of "The Idiot Boy": the blame "must soon alight / Upon *his* head, whom, in despite / Of all his failings, they love best." It is this relationship between human and animal consciousness that makes Benjamin an incomparable waggoner — "Benjamin, with clouded brains, / Is worth the best with all their pains" — but more like a genius on laudanum than a water-drinking bard.

Benjamin falls in with a sailor, who eventually lures him into a tavern. The sailor too travels with an ungulate, in this case an ass, but has no particular rapport with it, being perhaps of such a disparate calling. As Benjamin says, " 'That Ass of thine, / He spoils thy sport, and hinders mine.' " When in the tavern the sailor reveals an exuberant creativity in the form of the model ship he uses to recreate for the awed spectators the events at the Battle of the Nile (" 'You'll find you've much in little here!' "), this too is a different sort of creativity and calling. Having rigged the sails,

> He names them all; and interlards
> His speech with uncouth terms of art,
> Accomplished in the showman's part.

It is tempting to say that this is operation of *fancy,* the false secondary power that murders to dissect. In any event its uncouth terms and showmanship are not the language really used by men. This will suffice to show, perhaps, how Benjamin and the sailor displace the figure of the poet onto the figure of the prose writer.

Despite sharing the benign placidity of Johnny's pony and Benjamin's horses, the ass in *Peter Bell*[16] would appear to teach a different lesson, moral rather than ontological or poetological. The ass is much more ambiguously anthropoid than the pony, and it seems to enlist supernatural powers or guidance in order to teach the saving grace of sincere fellow-feeling.[17] The devotion of the ass to its dead master gradually steals upon the consciousness of Peter, who had been a sociopath heretofore (the word "brutal" comes to mind), resembling the patients of neurophysiologists who have pre-frontal lobe lesions or defects — persons who are reasonably intelligent yet incapable of feeling and unable to make useful choices or plans for the future: "nature ne'er could find the way / Into the heart of Peter Bell." The reverse of Johnny, Peter thinks differentially with no unifying feeling: a primrose — in a passage that mystified Jeffrey — is just a primrose, but "nothing more." (Note the apparent resemblance of this attitude on Peter's part to what I have been calling the privileged state of consciousness disclosed by lyric; but not attaching significance to an object is not the same as seeing the insignificance of things to be their fundamental unity. To perceive the unity of things *qua* things requires the power of non-cognitive feeling that in this chapter I have been associating with meter.)

Because its basis appears to be primarily moral, Peter's interaction with the ass would seem to be a different sort of man-beast relationship than the one in "The Idiot Boy"; but the two poems, written at much the same time in the same five-line stanza and featuring the same cheerfully garrulous, sometimes fatuous speaker, are meant clearly to be companion pieces. Unlike the pony, the beast of burden, descended from Balaam's ass (as has been pointed out), must inevitably carry a moral burden. Despite this emphasis, however, one still finds in *Peter Bell* the ontological reduction of the great chain of being to a level field proclaimed by Johnny to conclude "The Idiot Boy." Again, the focus is hoofed consciousness, wonderfully evoked by the speaker in calling the ass a "heavy-headed Thing." The lengthy Prologue to *Peter Bell*, with its flying boat, repudiates the visionary flights of romance or exotic narrative (the airborne machinery of Southey's long poems in particular) in order to tell a homely tale; but before the appearance of the boat—which has the shape if not the substance of a crescent moon—the first line of the Prologue contemplates a flight on Pegasus: "There's something in a flying horse." In pointed contrast, the first line of the poem proper makes the hoofed animal lowly and abject: "All by the moonlight riverside / Groaned the poor Beast / . . . As Peter struck, and struck again." The prematurity of the speaker plunging into his story *in medias res,* protested by an audience that wants its narrative to unfold in good time, is paralleled by what might be called frantic or manic meter. Just as the boy on the lake "struck, and struck again" when the cliff loomed in the boat-stealing episode of *The Prelude,* so here Peter turns the proper monotony of recurrence into violent aggression.

Soon it appears that this poem is, if not a critique, at least a reconsideration of the insights of those simpletons who in Wordsworth's time were more often called "naturals" than idiots. The problem that Wordsworth must now work through is that un-self-conscious oneness with the nonhuman world as exemplified by Peter, so desirable as an antidote to false urbanity and poetic diction, is an undeniable moral liability. Wordsworth does not flinch from this unpleasant reminder but reflects on it carefully in trying to account for his rather unusual anti-hero, who had always "lain beside his asses" without feeling any affinity with them:

> Though Nature could not touch his heart
> By lovely forms, and silent weather,
> And tender sounds, yet you might see

At once, that Peter Bell and she
Had often been together.

A savage wildness round him hung
As of a dweller out of doors;
In his whole figure and his mien
A savage character was seen
Of mountains and of dreary moors.

To all the unshaped half-human thoughts
Which solitary Nature feeds
'Mid summer storms or winter's ice,
Had Peter joined whatever vice
The cruel city breeds.

Like the Savoyard peasants whose very habituation to life in the mountains prevented their appreciation of the scenery according to the un-Wordsworthian Kant in the *Critique of Judgment,* Peter unites the flinty minerality of the nonhuman with the equally stony hardheartedness of complex society without mixing in the necessary softening of ungulate consciousness. Peter gets on the ass's back, like Johnny, but with opposite results: the ass does not respond to the tug on the halter (a tug Johnny never had to make), and Peter dismounts in frustration. There is the same focus in this poem on seemingly mechanized movement, but automated locomotion is replaced here by the automated rotation of ears and eyes — conduits of differential perception, again — in their sockets: "the Ass, with motion dull, / Upon the pivot of his skull / Turned round his long left ear," twice repeated, and then "he turned the eye-ball in his head." Movement in the absence of will is thus replaced by disjointed but willed movements that underscore the stubborn refusal to move as an integrated organism. In "The Idiot Boy," motion is unwilled, here immobility is an act of will.

Only when Peter makes the first gestures of assistance, striving to pull the dead man from the stream, does the ass join forces with him and minister henceforth to Peter's moral amendment. The ass kneels to allow Peter to get on his back, and from that moment the two become the centaur of "The Idiot Boy," with the same appearance of spontaneous, abstracted movement: as with the horse that thinks, "pensively his steps advance." But the ass continues somewhat mysteriously to function as a ministering agent, encouraging Peter to overcome habit and feel kinship with others with an anthropoid gesture for which asses are well known: "the Ass turned round his head, and *grinned, /* Appalling process!"[18] Peter bares his teeth and grins back, though he does not quite know why, thus registering the partial degree to which he has absorbed, or learned, from ungulate consciousness that sense of togetherness with other things and other minds that takes the form of ontological unity in "The Idiot Boy" and instinctive charity in the present poem. Mechanical regularity, agreement of gesture, induces a hypnotic sense of the same which, like meter, makes no sense but carries the burden of sense. With Wordsworth, or with what one is here tempted to call his theory of meter, the Foucauldian disappearance of man is heralded. It is Wordsworth's rebuke of Enlightenment anthropocentrism, and considering what man the social animal "has done to man"—as Wordsworth says elsewhere—who could regret it? As he wrote around this time:

> Why is it we feel
> So little for each other, but for this,
> That we with nature have no sympathy,
> Or with such things as have no power to hold
> Articulate language? (Alfoxden Notebook, 1798)[19]

Strange vocation for a poet, but undoubtedly Wordsworth's vocation at least from 1797 to 1800: to be the bard of disarticulation, of *homo infans.*

Like "Simon Lee," "Hart-Leap Well" begins by evoking the *Ritter* tradition — "The Knight had ridden down from Wensley Moor"—but this poem then immediately evokes instead the hypnotized space and pace of "Strange Fits": "With the slow motion of a summer's cloud." This is one of those amazing lines in Wordsworth that commentary nearly always glides past. (The moment when the running Simon Lee "reeled, and was stone blind" is another.) Sir Walter is clearly in a hurry to catch up with the deer, and he is about to call for another horse, yet the poem has captured him in a dream space, his "slow motion" anachronistically pointing forward to the device used for related purposes in the cinema: the slowing of subjective time or dream time at odds with the need for haste, or the ant-like progress of some vehicle viewed from a great height (as from the summer cloud itself), all of which leave a momentous outcome, climactic or catastrophic, hanging in suspense. The rider, once more, "is somewhere else." He is reveling in the glory of a "glorious day," overcharged with excitement like an overexcited poem, yet something external to him views him distantly from the very beginning, long before the narrative turns against him: something, for example, like meter. (This contrast is soon stated in a different way: "But, though Sir Walter like a falcon flies, / There is a doleful silence in the air.") This measured, decelerated perspective, from within which it will take many years to blight the scene of his triumph, all things being slowed in good time, is that of nature itself, moving steadily forward like a pensive horse. True, the centaur-like fusion of man and beast is still possible, but even while it retains the happy simple-mindedness of "The

Idiot Boy," it is now aggressive rather than peaceful: "Joy sparkled in the prancing courser's eyes; / The horse and horseman are a happy pair."

As the human ego prevails, animal consciousness literally falls by the wayside. The dogs, who resemble the pack of hounds fondly recalled by Theseus in *A Midsummer Night's Dream,* are in worse plight than Simon Lee in the moment mentioned above: "breath and eyesight fail; and, one by one, / The dogs are stretched among the mountain fern." At this point the horse too falls out of the narrative, leaving Sir Walter with the one remaining flicker of animal consciousness: "Sir Walter and the Hart are left alone." "Dismounting, then," ensues, but the horse has already been left out, and when it reenters the narrative its does so to reinforce the critique of the "happy pair" above: "Close to the thorn on which Sir Walter leaned / Stood his dumb partner in this glorious feat." Sir Walter now somewhat resembles Betty Foy, being as simple-minded as she, and as innocent of wrongdoing. Yet unlike her, he is unforgivably alienated from the ways of nature — within which the last groan of the deer makes the waters of the spring tremble:

> And now, too happy for repose or rest,
> (Never had living man such joyful lot!)
> Sir Walter walked all round, north, south, and west,
> And gazed and gazed upon that darling spot.

As is often pointed out, Sir Walter believes that nature is a vast pleasure ground provided for the privileged classes, hence naturally wants to commemorate his happiness with "a pleasure-house" on this spot, complete with a dubious "Paramour." Even though "pleasure" entails the decadence of a baroque taste at odds with nature (" 'A cunning artist will I have to frame / A basin for that fountain in the dell!' "), Sir Walter does not see himself as cruel, and certainly not alienated, because he views the beast he has destroyed through the eyes of the heroic tradition as a noble antagonist, Saladin to his Lion-heart, hence a kindred spirit: "And, gallant Brute [Stag 1827ff.]! To make thy praises known, / Another monument shall here be raised."

The reader will not be surprised to find me recalling "Kubla Khan." Kubla, like Sir Walter, is an alienated artificer who harnesses nature instead of accepting it as it is, with the result that his creation descends into a "sunless," "lifeless" sea. To be sure, Coleridge wants to say that that sea is life — or nature — without imagination, but I hope to have indicated earlier how he differs from Wordsworth about this. Kubla has no use for nature as it is because he thinks it lifeless. Just so, but with a different and pointedly responsive agenda, everything in the second half of Wordsworth's poem dies and nothing grows in the vicinity of Hart-Leap Well. Yet Kubla's is unquestionably an act of creative heroism, an imitation of divine creation itself that cannot really be called a parody though it is perhaps tinged with blasphemy. His very loneliness, attuned to the demonic, is divine. If it has an accompaniment, a "measure" that can offset the caverns measureless to man, it is that of the damsel with a dulcimer. The measure of "Hart-Leap Well" needs to be understood by contrast as a sequence of successive paces, strides, and leaps, all of them destroyed. The creator having violated the regularity of nature, the timing of what he makes, with its dancers, minstrelsy, and "cunning," can only be arabesque. Kubla's is an experiment in the organic, subduing the diversity of the natural to the shaping spirit of imagination, even though the imagination is mediated by the decadence and loneliness of an opium dream. A *paradis artificiel,* yes, a hothouse growth; but it is not in this poem that an albatross or Hart is killed. Hence it is not to "Kubla Khan" but to the conclusion of the *Rime* that Wordsworth alludes in concluding "Hart-Leap Well" with a lesson to be taken from "Nature":

> "One lesson, Shepherd, let us two divide,
> Taught both by what she shows, and what conceals;
> Never to blend our pleasure or our pride
> With sorrow of the meanest thing that feels."

If all three poems are about creative failure — "here a mansion stood, / The finest palace of a hundred realms!" — they are nonetheless allegories of imaginative possibility, and respect their protagonists accordingly. To allude again to Stevens, in Wordsworth we have to do with the noble rider, the sound of words, and the suppression of measure in transport. The astonishing three leaps of the dying deer, the last steps taken by any animal in the poem ("neither dog nor heifer, horse nor sheep, / Will wet his lips within that cup of stone"), are leaps that exceed bounds. Sir Walter tries to make them measures by erecting pillars over their imprints, but this can only be the pseudo-Palladian equivalent of what Wordsworth describes, in the "Preface," as meter ill-advisedly accompanied by "artificial distinctions of style." One is not to think, for example, of trimeter. Yet there is a connection, unbeknownst to Sir Walter, between Hart and Heart. "My heart leaps up." The deer in tune with its environment, the "unoffending creature" promoted by nature in death to be the retributive genius of the place (like Wordsworth's Danish Boy), may have used those last leaps, the poem says, to return to the spring by which it was born, its inspiration, origin, *fons Bandusiae.* The hart leaps up until it leaps no more, but it cannot be forced to race ahead of measure, as the physiology that under-girds the poet's overbalance of pleasure needs healthy regulation, whether it be the moderation of transport or the aerobic enlivening of lethargy.

*The White Doe of Rylstone* seems to me to be about gender. The affinity of Emily and the doe, the appearance of effeminate pacifism that belies Francis's bravery (making him an odd precursor of Byron's Sardanapalus), are emphases directly linked to the poem's meditation on the masculine gendering of human agency. In 1837, Wordsworth set a context for these concerns by choosing as epigraph the now-famous passage about agency from *The Borderers* that was then unknown. The passage is spoken by the villain Oswald at the height of his homosocial plot to lure Marmaduke into performing an arbitrarily evil act. He is foiled in that Marmaduke's "act" as it turns out is not one of commission but omission: forgetting to leave Herbert the scrip of food. It is not an act at all. Just so, as Wordsworth argues in the Fenwick note, no *act* performed in *White Doe* has any bearing on its celebration of passive Christian suffering.[20] The downfall even of Francis is his determination to act, his agreement (at his father's behest much as Marmaduke's is at Oswald's) to seize the banner and return it to Rylstone-hall. The six lines from *The Borderers* ("Action is transitory — a step, a blow," etc.), in which evanescent action and its arbitrary effects are contrasted with the permanence of suffering, are here supplemented with newly written lines describing the solace of Christian patience, with the soul's passage to "peace divine." What I wish to underline in these new, very late and very orthodox, lines is the expression "with patient steps of thought."

Even the next words, "Now toiling," detract from what I think Wordsworth is instinctively doing here, as their emphasis on the difficulty of transcending earthly care does not fully correspond to the curative effect of Emily's companionship with the doe after her initial period of inconsolability. The contrast between these patient steps, however, and their intermission, "wafted now on wings of prayer," is at the same time, interestingly, a contrast between the doe and Emily in this very relationship. The step of the doe (its "steps of thought," as in "a horse that thinks"), its placid, benign pace which does not toil, sustains flights of prayer even though hoofs and wings diverge: the rider is somewhere else. This is the contrast upon which Wordsworth insists in the prose epigraph to all editions, beginning in 1815, taken from Bacon's "On Atheism":

> They that deny a God destroy Man's nobility; for certainly Man is of kinn to the Beast by his Body, and if he be not of a kinn to God by his Spirit, he is a base ignoble Creature. It destroys likewise his Magnanimity, and the raising of humane Nature: for take an example of a Dogg, and mark what a generosity and courage he will put on, when he finds himself maintained by a Man, who to him is instead of a God, or Melior Natura.

Bacon here takes us back to Sidney's horseman and horse, which it seems to me has little enough to do with Wordsworth's account of Emily and the doe, simply because there is no sense of the "infected will" that undermines agency in either; but then comes an odd turn of thought in Bacon's text that amounts almost to a digression, turning the duality of the divine and the beast in man into a differential equation (and a chiastic one at that): Dog(g) is to man as man is to God, giving the altered impression that dog and God have as much in common as man has with either. In the syncretistic explanation of the scape*goat* across cultures with which Frazer is associated — and on which tragedy has been said by many to turn — Wordsworth's poem comes into at least partial focus: in the fictitious present time of the narrator, the subhuman doe is an otherworldly sabbath visitant, the saintly Emily is in the tomb, the bleeding body of Francis, full of punctures, has superimposed real stigmata over those originally painted on the banner by Emily, and all three are bound together by this imagery in a single sphere of holiness. As Wordsworth explains (*White Doe*, 63), "the anticipated beatification, if I may so say, of her mind, and the apotheosis of the companion of her solitude [earlier but not here called 'the inferior Creature'], are the points at which the Poem aims."

Or, to put this in terms more congenial to the earlier and less conventionally pious poet, all three belong to the same order of being, one which, *pace* Bacon, is *not* hierarchical. I would suggest that even in a poem as late as this one (1807–09), the blessed sphere in which these three figures move together is the sphere in which the concept of the human is sharply dissevered from the concept of agency, hence in a certain sense dissevered even from the concept of God understood as Creator. To be sure, as has often been pointed out, Emily's heroism, descended from Milton's "They also serve who stand and wait," involves a choice that is more difficult and steadfast than the choice of violence. But it is nevertheless a Keatsian "passive attending upon the event," a different sort of creativity from any ordinary investment of power in volition: "but on my mind," says Emily, "A passive stillness is enjoined." This is what Wordsworth vehemently insists on as the motive and theme of the poem that he considered "in conception, the highest composition that he ever produced."[21]

To confine ourselves more closely to the topic of this chapter, however, we may ask, what then does the doe, with its steps of thought, contribute? This doe reflects the same flirtation with anthropomorphism we find in the ass in *Peter Bell*, perhaps also the hart in "Hart-leap Well" (at least from the viewpoint of the shepherd's superstitious folkways: "What thoughts must through the creature's brain have past!"): "harbors she a sense / Of sorrow, or of reverence?" But as always Wordsworth finesses this possibility, refusing to take sides in the same way that certain ghost stories refuse to take sides. The doe walks among the baronial tombs, but "As little she regards the sight / As a common creature might." Not even that settles the matter, of course: as in that case she is *not* a common creature; and, if she is not, may not her indifference to these tombs simply reflect her single-mindedness in approaching Emily's "grassy grave," which for its part, as if to bring the two orders of being together from the outset, seems "shy of human neighborhood"? The doe in this pious poem undoubtedly moves under divine auspices, yet without ceasing to be a doe, and the speaker is at pains to dispel "superstitious fancies strong, / Which do the gentle creature wrong."

The distinction is carefully drawn, in Wordsworth's dismissal of the parishioners' beliefs about the doe, between the doe in imagination and the doe in fancy. Francis later in the poem is closer to the truth about the doe than the latter-day churchgoers of the speaker's present time, but he naturalizes her too much by failing at least on this occasion to link the natural order with Providence:

> Even she will to her peaceful woods
> Return, and to her murmuring floods,
> And be in heart and soul the same
> She was before she hither came.

It may be from his perspective, indeed, that her behavior is recalled during his last instructions to Emily: "the milk-white Doe — / The same who quietly was feeding / On the green herb, and nothing heeding." Francis himself enters the doe's order of being while trailing the renegade army; through his posture of inaction he becomes a creature of the field, a ruminant, or at least the attendant of such of creature:

> He there stands fixed from hour to hour:
> Yet sometimes in more humble guise
> Upon the turf-clad height he lies
> Stretched, herdsman-like, as if to bask
> In sunshine were his only task. (MS. 62 revision; *White Doe*, 47, 315)

Emily and the doe meanwhile at times become figures in a medieval tapestry, the doe transfigured almost into a unicorn, as in the recollection of Emily's father (for whom the tableaux of tapestry are ideologically congenial) on the eve of battle: "I overheard her as she spake / Sad words to that mute Animal, / The White Doe, in the hawthorn brake." Wordsworth does not often use the word "animal," much preferring "creature," and is more likely to use it as an adjective, as in "Animal Tranquillity and Decay," indicating a state of consciousness that is marginally human rather than nonhuman. In *White Doe*, this marginal state is sacralized, yet without leaving the borders of ordinary human reflection. The holiness of simplicity becomes, in later Wordsworth, the simplicity of the holy.

For a period after the doom of her family is completed, Emily and the doe revert to their separate states of being, Emily in her distraught human solitude, the doe in a herd: "A troop of deer came sweeping by." But then, like the single tree of the Intimations Ode, but also like the ship arbitrarily singled out for attention in "With ships the sea was sprinkled," one deer stands out: "One, among those rushing deer, / A single One... / fixed her large full eye / Upon the Lady Emily." The peculiar insistence, stressing the subjectivity of selection, with which objects are *singled* out, "of many, one," paradoxically serves as much to naturalize the doe as to make her unique. But then, as their identities begin to reunite, the doe, no longer racing with the herd, approaches Emily with "steps of thought": "A little thoughtful pause it made; / And then advanced with stealth-like pace." This means primarily, of course, that the doe after this separation has become timorous in the presence of human beings; but there is also the sense that the doe is beginning to exert an influence, subtle and for a time unfelt, that will culminate in their recognition and reunion ("O Pair / Beloved of Heaven, Heaven's chosen care"), but which first operates in a subliminal way. I would suggest once again that this "stealth" is the influence of meter on passion.

"Attended" thus "by the soft-paced doe," Emily grows used to a companion that moderates the excesses of grief. It is at this point that Wordsworth reintroduces the hierarchical sense of the man-beast relation that informs his epigraph from Bacon, as Emily for her part vouchsafes "Communication, like the ray / Of a new morning, to the nature / And prospects of the inferior Creature!" Certainly the doe is inferior, precisely in the degree to which metrical consciousness is inferior to reflective consciousness, there being no cognitive gradation to form a bridge between them, as the indifference to imitative form in Wordsworth's theory of meter makes clear; yet in each other's company they belong to the same sphere, their moods and their ways of being in the world tempered by each other to the point of unity. Emily soon dies because she is "faintly, faintly tied / To earth," and although the doe lives on the speaker confers upon it a similarly euhemeristic tribute: she "bears a memory and a mind / Raised far above the law of kind."

The concluding lines of the poem, which afforded Jeffrey a good chuckle, would seem to belie the sense I have tried to develop in this chapter that the steady pace of hoofed animals in Wordsworth thematizes the chronometric aspect of the ontic awareness, awareness of being in (a spot of) real time, that is disclosed in the lyric moment. After all, here we find the speaker saying that when Bolton Priory looks down on the doe in the churchyard, it smiles "[a] gracious smile," and "seems to say," like a Grecian urn, " 'Thou, thou are not a Child of Time, / But Daughter of the Eternal Prime.' " Not Wordsworth's finest hour, to be sure, but it does afford a very precise means of gauging how far he has come, as a theorist of lyric, from "We Are Seven" and "The Idiot Boy." The little girl of "We Are Seven" is a child of time, much to the speaker's frustration, but she makes us sense that insight resides in immanence rather than transcendence. Johnny and the pony combine to show that time is the scene of mutability *only* for those forms of enlightenment consciousness that insist on difference. By 1807, Wordsworth no longer fully trusts *das Kind im Manne,* whether as child, as idiot, or as the marginally human of any other kind, precisely because such figures are children of time, and not at all necessarily "in Abraham's bosom all the year," God being with them when we know it not. We have moved, again, from the holy simpleton to the simplicity of the holy, and it can no longer be the primary function of metrical verse to *keep time.*

In alluding to "It is a Beauteous Evening" above, I have pushed the date at which I think this change begins to overtake Wordsworth from 1807 back to 1802, although at that period the change cannot be called definite or decisive. It is simply the point at which eschatological time begins to take precedence over being in time. This change is accompanied, in the ballad-like poems, by a shift from the child's perspective (as in "Anecdote for Fathers" and "We Are Seven," where the child's refusal to make distinctions furnishes a lesson) to what one needs rather sadly to call the adult perspective. This is clear from the difference between "The Idle Shepherd Boys" (upbraided "gently" by the bard) or "The Two Thieves" (a senile kleptomaniac and his grandson, beloved and forgiven by the parish in admiration of their innocent devotion to each other), both of 1800, and "The Beggars" of 1802, in which the adult speaker says to the children of nature who have accosted him, " 'Hush, boys! You're telling me a lie,' " and nothing in the poem reproves him for his didacticism. This latter poem in itself in some ways revisits "We Are Seven," as the concluding dispute is about whether someone is dead or not, and the speaker's exasperation, this time sanctioned, is much the same.

I wish to pause instead, though, over another poem of 1802 about an adult's encounter with a child that recalls "We Are Seven," "Alice Fell," in part because it features a horse-drawn carriage. These horses speed along to escape bad weather, and they stop, twice, at the command of the speaker. They are indeed at his command, and when they resume their pace a second time they "scamper" like mice. The command of their progress, while evidently in the speaker's absolute possession, is nevertheless indirect; it is mediated by an actual driver, the post-boy. The distance is here sharply increased, that is, between conscious agency and locomotion, and there is no question of the centaur-like bond of man and beast that I have traced in other poems. The speaker then finds that a child's cloak has become entangled in the wheel of the carriage; as the burden of the poem henceforth concerns this cloak and finding a replacement for it, it is hard to resist allegorizing, long before I. A. Richards, that the tenor has been chewed up by the vehicle.

Sign of the girl's poverty, her abjectness, the cloak is also therefore a synecdoche, making the girl's relation to the carriage in turn problematic. She has been sitting outside at the back with bad weather coming. The speaker then exercises the same authority over her (though more benign and charitable) that he exercised over the post-boy and the horses, and bids her join him inside the carriage. The poem's journey resumes, but its movement does nothing to alter the overbalance of emotion in its titular character, on whom the speaker's interrogation (recalling comparable quizzings of 1800) likewise has little effect. Halted at the tavern, the speaker orchestrates a final act of charity:

> And I gave money to the host,
> To buy a new cloak for the old.

> "And let it be of duffil grey,
> As warm a cloak as man can sell!"
> Proud creature was she the next day,
> The little orphan, Alice Fell!

The adult speaker is the hero of the poem; this child has nothing to teach him, in sharp contrast with earlier children. Yet despite having received a new gray "fell," this "creature" is not just a creature; it is not just a question of being carried by the sheltering wisdom of the poem rather than carrying it, as other creatures carry it. What steals into this conclusion is a completely gratuitous hint of lost innocence that reinforces our sense that the child has lost authority. The "mature Wordsworth" now keeps time, chronicles pauses, halts, and days not chronometrically but teleologically (before, after), and simplicity is now somehow tainted, the child now parentless, deracinated, disemparadised. Now "proud" of her appearance, like Eve, Alice fell.

Having argued that Wordsworth's poetry is chronometric — that it keeps time rather than defying it — I need to say a word about the sonnet, a form of which Wordsworth is a master comparable only to Shakespeare, Milton, and perhaps Keats in English, an evaluation he himself no doubt shared. There is no question that in one register at least Wordsworth thought of the sonnet as a containing form, the more efficacious for being close-fitting: "Nuns fret not in their narrow rooms." Wordsworth certainly does agree with sonneteers from Shakespeare to Rossetti that the form is, as Rossetti says, "a moment's monument," and there is plenty of material in Wordsworth's sonnets to add to self-referential figures of spatial miniaturization in sonnets such as gems, flowers, and stars discussed admirably in this regard by Jennifer Wagner.[22] What happens then to time, and to the role of meter as I have described it?[23] Before turning to examples, I would remark only that when he writes sonnets Wordsworth goes back to the early modern practice (to which the generation of Meredith and Rossetti also returned) of writing them in clusters and sequences. I say "clusters" because even sonnets that are not declaredly written in sequences (as are the River Duddon sonnets, the Ecclesiastical Sonnets, and those "On the Punishment of Death") are mainly written in groups: the Political Liberty group, the Trip to Calais group, the Spanish Campaign group, and so on; and these groups too can profitably be read as sequences. In other words, a sonnet is undoubtedly a distillation of cloistered liberty, less being more, but it is also to be understood as a pause in an ongoing argument, like a verse paragraph. Its Petrarchan octave-sestet and rhyming intricacy is offset by its stanzaic repetition, by a regular unfolding of iambic pentameter that levels off the peaks and troughs of reflection as effectively in this short form as in the self-dilating conversation poem — to which genre the endless "Poem to Coleridge" belongs.

The self-thematization of the sonnet as a narrow space or miniature object is common, then, but consider this sestet from one of Wordsworth's earliest sonnets, "When slow from pensive twilight's latest gleams," probably begun in 1788:

> The lonely grey-duck darkling on his way
> Quacks clamorous; deep the measured strokes rebound
> Of unseen oar parting with hollow sound
> While the slow curfew shuts the eye of day
> Soothed by the stilly scene with many a sigh,
> Heaves the full heart nor knows for whom, or why.

The focus here is on recurrent sound ("rebound," "sound"), which can take the form, or rather linearity, of "measured strokes." In looking back to Chapter 5, with its discussion of the sonnet written at the same time ("Calm is all Nature as a resting wheel"), and forward to Chapter 8, for which the discussion of *rowing* as a figure for meter is reserved, I wish to argue that the theme of measure in these lines moves the speaker forward to an acknowledgment of the indiscriminate which is strikingly different from the speaker's implication in the sestet of "Calm is all Nature" that his woes have some specific cause. Here the heave of the heart itself, with "many a sigh," becomes metronomic and concedes the disappearance of any objective correlative to feeling. Thus not only does this sonnet in itself figure forth the role of meter as described in the later "Preface," but the two sonnets together might well be read as a sequence in which specification (which is already coyly evasive) gives way to feeling without knowledge.

The paradox in Wordsworth's view of the sonnet form can be distilled in the word "composed," as in "Composed upon Westminster Bridge." "Composed": shaped, historicized, turned into that handy synecdoche for poetic form called a sonnet, but also calmed, stilled, wisely passive and even numbed, like the "maid [made] compos'd" of Collins's "Ode to Evening." Here the heart that heaved in the juvenile sonnet is "lying still." The theme of indiscrimination is unquestionably paramount (this is one of those magical poems, like "To Autumn," which all acknowledge admiringly to be "about nothing"),[24] but it would seem to be in the service of suspended time rather than metronomic time, arguably in keeping with the formalism of sonnet-writing. In *The Country and the City*, though, Raymond Williams usefully offsets this view by declaring that Wordsworth's suspended moment is not formal but is rather a percept of universal scope meant to be common to all (the poet being, after all, a man speaking to men):[25] this experience in other words is not a fiction, not a mystification, but simply what we all have felt in gazing on a cityscape at a certain auratic distance.

Before turning back to the question whether metronomic time can be involved in such a poem, it is worth pausing over Williams's interest in the universality of this experience to ask whether there is a relevant politics to be discovered in this poem. In the sonnet called "London" addressed to Milton, Wordsworth calls that specific city "a fen of stagnant waters," and it is in this expression that we can find a key to the catalog of which the London skyline is "composed" in "Upon Westminster Bridge." It is Milton's "Rocks, Caves, Lakes, Fens, Bogs, and shades of death" which not only links Wordsworth's city with "valley, rock, or hill," but also shows us *how* the city could be "[o]pen unto the fields" even though no fields were visible when one looked back toward the city from the bridge. (The houses "were spread out endlessly," writes Dorothy Wordsworth on this occasion.)[26] As a litany or catalog anticipating Wordsworth's, Milton's line lends both a model of structurelessness, its relatively formless spondaic linearity, and also a mode of indexical neutrality, to the intent of Wordsworth's semantic underdetermination. Milton's line helps Wordsworth to say that things as they just are, whether natural or man-made, are somatic, not semantic. But the link to *Paradise Lost* has another function. Sonnets, as I remarked in Chapter 1, frequently end with a dying fall or understatement in imitation of the frequently inconsequential last lines of traditional epic. That does not happen here, but the republicanism or universalization of Williams's insight points to another connection: Wordsworth inherits Milton's view that the noblest purpose of the sonnet is the celebration of a whole people's political liberty. In other words, a sonnet is not just a miniature but a microcosm; it is the distillation of that which unfolds in time on a scale that seems boundless, as in epic — and seems to extend beyond endings because those endings are calculated not to seem conclusive.

"Composed upon Westminster Bridge" is part of a sonnet group that includes all the Calais sonnets, and looks toward a time that is "calm and free." It is written during a hiatus in the hostilities with France when peace seems within grasp and London can be hailed proudly as a symbol of freedom, with the river gliding "at his own sweet will" through time. What is laid to rest here, and what discloses the only tangentially political nature of this freedom, as most commentary on the poem has implicitly recognized, is the purposeful bustle of life when the city is awake — as in the exhausting phantasmagoric vision of London in *Prelude* 7, when everything, like the cloak of Jack the Giant-killer labeled "Invisible," is overburdened with the kinds of signification that call attention to their arbitrariness. This sonnet then may be a moment's monument but it is also part of a journey. There is conflicting evidence about when it was "composed" (September or July, 1802 or 1803), but we know when and where, and in what circumstances, what Helen Vendler would call its "experiential beginning" took place.[27] Wordsworth and his sister were in a "diligence," the shuttle carriage to Dover, crossing a bridge between past and future, in this case between the past with Dorothy and the future with Dorothy and Mary, the past with Annette Vallon — to be visited in Calais under Dorothy's chaperonage — and the future with Mary Hutchinson. They must have felt even more strongly than usual that they were keeping time; so much so indeed that the horses audibly drawing the diligence forward, hoof after hoof, just go without saying.

# 7

## *The Poem to Coleridge*

> *Scattering thus*
> *In passion many a desultory sound,*
> *I deemed that I had adequately cloathed*
> *Meanings at which I hardly hinted, thoughts*
> *And forms of which I scarcely had produced*
> *A monument and arbitrary sign.*
> —Peter Bell MS, *Fragment (a), 8–13*

In saying that "The Poem to Coleridge," the working title by which *The Prelude* was always known in the Wordsworth circle, needs to be taken still more seriously than it has been, I don't mean that the title suggested by Wordsworth's wife and agreed upon by all involved when the poem was published in 1850 is wrong or even misleading. But before turning to the title that makes *The Prelude* a conversation poem, it is worth stressing why "The Prelude" is indeed a good title. It does not just promise whatever long poem it may be that Wordsworth has in mind — by Milton left unsung, for example, or else something comparable to "Michael" or "The Ruined Cottage" but more sustained [I, 221–24]). It promises what is coyly described in Book I as one possibility among many, albeit his "last and favorite aspiration" (I, 228): the great philosophical poem that Coleridge wanted him to write with "Orphean lyre" (I,

234).[1] This was to be a grand versification of the ideas that Coleridge supposed them to share in common, or supposed himself in any case to have taught Wordsworth to understand and believe. (I have pointed to Coleridge's earliest doubts on this score in my chapter on "The Rime of the Ancient Mariner.") This prospect is an "awful burthen," though (I, 235), which the poet professes himself eager to postpone until he is mature enough to understand what Coleridge wants him to say. His self-inventory of 1799 is already a prelude in this sense—though it is not addressed to Coleridge until the end—when, as yet somewhat enigmatically, the poet opens with what would continue to be the crisis point of Book I in later versions: "Was it for this?" Was it just to end up sitting by a foreign stove with nothing suitably profound to say that he was so generously endowed in childhood with a poet's sensibility? Well, perhaps he can find his theme—returning to the poem in 1804—by dwelling first on this very endowment. (For he has long been certain of his vocation, more certain by far than Coleridge ever was of his.) Perhaps somehow within this preliminary survey of his past, "the growth of my mind," but also, with hope, "the growth of a poet's mind," any poet's—perhaps within this prelude he will uncover the very ideas Coleridge wants him to express. Were that the case, and were it not quaint and pedantic, nay, Coleridgean, to do so, some future executor could then call his poem *The Prolepsis.*

The 1799 version is already a prelude that concludes with an address to Coleridge, but it does not yet aspire to be proleptic. It is strictly a review of credentials (Clifford Siskin calls even the later versions a "resumé")[2] for what remains an implicit task, sure to be more worthwhile, whatever it is, than "this." Freezing in Goslar, Wordsworth can have no distinct conception of what Coleridge is learning in Göttingen. The fuller and more consecutive account of the poet's personal history is added in 1804 to give space and occasion for the task now to be anticipated, the task expressly urged upon him by Coleridge, as Cowper's was by Mrs. Unwin, and promised to Coleridge as a treat to look forward to during his wished-for rehabilitation abroad. (Already in 1799, with Coleridge then en route to London, Wordsworth is somewhat officiously praying, "Health and the quiet of a healthful mind / Attend thee" [II, 510].) The task in this expanded form can now perhaps be realized in prophetic moments, or couched in stirring symbolism, or at least, the poet hopes, taken as it were by surprise. Important in this girding of the loins is the hope that, in keeping with Coleridge's belief in a transcendent imaginative principle in which gifted minds participate, Wordsworth's autobiography can also be enthymemic, a psychological prolegomena to any future Coleridgean metaphysic. "Blest the infant Babe" and all the other passages in which Wordsworth is careful not just to talk about himself are composed to this end.

Interesting, however, that Coleridge in 1807, although lost in something beyond admiration ("when I rose, I found myself in prayer" [112]), nevertheless rejects Wordsworth's bid for this power of generalization: in its subtitle, "To William Wordsworth" responds to "the recitation of a poem on the growth of an individual mind" ("of His Own Mind," one manuscript reads).[3] It *is*, Coleridge says, a "prophetic lay" (3), but prophetic only of "a [single] Human Spirit" (6). Not Coleridge's philosophy but simply the consecration of Wordsworth's own genius is prophesied ("With steadfast eye I viewed thee in the choir / Of ever-enduring men" [49–50]), in contrast with which, "with a heart forlorn," Coleridge must now utter his own version of "Was it for this?" All his youthful hopes have resulted in death-in-life (61–75), including perhaps the youthful hope that Wordsworth would some day be his poetic mouthpiece:

> and all,
> Commune with thee had opened out — but flowers
> Strewed on my corpse, and borne upon my bier,
> In the same coffin, for the self-same grave! (72–75)

This last line is difficult to construe ("self-same" as what?) unless somehow against the apparent sense of the passage Coleridge can be seen burying Wordsworth alongside himself. "Commune with thee" is strikingly ambiguous: we expect Coleridge to say generously, as in effect he does in the lines preceding these and elsewhere, "what I was taught by you," but here he allows the reading, "what I told you." *That* is what must now be buried because it is dead in him who can no longer speak it, and likewise in him who could speak it but has apparently failed to heed it.

Coleridge's *hommage,* which includes an excellent brief description of *The Prelude*'s contents, does touch upon one matter of doctrine, the eolian harp or correspondent breeze theme with which Wordsworth's poem begins and to which he frequently recurs. Even in "Tintern Abbey" this theme of mutuality — "what they half create, and half perceive" — reflects Wordsworth's effort to make the imagination seem less Hartleyan and more creative, more of a visionary gleam in the head than he often supposes it to be — though in that poem only "they," the outer senses of eye and ear, are involved. That is, this theme, call it the Abrams theme after its most distinguished modern expositor,[4] reflects Wordsworth's effort to agree with Coleridge. But if we are to see why Coleridge does not consider even this theme, rightly or wrongly expressed, to be proleptic of the great philosophical poem, we have only to learn what he wanted Wordsworth to say by glancing at the opening words of "Frost at Midnight," the poem to which "Tintern Abbey" makes answer: "The Frost performs its secret ministry, / Unhelped by any wind." Very positively and precisely, Coleridge here *states* (there is no other word for it) that this frost is neither an eolian harp nor a correspondent breeze, both of which need wind. That is his point. The thin blue flame on the grate burns mysteriously without a fuel source, harbinger of a visitor who may arrive unbidden. The baby seems to breathe without agency, its lungs sleeping like all the rest of him. Whatever its beauties and consolations, however inexhaustible its materials for symbolization, nature for Coleridge is not integral to the imagination's alchemy. Yes, Hartley will grow up to revel in the natural world, seemingly like Wordsworth's Dorothy, but Hartley will enjoy the objects of Wordsworth's eye and ear, "lovely shapes and sounds," solely as though they were a book, "intelligible / Of that eternal language, which thy God / Utters." Neither "Tintern Abbey" nor *The Prelude* (with notable small exceptions proving the rule) says anything of the kind.

What *The Prelude* does in fact say, or whether its genius lies in its eloquent forbearance from saying anything at all, remains to be seen. Perhaps the best entrée to its labyrinth of obliquities, however, might be a review of all the places where Wordsworth is doing his best to express Coleridge's ideas, first pursuing the Abrams theme where it recurs in this poem, and then turning to the justly celebrated attempts to envision the imagination as an autonomous shaping power that escapes the limiting influence of nature altogether—Simplon, Snowdon, the Spots of Time passage. For these two themes, the correspondent breeze and the transcendental imagination, are not the same doctrine, though the former may sometimes be supposed a tentative step toward the latter; to say that the imagination and nature interact is decidedly not to say that the imagination sublates nature. The Abrams theme, which can be but need not be read as pantheism, implies some sort of monism no matter how it is read. The Lockeian model of mind allows for the agency of the understanding in reassembling sense data, yet remains unicameral and material, as Cathy Caruth has argued in a book whose trajectory passes through Wordsworth from Locke to Freud.[5] Coleridge I think agreed with this, hence believed, again, that Wordsworth could not get to Snowdon or Simplon, where "the light of sense goes out," from that starting place:

> Theme hard as high!
> . . . . . . . . . . . . . .
> Of tides obedient to external force,
> And currents self-determined, as might seem,
> Or by some inner power; of moments awful,
> Now in thy inner life, and now abroad,
> When power streamed from thee, and thy soul received
> The light reflected, as a light bestowed— (10–19)

The theme is hard, and Wordsworth didn't get it, but he should be sincerely praised, regarded even with awe, for describing with such bewildering, seductive eloquence the illusion of transcendence that even Associationism such as that of the devout David Hartley is able to convey: it is only "as might seem," however, that one can speak of thoughts independent of sense perception; and the "light bestowed" is either just the light given to the senses or it may seem "as" *though it were* bestowed by a supernatural agent. In all this there is no firm basis for a transcendental "logic" (as Coleridge called his own proposed magnum opus in prose), but only the rhetorical power that promotes conjecture to an article of faith. Ordinarily one could ask no more of a poem, as Coleridge no doubt would agree, but Wordsworth's assertions as Coleridge sees them are meant to be the psychological basis for a "philosophical poem," and Coleridge isn't fooled.

Like the inner breeze that vexes its own creation in Book I, what we half create doesn't always accord smoothly with what we half perceive. In youth, says Wordsworth after he has decided in Book II that he really must recount the sequential stages of his mental development, distasteful as it is to do so — in youth "A plastic power / Abode within me" (plastic being a Coleridgean keyword) which was sometimes "at war" with "the external things" to which it was more often "[s]ubservient strictly" (II, 381–86). This is a complicated gambit: the anchorage of things as they are is needed for the most part to show that the mind is not merely raving, yet the occasional friction with the external is needed to show, one hopes, that the mind has a transcendent home, and shapes that which has not necessarily shaped it in advance. Yet the Lockeian model, as I have said, already allows for this independence without implying a ghost in the machine.

What then of Simplon? The great Crossing the Alps showcase is prepared for by the passing encounter with Mont Blanc, which, once beheld, made the poet and his companion grieve "to have a soulless image on the eye" (VI, 454). Not Burke but Kant, presumably as explained by Coleridge: not mountains themselves but rather the realization of our capacity to think the infinite when we find that mountains are finite, that and only that is the sublime. This insight is repeated in the whole narrative of Crossing the Alps that surrounds the apostrophe to the imagination — but with an important change inherent in the rhetorical amplification of the insight. Yes, the imagination is "unfathered" (VI, 527), hence arises independent of, though prompted by, our disappointment with the finitude of material things. But Kant had not been thinking of the *imagination* in this context; he had been thinking of an a priori Idea of Reason, an abstract idea that could be disclosed, for example, in contrast with the sight and the soulless after-image of Mont Blanc. The imagination for Kant

(*Einbildungskraft*) is quite different; it is the mind's power to synthesize imagery, and remains in Kant the sort of eighteenth-century capacity (not a faculty but a handmaiden of faculties: the understanding and the judgment) that would be familiar to Addison or Akenside. Imagination must involve synthesizing imagery for Coleridge too — and for Wordsworth hoping to please Coleridge, here and in the 1815 "Preface" — if it is to be "esemplastic," the crucial remaining question then being, from what source does this imagery and the power to shape it derive? If from the senses, then nothing is gained for the claim of idealism; but if not from the senses, then the source must be apocalyptic, a repetition of the Logos, the divine fiat, in the finite mind, hence unified by way of Schelling and the idealists with Kant's transcendental Reason. That is what Wordsworth strains brilliantly to show.

Note to begin with that Wordsworth has not actually seen the pinnacle of the Alps, whatever it might mean to see it, and indeed has been left without any clear notion of it. As the correct downward path indicates, to "cross" the Alps is not in fact to pass over a pinnacle at all. What he has been deprived of, in other words, is not a sensory image but rather a pure idea that could not have been accompanied by an image and would in fact have been distorted and confused by an image. Thus when imagination lifts itself up to halt the poetic traveler (like the admonition of a churchyard epitaph), it comes to the aid of, or to supplement, a frustrated idea and not an inadequate image. Now, I agree with Empson that when Wordsworth ambiguously says "the light of sense / Goes out in flashes" (VI, 534–35; goes out like a guttering candle, but conversely goes out over the world like a rotating beacon), he inadvertently reveals his persisting empiricism;[6] and in a sense, having said that, I have already anticipated Coleridge's disappointment. But let us give Wordsworth's poetic tactics their full due. It is, again, to supplement an imperfect idea and not to transcend an imperfect image that "the light of sense goes out." The whole course of the experience has been ideal, that is, and imagination with its asserted autonomy simply eliminates such confusion as sense impressions might now cause: the confusion, for example, of beginning to form a visual impression of what crossing the Alps might be like as one retraced one's steps down the path and followed the brook, as directed. But the imagination does not halt the traveler in order to supply an idea of Reason. It supplies, rather, a copious imagery that the eye cannot see and could never have furnished, "[t]he invisible world" (VI, 536) which is, as in the Intimations Ode, "our home." Wordsworth avoids the mistake of describing this world, and the emotion that comes with the invisible imagery is a *feeling* of expansive self-sufficiency so great that "like the overflowing Nile" (VI, 548) it hides the parallel *idea,* the principle of cognitive autonomy, that has inspired it. This shows it to be a transcendental aesthetic, a purposiveness that masks the purposefulness of transcendental reason, and liberates the imagination from its empirical fetters.

Modern criticism has shown how easy it is to deconstruct this undoubtedly subtle and interesting line of poetic thought (de Man, Ferris),[7] or to lay bare its imaginary in the political unconscious (Liu).[8] But such arguments suppose in common that it is something not subject to control in the poet's discourse, however defined, that undermines what he believes. Coleridge, however, whose powers of deconstruction rival anyone's, does not pointedly ignore the Wordsworthian rhetoric of transcendence in his hymn of praise for any such tough-minded reasons as these. He doubts, rather, what everyone since has taken for granted: that Wordsworth, whom he has called "half an atheist," believes or at least has his heart in what he is saying. Here the psychologically oriented wing of the Yale School (in this instance especially Weiskel)[9] seems to me to be closest to the truth, and implicitly to voice Coleridge's frustration. Without ever declaring that Wordsworth is straining beyond the limits of his authentic and radically original poetic perspective in such moments (I am afraid I am alone in saying that), these critics acknowledge that the descendental pull of the natural sphere is so strong in Wordsworth that it renders transcendental belief staggeringly difficult ("awful burthen," "theme hard") to achieve and sustain.

The Gorge of Gondo is an infernal descent, an apocalypse gone bad, as for all the unfortunate hell-bound souls depicted in Early Modern altarpieces. The "slackening" (VI, 549) that ensued upon the peasant's tidings, a Low Church term denoting neglect of religious and moral zeal (the boy Luke in "Michael" began to "slacken in his duty" [443]), is soon "dislodged" (VI, 551), only to be replaced at the bottom of the gorge by another "lodging" (VI, 573) that is worse yet. The "narrow chasm" (VI, 553) of Homer's and Virgil's Descents is passed through, and leads downward into the atmosphere of Dante: "this gloomy pass" (VI, 554). Could the confusion about crossing the Alps have been a *selva oscura,* passed through by Wordsworth, as in all other Spots of Time, *without a guide?* "Hastily rose our guide, / Leaving *us* at the board" (1850; 566–67, emphasis mine). For this pilgrim, an as yet radical Protestant venturing through vast seas of thought alone, the plump and cheerful Robert Jones (see "A Character") is the perfect anti-Virgil. Coleridge is not there; and Wordsworth finds himself to have plummeted from the enthusiastic vision of the autonomous creative Imagination that had been his absent guide's metonymic sign, framed as an epitaphic *Denkmal,* downward to the sickness-unto-death of the "hospital (as they are named)" (VI, 574). This "dreary mansion" (VI, 577), dreariest perhaps of the many in his Father's house, so oppressed Wordsworth's spirit that he could not be prevailed on to reenter it when he returned in 1820.[10] As the "blank misgivings" of the Intimations Ode suggest, together with the idealism vertigo to which he confesses in the Fenwick headnote that explains such misgivings, the apocalyptic thought of transcendence for Wordsworth takes a tremendous psychological toll. It is un-natural. "Uprisen betimes" or not (VI, 581), one does not wish to have lain, an estranged consciousness, "among weary bones" (VI, 580). Happier far the "innocent sleep" (VI, 579) of sheer immanence. Coleridge's silence about such deliberately climactic moments, crafted for his approval, may imply his awareness that Wordsworth has, as his anecdote confesses, taken the wrong path.

As all have recognized, Simplon is the midpoint of the poem (its *cammin mezzo*), while Snowdon is its final, paradisal ascent, this time a pinnacle achieved rather than a pass negotiated. Again Wordsworth's most urgent task is to find a way of describing the imagination that will please Coleridge. Robert Jones is again his companion, now on his own, Welsh, turf; and again there is no guide present on "the lonely mountain" (XIII, 67), though a "conductor" (XIII, 18) has fallen behind at the point when "I, as chanced, the foremost of the band" (XIII, 35) burst upward out of the mist, and "a light," like the earlier "light of sense," "upon the turf / Fell like a flash" (XIII, 39–40). The grandeur of the scene is extraordinary: the pale fire of the moon, the mountaintops like a pod of leviathans turning the mist into an imaginary sea that seems more real than "the real sea" (XIII, 49), the vast yet composed "universal spectacle" (XIII, 60) — all this suggests the thought elaborated on by the poet's ensuing "meditation" (which "rose" as Imagination had earlier risen in the path [XIII, 66]): the thought that the world is but a copy of what the divine power of the imagination creates and beholds as an image of itself. Here the influence, with the poet emerging from the mist as from a cave of illusion, would seem to be Plato rather than a mediated Kant; but to elide the two would be quite suitable for the synthetic plan of Coleridge's Logic. Apocalyptic tumult is this time carefully excised from the revelation, enabling the pervasive exaltation of an ultimate rhetorical triumph.

Yet the argument of Snowdon is patently weaker than that of Simplon, because the scene Wordsworth has witnessed this time is never anything other than a scene, a visual and auditory panorama given by the senses which neither originated in nor becomes an imageless idea. What this scene is a "perfect image" *of* — "a mighty mind" (XIII, 69) — can "hold communion with the invisible world" (XIII, 105), but the scene is not itself invisible. It has afforded, precisely, a natural revelation, and it is amazing how often, in the circumstances, Wordsworth reiterates that point: "in that breach / . . . had Nature lodged / The soul, the imagination of the whole" (XIII, 62–65); "One function of such mind had Nature there / Exhibited by putting forth" (XIII, 74–75);

"The power. . . / which Nature thus / Thrusts forth upon the senses" (XIII, 84–86).[11] The insistence that in inspired poets Coleridge's imagination repeating the divine Logos completely dominates and transforms "the outward face of things" (XIII, 78) is derived repeatedly from the natural scene rather than from the transcendent source that is supposed to eclipse that scene — just as, ominously for the argument to come, the natural mist usurps the natural sea. What is not natural here? Something that can only appear if nature is a book, as normally during Wordsworth's Great Decade it is not. And in any case, Coleridge thinks, and thought already in "Frost at Midnight," that if this book is to be credited, supplementary revelation is required. It is not enough to hearken to "sounds that are / The ghostly language of the ancient earth" (II, 327–28).

"There are in our existence spots of time" (XI, 237). Why? For one thing they harbor "a renovating virtue" (XI, 259), good to recall in those Miltonic moments when one is fall'n on evil days, 'mid evil tongues: "false opinion and contentious thought / Or aught of heavier or more deadly weight" (XI, 260–61). In "Tintern Abbey," the "serene and blessed mood" in the city, beneath "the weary weight of all this unintelligible world," "amid the many shapes / Of joyless daylight," "the fretful stir / Unprofitable" marred by "evil tongues," "the sneers of selfish men," "all / The dreary intercourse of daily life," is clearly the recollection in tranquility of a Spot of Time. Notice however that both these passages concerning what we would call bad days at the office focus upon two particular aspects of our workaday discomfort: the failure of reflection (false opinion, contentious thought, the unintelligible world) and an accompanying sense of burden (heavy or deadly weight, weary weight). In the one case the burden is "lightened" owing to the spot; in the other, recalling the spot lifts us above the world's weight by means of the "feeling" (XI, 270; "knowledge" by 1850 [XII, 221]) that "the mind / Is lord and master, and that outward sense / Is but the obedient servant of her will" (XI, 270–71). That would appear to be what Coleridge wants to hear.[12]

But this is a weight! What does it mean to illuminate ("lighten") a weight? The subtle pun in "Tintern Abbey" overcomes the apparent catachresis and discloses rather that what was heavy is now made light. There need be no question of enlightenment at all; rather, whenever the burden of unintelligibility is *lifted,* we simply become indifferent to it and realize that we can live with unintelligibility after all, perhaps even that unintelligibility itself harbors the truth we have sought. It is not that thought fails, but that thought is itself the culprit. Not true "opinion" as opposed to false (could there be such a distinction) but a serene and blessed mood is what the Spots of Time are good for. They provide not enlightenment but a critique of enlightenment, of the sovereign mind; and it is rigorously in keeping, therefore, that as we read them more and more carefully we come to realize that they mean absolutely nothing at all. In 1799, the era of "Tintern Abbey," when Wordsworth first writes that there are in our existence Spots of Time, and when the looser organization of his memories makes it somewhat clearer that this declaration refers to nearly all the enchanted moments he is piecing together, not just to the Hanged Man and Waiting for Horses spots that follow it — on that occasion we hear nothing about the mind being lord and master, but only that our minds "are nourished and invisibly repaired" (1799, I, 294). They are relieved of thought-strain. There is one other "lord and master" in 1805, and that is the idealized shepherd of Wordsworth's boyhood (VIII, 393), but the sovereignty of this figure is reflected in the Rousseauian grace of doing nothing in the state of nature, "that majestic indolence so dear / To native man" (VIII, 389–90). "[S]talking through the fog" (VIII, 401), the shepherd remains in the mist from which Wordsworth will so dramatically emerge on Snowdon. "We are in a Mist," said Keats acutely, the burden of the mist-ery ringing in his ears: "To this point [but no farther] was Wordsworth come . . . when he wrote 'Tintern Abbey.' "[13] Wordsworth on Snowdon rises above the mist, anticipated in this by the shepherd and his dog described earlier in Book VIII (recall the "shepherd's cur" barking during the ascent of Snowdon [XIII, 23]); but like them, "inhabitants / Of an aerial island floating on" (VIII, 97–98), he has lost touch with terra firma, a Projector on Swift's floating island.

Snowdon and Simplon, peak and pass, are revelation or "spot" moments that come furnished with explanations, cogent or otherwise. Most of the Spots of Time do not. As I have argued elsewhere, their focal objects "rise up" as obstacles to which the rhetorical structure of the eighteenth-century sublime moment of "opening" or clearing is adapted, obstacles bringing about an ascetic clearing of the mind that is not revelatory but de-signifying.[14] A spot is not transparent. Exceptions other than Snowdon and Simplon may seem to be those "breathings" and shadowings in the wake of childhood misdemeanors (woodcock-stealing, nest-robbing, boat-stealing) that the child interprets as nature's form of penal correction. I place emphasis on the child's interpretation here, however, because such lively *ad hominem* forms of personification are presented as a child's reduction to meaning of something in itself wholly obscure. In childhood alone "the speaking face of earth and heaven" is the "prime teacher" (V, 12–13). None of the spots experienced in adolescence and later are accompanied by this simple ministry; and indeed some of the childhood spots recorded later in the poem occur without it as well.

The "powers," "spirits," and "genii" that populate the Two-Part *Prelude* but are replaced by the still slightly personified "Nature" in 1805 ("led by her" [I, 372]) confer "meanings of delight, of hope and fear" on the world (1799; I, 197). Not I think through any change of viewpoint but with greater circumspection, Wordsworth in 1805 makes the "presences of Nature" (I, 490) inspire emotions alone ("triumph, and delight, and hope, and fear" [I, 500]) rather than concepts attached to emotions. Typically what seems to be meaningful in nature ceases to be so when better understood. The colloquy with the owls in "There was a Boy" begins as a staged exercise in communication with the nonhuman, forcing the issue: "[t]hat they might answer him" (V, 399). With this stimulus the owls seem indeed to be "[r]esponsive to his call" (V, 401), but this moment is not yet the Spot of Time. The arrival of the Spot requires the severance even of a phatic tie with nature, not to mention a semantic one: "when it chanced / That pauses of deep silence mocked his skill" (V, 404–05). Only after this does the memory fragment itself deepen, substituting the agnosticism of an "uncertain heaven" (V, 412) for the child's faith in talking animals. The silence, characteristic of Wordsworth, is the ontological equivalent of death, of being dead, that is, with all beings suspended ("hung" [V, 406]) in a state of insentience; and the revelation is sadly literalized when the boy is taken from his mates, just as he had already been estranged from the jocund din of the owls. His death at ten is the death of the poet's trust in the anthropocentric community of things, and today the adult poet stands "[m]ute" (V, 422) joining the somatic unity of the things that are silent and inert in the Hawkshead churchyard, possessed of a negative knowledge that is literally superior to — "hangs / . . . above" in an emblem of its own suspense of knowing (V, 417–18) — the semantic knowledge taught to children like the Winander boy at "the village school" (V, 418).

This famous Spot, one of the few *Prelude* fragments that Wordsworth published separately (in the 1800 edition of *Lyrical Ballads*), appears in the intricately organized Book (V) called "Books." The Boy of Winander is exhibited in happy contrast with the "child, no child / But a dwarf man" (V, 294–95), steeped in book-learning, who is the subject of one of Wordsworth's ungainly satiric anatomies. Not even I am tempted to say that this child, whose complex relation to the boy programmed in every detail by his tutor in Rousseau's *Émile* has often been remarked upon, is the youthful Coleridge. It should be recalled, though, that Wordsworth — and Coleridge himself — never missed a chance to regret that Coleridge, already a prodigy of learning at Christ's Hospital, was a child "in city pent" and not a child of nature. Book V, which announces itself as a celebration of reading to offset the preponderant emphasis hitherto on education by nature, proves to be nothing of the kind, either as a whole or in any one of its gestures of apparent homage to the recorded wisdom of books. To the question of books and reading we shall return by way of the other Book V spots, the Dream of the Arab and the Drowned Man. But first, to keep track of our emphasis on *The Prelude* as a poem that compulsively quarrels with Coleridge (even, as we have seen, in those passages that attempt to versify his views), it were best to continue approaching its critique of enlightenment in terms of its psychology of perception. The intellectual rift is not caused solely by Wordsworth's failure to show convincingly that the transcendent mind is lord and master of sense experience; the far more radical problem is that Wordsworth can give no adequate account, not even a Lockeian one, of how the mind can reflect experience at all. (I would like to think that this is what Arnold means in saying there is "no philosophy" to be found in Wordsworth.) Wordsworth's critique of enlightenment is grounded in eighteenth-century thought (the materials of the indispensable Basil Willey "background" books) and is largely unrelated to the problem of idealism except in occasional but uncharacteristic Platonizings. As the relation between the uncertain heaven and the steady lake will already suggest in the Boy of Winander, Wordsworth undermines the very idea of reflection.

The climactic moment of *The Excursion* concerns a lordly white ram perfectly reflected in the pool beneath him—a passage written originally for *The Prelude* but found unsuitable. As I shall argue in the next chapter, the white ram passage too proves far from satisfactory as a triumph of reflection; but one sees immediately nonetheless that there is nothing like it in *The Prelude*. As I said in Chapter 1, the Skating episode is about the achievement of a vertiginous epiphany by severing all ties with community, and even with ideas of socialization; yet it too entails a figure of reflection. Just as the Winander boy is taken first from the owls and then from his mates, so the child of Book I first avoids going home, then even in the moment of playing at squirearchical pastimes becomes an "untired horse," "all shod with steel" (I, 459–60), then skates away from everyone and everything—reaching this final moment of solitude through a severing symbolic gesture: "to cut across the image of a star" (I, 477). In revisions Wordsworth keeps tinkering with the word for the star's double: it was a "shadow" in 1799 (I, 173) and becomes a "reflex" in 1850 (I, 450). As no striking semantic change results from these choices, one can only conclude that the place-holder, if not the specific word, holds special significance for Wordsworth, so closely does he reexamine it. He can't get away from it: in order to achieve the spot experience of unity with all existing things in their sheer somatism ("all was tranquil as a dreamless sleep" [I, 489]), he needs to slice through reflection, however one may describe it. There can be no doubling of subject and object, no specular model of any kind, because Wordsworth's way of experiencing unity "cut[s] across" the subject-object relation itself.

But what about the boast that would seem to justify an autobiography, the boast that one can form an authentic subject-object relationship with one's own past, so vivid that one seems "Two consciousnesses — conscious of myself / And of some other being" (II, 32–33)? This is not a transitory claim: "at this hour / the heart is almost mine with which I felt . . ." (I, 517–18). On the other hand, however, "[w]e see but darkly / Even when we look behind us" (III, 491–92). Wordsworth candidly reviews his efforts to recall the past, freely acknowledging everywhere at work what we would call screen memory ("what may rather have been called to life / By after-meditation" [III, 647–48]), in a classic figure of jumbled reflection, dignified as an epic simile:

> As one who hangs down-bending from the side
> Of a slow-moving boat upon the breast
> Of a still water, solacing himself
> With such discoveries as his eye can make
> Beneath him in the bottom of the deeps,
> Sees many beauteous sights — weeds, fishes, flowers,
> Grots, pebbles, roots of trees — and fancies more,
> Yet often is perplexed, and cannot part
> The shadow from the substance, rocks and sky,
> Mountains and clouds, from that which is indeed
> The region, and the things which there abide
> In their true dwelling; now is crossed by gleam
> Of his own image, by sunbeam now,
> And motions that are sent he knows not whence,
> Impediments that make his task more sweet;
> Such pleasant office have we long pursued
> Incumbent o'er the surface of past time —
> With like success. (IV, 247–64)

Wordsworth here compares himself with one of the searchers looking for the Drowned Man in the next Book, "hanging," like them and like the Boy of Winander, in the suspense of realizing that a relationship of mutuality — the responsiveness of the owls, the reflection of a living face in the water — has been severed. In this passage the confusion is pleasurable because soothingly phantasmagoric; but in the intermingling of what is seen, what is reflected, and the viewer's own intervening image — which *crosses* the scenery just as the skater crosses the image of a star — in this intermingling any possibility of considering reflection to be a model of thought, what I see doubled as what is really there, whether in the form of memory or observation, is dissolved in confusion like the scene itself.

Book VII, the London whirligig of far more frantic phantasmagoric spectacles in the absence of nature's stillness, provides a running commentary on what it means to reflect on what we see. Jack the Giant-Killer in Sadler's Wells is a ludicrous reminder that according to the reflective model of knowledge which aligns sight with recognition, we don't see things but signs of things and without the signs would see nothing at all, things as they are being to all intents and purposes enshrouded in a "coat of darkness": "his garb is black [black as death, 1850], the word / INVISIBLE flames forth upon his chest" (VII, 304, 309–10). Things in themselves, before they are known by labels, are as the moon is, " 'Hid in her vacant interlunar cave' " (VII, 307), to Milton's blind Samson — than whom there is no literary or biblical figure with whom Wordsworth more strongly identifies. The figure of Homer or Milton, the blind epic poet who sees more clearly, becomes, in Wordsworth's turn, the seer fated to pull down the house of illusion. His moments of insight are achieved in the absence of a guide, even though the fear of blindness inclines him to want one, someone like the Dora-Antigone of the later poem (1816) that opens with the opening lines of *Samson Agonistes:* "A LITTLE *onward lend thy guiding hand /* *To these dark steps, a little further on.*" In *The Prelude,* the ostensible guide is the absent Coleridge: "O honored friend, / Who in my thoughts art ever at my side, / Uphold as heretofore my fainting steps" (III, 199–201). It is the absence of that guide — honest James in the Hanged Man, the as yet unchosen wandering cloud of the Glad Preamble (I, 16), the mountain trail guides we have mentioned, "a track / To guide me" on Sarum Plain (XII, 315–16), or the Arab galloping ahead in the Dream of the Arab — that enables this latest blind poet to see.

In Book VII, he sees himself in this role most clearly, and at the same time most clearly sees the limits of reflection, when he encounters the Blind Beggar, who wears, like Jack the Giant-killer, a sign that says who and what he is. London in general is known through signs that confer meaning on the face of things, as in this Dantesque passage:

> A weary throng,
> The comers and goers face to face —
> Face after face — the string of dazzling wares,
> Shop after shop, with symbols, blazoned names,
> And all the tradesman's honours overhead:
> Here, fronts of houses, like a title-page
> With letters huge inscribed from toe to toe[.] (VII, 171–77)

Poverty and disability are everywhere marked by the poverty of signs: "Another lies at length beside a range / Of written characters with chalk inscribed" (VII, 221–22). But despite the signage diversifying the bright commodities of early industrial consumerism, and despite the accompanying affectation of singularity in personal appearance among the *flâneurs* of the day, Wordsworth remains a connoisseur of in-difference. The passers-by are so many seashells or daisies if you see through the signs that purport to make them different. When in the mood to meditate more feelingly about what the identity of all he sees might actually consist in — " 'The face of every one / That passes by me is a mystery' " (VIII, 597–98) — he is openly disillusioned with signs, "beyond / The reach of common indications" (608–09), and ready to meet the blind beggar:

> Upon his chest
> Wearing a written paper, to explain
> The story of the man, and who he was. (VII, 613–15)

Such an account must have been more ample than most, and certainly more informative than the ludicrous "INVISIBLE," yet this "upright face" (VII, 612) resembling Rilke's not only sightless but headless Archaic Torso, "from another world" tells the sighted gazer that he must change his life (VII, 623), must accept the truth that can only come naturally to the blind. Signs are not what they signify: "in this label was a type / Or emblem of the utmost that we know / Both of ourselves and of the universe" (VII, 618–20). Hard lesson for the poet, whose very critique of signification must confess its reliance on types and emblems.

The blind Milton and the sighted Newton were the poet's presiding genii at Cambridge, but for Newton's enlightenment contributions to fit the pattern we are tracing his living face, with its famous optics, must be reduced to its blind simulacrum (another type or emblem), "where the statue stood / Of Newton with his prism and silent face, / The marble index of a mind for ever / Voyaging through strange seas of Thought, alone" (1850, III, 60–63). It may be objected that if the secrets of nature, of human nature and being, remain obscure, social nature by contrast, at least in its preferred village form, is easily legible: "The face of every neighbor whom I met / Was as a volume to me" (IV, 58–59). But this copious local knowledge in turn dissipates when the broader social scene fraught with its portentous historical destiny, in this case the scene of the September Massacres at the Place de Carrousel, comes under the poet's gaze:

> Upon these
> And other sights looking as doth a man
> Upon a volume whose contents he knows
> Are memorable but from him locked up,
> Being written in a tongue he cannot read (X, 48–52).

Equally hard to read ("Long time / Did I peruse him" [IV, 419–20]), obstacle rather than transparency (propped up and upright like the Blind Beggar — and like the Drowned Man breaching the surface of the lake), the Discharged Soldier appears, his visage as dead as Newton's in marble, showing "ghastly in the moonlight" (IV, 411). He appears as an admonishment, though whether the politics surrounding abandoned veterans (the indignation of "Guilt and Sorrow" is here at most only implicit), the thoughtless manners of the collegian on vacation (Why don't you beg if you're so feeble?), or the simple failure to understand in itself is the focus of this admonishment remains unclear. True it is, though, as the 1798 version of The Discharged Soldier emphasizes, that the admonishment seems to come from some other order of being: the ghastly soldier who seems indifferent to all things including his own plight is "a man cut off / From all his kind, and more than half detached / From his own nature." He has ceased to belong to or to care about the realm of signification, and speaks as it were from beyond the grave in "a tone / Of weakness and indifference, as of one / Remembering the importance of his theme / But feeling it no longer" (IV, 475–78). It remains to consider what kind of transition this figure provides to the theme of reading and books that ensues and for the first time suspends the narrative of the poem.

Ostensibly, the Discharged Soldier at the end of Book IV brings to a conclusion the reflections on suffering that may be called personal — "Enough of private sorrow" (MS. W) — and introduces those painful feelings that one may experience in behalf of all humanity, for example the feeling at the beginning of Book V that books, which should be immortal, are made out of perishable materials.[15] This sentiment is curiously derailed by the same idealism vertigo one senses in the "blank misgivings" of the Intimations Ode, so that what begins as a complaint that books can't last becomes a complaint that when we become immortal we won't be able to enjoy "such garments" (V, 23), the perishable pages and bindings and printed verbal signs (such as poems) he has just decried. If the inaccessible thing in itself in Wordsworth is indicated by the keyword "naked," among others, "garments" is one of his most interesting signs for a sign, for the way the thing in itself is concealed by its designated identity. The burden of knowing — not the weary weight of not knowing — makes a nuisance of the self as much as of the labels affixed to others: "the very garments that I wore appeared / To prey upon my strength, and stopped the course / And quiet stream of self-forgetfulness" (IV, 292–94). The zero degrees of selfhood, aimed at in so many of the spots, are nakedness and death — hence the sad disservice done to Wordsworth by insisting, with Hazlitt and Keats and every anti-romantic reader from their day to this, on his egoism.

It is to insist on the antithesis of nakedness and clothing (developing the conceit of wearing bareness like a garment in the Westminster Bridge sonnet) that the Drowned Man spot, appropriated by Wordsworth in 1805 for the Books topic, is introduced by staging the detachment of signs from things that alone, and paradoxically, makes intelligibility possible: "I saw distinctly on the opposite shore / A heap of garments," and these signs not accidentally seen at a distance, across a gulf, already "distinctly" supply the supposition of "one who was there bathing" (V, 460–62). As a span of time passes to reinforce the spatial gap, knowledge becomes certain: "The succeeding day — / Those unclaimed garments telling a plain tale . . ." (V, 467). Were all this to be understood as a philosophical parable (suitable in form though decidedly not in content for the projected *Recluse*), it would amount to saying that the nature of objects becomes clearest when they are themselves absent, and when the signs that identify them in turn are distant in space and time and "unclaimed" — no longer camouflaged *as signs* by attachment to the objects their estrangement clarifies. When the drowned man "bolt upright / Rose with his ghastly face, a spectre shape" (V, 471–72), having been probed for with "grappling-irons and long poles" (V, 469) as if by strenuous thought probing the depths, he proves a spot-object that most closely resembles the Discharged Soldier with *his* ghastly face, though in being upright and uprisen he has much in common with the looming mountain in Book I, with the recollection that "[d]oth here rise up against me" in Book IV (316), with the Imagination uprisen in Book VI, and the Blind Man propped upright in Book VII. But among these figures the Discharged Soldier and Blind Man are most closely related, each admonishments as though "from another world" about the limits of what we can know. In the lines added to the 1799 Drowned Man spot in 1805, yoking this episode to the theme of Book V with obvious strain, Wordsworth says it was because of books that he was not bothered as a child by this and other gothic nightmares made real. Gruesome things were made familiar by fairy tales and romances. But this further instance of familiarization with things by means of signs is yet another form of distancing, an "ideal grace" conferred on the grotesque and immediate which can only serve further to alienate consciousness from actuality (V, 479).

"Books" always do that. That the Dream of the Arab was in 1805 assigned to a "friend" (V, 49) who must have been Coleridge helps show how we can understand this dream as an introduction to the theme of reading. As a prodigious reader, Coleridge may or may not be a friend of the false secondary power whereby we multiply distinctions; but it is well to remember that the virtuoso polymath anatomized in Book V is none other than the learned boy who "can read / The inside of the earth, and spell the stars" (V, 332–33). How can reading be rescued from satire? The dreamer in his cave by the sea (sequestered and lulled by oceanic sound as effectively as the boy Marcel reading in his room) is reading, or more precisely has ceased to read, *Don Quixote*. From this source arises the gaunt figure of Quixote with his lance who sometimes is and sometimes is not also an Arab, probably Cide Hamete Benengeli, the Arab whom Cervantes' narrator encounters in Barcelona and entrusts with translating the continuation of the Quixote story that he has found there —but whom he *mistrusts* thereafter and blames for any inaccuracies the reader may find in the text. It is this quixotic Arab who explains to the dreamer that the stone and shell he hopes to save from the coming deluge are Euclid's *Elements* and an "ode in passion uttered," respectively. The ode, a song of the earth prophesying its own dissolution in the flood, speaks "an unknown tongue, / Which yet I understood" (V, 94–95), an oddity for one normally so skeptical about grasping even languages that are known —unless we remember that he is, after all, dreaming, and that Coleridge, if the dreamer be he, had by then sadly become a waking dreamer. This episode is not composed as a waking meditation, nor could it be; the situation as represented concerns a person having a dream (and we know that dreaming is as delusive as madness or the *malin génie* for the first dreamer of this dream, Descartes),[16] a dreamer who is being instructed about the importance of books by the unreliable translator of a torn manuscript found in a bazaar and a paranoid delusive whose particular psychosis consists in *thinking that what he reads in books is true*. What this madman tells the dreamer is that a stone and a shell, the always reliable mineral basis of Wordsworth's ontology, are not a stone and a shell but books. The simple converse, in an awakened state from which the learned boy soon to be described must be excluded, the lesson that the child of nature must learn from the silence of the owls, is that one can read books about as well as one can read stones and shells.[17]

"Not that I slighted books" (III, 371); but he does seem to like them best when they become objects in the natural world like stones and shells. When his aging guardian Ann Tyson used the Bible she had been reading for a pillow on Sunday afternoons, that is when Wordsworth "loved the book" (IV, 220). Even the metaphor of reading is so troublesome that a long passage of 1805 (VIII, 64–11) attempting to explain how the love of nature leads to the love of man in terms of learning "to read the inner mind" is cut from 1850, as if to confess that the inadequacy of the metaphor signals the difficulty of the theme itself. Truly praiseworthy books, like fairy tales and the Arabian Nights in childhood, can be valued because they so clearly make no claim to be true, requiring a willing suspension of disbelief that goes without saying:

> Ye dreamers, then,
> Forgers of lawless tales, we bless you then —
> Impostors, drivellers, as the ape
> Philosophy will call you — (V, 547–50)

These books and only these serve the same purpose that is served by the negation of the ego — "self-forgetfulness" — in the Spots of Time: "The child whose love is here, at least doth reap / One precious gain — that he forgets himself" (V, 368–69). The "ape philosophy" is meanwhile busy with reflection, and the intimate connection between truth-claims and the ego is most obvious in books, whose admirers are "fed"

> By the dead letter, not the spirit of things,
> Whose truth is not a motion or a shape
> Instinct with vital functions, but a block
> Or waxen image which yourselves have made (VIII, 431–36)

The poets preferred by the adult reader seem marked by the same exemption from truth-claims as children's books, and Wordsworth at the time of his sojourn in France cared little for any reading that did not claim this exemption, "even the historian's tale / Prizing but little otherwise than as I prized / Tales of the poets" (IX, 207–09). As though Book V and much of Book VIII were not sufficient, the attack on "that to which alone we give / The name of education" is renewed in Book XII, when he thinks "above all / How books mislead us" (XII, 169–70, 206–07).[18]

He knows well enough that *The Prelude* in its turn misleads us, and hopes in some degree that it will mislead at least one reader, Coleridge, but he can never feel comfortable with an original insight so subversive — of religion in any conventional sense and of the enlightenment construction of meaning, as well as of friendship — that a "book," any book, must inevitably lead us away from it. Thus far in this chapter the ontic theme has appeared only as that which lingers when Wordsworth's surprising, even inadvertent negations have done their work. It remains to bring this theme once again to the fore as that which is compulsively affirmed in and as the vacancy of visionary dreariness in *The Prelude*.

I have been something of a quoting fool for the last few pages because, despite the tedium of this sort of cento-writing for writer and reader alike, I have not wanted to let stand the viewpoint, easy to espouse, that Wordsworth's distrust of knowledge understood as semiotics, a world of signs, is merely a casual or skin-deep "romantic" metaphor, bound to turn up here and there but scarcely of central importance. It is absolutely integral to the form of truth that the poem "to" the polymath Coleridge discloses. Wordsworth's surprisingly copious animadversions (Lockeian? Saussurian? Derridean?) on books and signs warn us that this truth can no more be identified in words than any other. It can however be triangulated as an association, an alignment, of bedrock existences, each in themselves at once indisputably present and, as Hartman would say, "unremarkable," comprising the part of lived experience that must be felt as pre-significant yet determinate, perhaps determinate because pre-significant.

As in reading "Tintern Abbey," we are steadily brought up short in *The Prelude* by the immanence of death in every moment or "spot" revelation, and I think it is that that pained Wordsworth most about what he had uniquely to say. The moment of denial that sets the stage for the poem's final peroration puts the problem clearly. Never, he says, speaking chiefly in a moral register of yielding to selfish habits that a hedonistic philosophy would justify—never has he permitted himself to

> Oppress [his mind] by the laws of vulgar sense,
> And substitute a universe of death,
> The falsest of all worlds, in place of that
> Which is divine and true. (XIII, 140–43)

Lakes, fens, bogs, a universe of death: could Milton's hell be Wordsworth's Lake District—revealing once for all what his "strong misreading" of *Paradise Lost* consists in, more radical even than the interiorization of Milton's epic promised in the "Prospectus to *The Recluse*"?

To focus the centrality of death—unrelieved by piety—to the structure of the spot moment, we may choose a spot from the "Five-Part *Prelude*" manuscript materials that was rejected for 1805, not omitting to consider why it did not make the grade:

> One evening, walking in the public way,
> A peasant of the valley where I dwelt
> Being my chance companion, he stopped short
> And pointed to an object full in view
> At a small distance. 'Twas a horse, that stood
> Alone upon a little breast of ground
> With a clear silver moonlight sky behind.
> With one leg from the ground the creature stood,
> Insensible and still; breath, motion gone,
> Mane, ears, and tail, as lifeless as the trunk
> That had no stir of breath. We paused awhile
> In pleasure of the sight, and left him there,

With all his functions silently sealed up,
Like an amphibious work of Nature's hand,
A borderer dwelling betwixt life and death,
A living statue or a statued life. (MS. W., 57–73)[19]

The writing is somewhat matter-of-fact, but Wordsworth could easily have polished it; and there is something in its very directness (the quality that caused Empson to prefer the style of 1805 to that of 1850) that places the unadorned fact of this perception in relief: "Mane, ears, and tail as lifeless as the trunk." As it stands, then, this "spot" has three features that set it apart from others (but not, interestingly, from the rejected white ram passage, which it does closely resemble): its object is an animal, not a dehumanized person or a silent landscape (from 1805 on, one dismounts from a horse or waits for horses in the spot moment, and the "single sheep" of Waiting for Horses is the only animal in any spot); it is not "worked up" even with the excited punctuation Wordsworth sometimes uses to gesture toward meaning; and it includes a companion, albeit a casual one, who functions as a guide. This means that what the peasant points to, what he has the sensibility to recognize, is an experience common to all, too plainly in view ("full in view / At a small distance") for the poet's mediation or meditation to be required. The manner of its being said, like its backlit silver frame that no one could possibly miss, shows it to go without saying. And what is "it"? The fact that life is "animal," and that living bodies suspended in motion ("laid asleep / In body") show that the somatic basis of life is barely distinct, as a border condition, from the somatism of death. It shows too directly and declaratively what the ultimately published Spots of Time keep at a distance, though still in view.

The disclosure of things as things, not as entities in a vertical chain of being ranged from inanimate to animate to reflective to celestial but as these varied entities in their inanimate or suspended moment: that is the sole function of the Wordsworthian imagination. Unlike Coleridge's esemplastic power, it does not create unity but discloses it, precisely by forcing aside, or seeing beneath, the reconciliation and synthesis of difference with which Coleridge's definitions (and some of Wordsworth's too in the 1815 "Preface") are concerned. Coleridge is addressed on the famous morning of Wordsworth's "election" as a poet: "Ah, need I say, dear friend, that to the brim my heart was full?" (IV, 340–41). He has been up dancing all night, and in one of his most knowingly Freudian moments confesses to such "vulgar laws of sense" as the "[s]light shocks of young love-liking" which will give way, in the morning, to what is not only sublime but a sublimation. His heart is full, but why, and with what? The magnificent scene before him in a way seems human: "The sea was laughing" like the girls the night before, and he is connected to it by means of this sublimation. Yet the landscape seems to do its work, as usual, by dissolving difference rather than as a "multëity in unity." If the sea is anthropomorphic, that is to show that all things laugh, not just human things, the point being not that all things are human or even divine but just that they are all the same — here in their laughing moment, at other times wearing in common the face of death. The 1850 revision of this scene *composes* it — as Empson complains in his radio talk defending the 1805 version of the poem (see Chapter 5, 000) — carefully locating its components in painterly and instrumental relation to each other. In 1850 the mountains purposefully "shone" bright, for example, but in 1805 they just "were" bright. All the emphasis in the first version is thrown on sameness of being, so that "solid" mountains merge with clouds in being as "bright" as they are; and the lower regions are pervaded by a "sweetness" about which there is nothing unique but which belongs to a "common" dawn — an amazingly counterintuitive use of this keyword (retained in 1850) for the designation of such a special moment. Apparently what is revealed through the sheer intensity of this sense of unity is that the experience of unity itself is not special at all but can be common. In this brilliant dawn, in which here too it is bliss to be alive, there is nothing new under the sun. With this understanding the young man realizes that his excitement has a permanent basis, and signals a lasting vocation: "On I walked / In blessedness, which yet remains" (IV, 344–45).

Another way of reading the instinctive revision of Milton's "universe of death" is to take note of Wordsworth's telltale restatement of the end of *Paradise Lost* with which he begins, twice, in Book I. If the "world" was all before Adam and Eve, entailing the fall into socialization (not the fortunate part of the Fall) that stretches ahead, Wordsworth upon escaping the city and entering rather than leaving his preferred home declares that "[t]he earth is all before me" (I, 16). It requires only a hint from Heidegger to see that the Miltonic projection of a socialized world has been reversed, and that nature for Wordsworth is much more decidedly that which is not the social than it is conventionally. "Nature" really is a being toward one's own death, one's existence in a universe of death. By the end of this first trial run, which features choosing rather than a drifting toward a destination, the direction can be announced: "The road lies plain before me" (I, 668). It reposes ahead as the level plain of existence-in-itself. Home at Grasmere is a very different place from the transcendental home of the Intimations Ode, as Wordsworth says not just incidentally but insistently. When the homeward movement is repeated in Book IV, not to Grasmere but to its equivalent, Hawkshead, an escape this time from the socializations of college life (thinking, drinking), the "road" has become unmistakably Stygian. Windermere, southern gateway to the Lake District, becomes a "river" in 1850 (IV, 6), and "the old ferryman" of 1805 (IV, 7) becomes "the Charon of the flood" in 1850 (IV, 14). In either identity the ferryman carries the poet "home / To that sweet valley where I had been reared" (1805, IV, 10–11). In his end is his beginning.

The next homecoming, this time after the turbulence of France, echoes these notes — "When to my native land, / . . . I returned" (X, 201–02) — but by then has acquired a new resonance from the peculiar story that precedes it, Vaudracour and Julia. I am not sure it has been noticed how often Wordsworth alludes, during the course of that narrative, to the wonderful epic anticlimax with which Milton concludes *Paradise Regained:* "Home to his mother's house he close returned." Having confirmed his identity as and with the Father, the Son now puts off divinity, as he must, and repairs to the lowly dwelling of his mortal mother. Here are the two identities of the Child in the Intimations Ode, one trailing clouds of glory and one embraced by mother earth. But in Book IX the allusion is reserved for Vaudracour, always in reference not to homecoming but to paternal bondage, to the site of the patriarchal prohibition of his happiness: "Home to his father's house did he return"; "Obtaining his liberty on condition / That to his father's house he should return"; "scarcely could at length / Tear himself from the cradle to return / Home to his father's house"; "and thus reached / His father's house, where to the innocent child / Admittance was denied" (IX, 656, 763–64, 867–69, 890–92). The effect of this repetition against the backdrop of Milton's succinct yet theologically sweeping closure can only be to suggest that the social order under the sign of patriarchy simply disallows the possibility of the Son's transcendent identity in Milton. Vaudracour will go home to his mother's house soon enough, and he arrives there, proleptically, along the road of in-difference taken by Wordsworth's ordinarily happier "marginals." A chance visitor "reached / The house and only found the matron there," and in this place of retirement, Stygian or Lethean again, "in those solitary shades / His days he wasted, an imbecilic mind" (IX, 918–19, 934–35). We can only speculate on the variety of patriarchal bans Wordsworth may have experienced in France, but the guillotine is an arresting symbol for them all. Happier far his mother's house, or spinster guardian's, or sister's.

Vaudracour's is not one of Wordsworth's happily imbecilic minds, secure in its animal tranquility and decay, though it may be mercifully imbecilic. Even so, he embodies, in this "home," the embrace of all things by earth. Here again we find Wordsworth's leveling instinct, which for him, as he admits, does not arise initially as a philosophy of human society (republican politics) but as a philosophy of nature which in its turn implies, or at first blush in any case implied, a republican politics. This too has to be said directly to Coleridge, for whom the shape of things, in themselves an "inanimate cold world" ("Dejection"), can only be constituted by the human imagination, and who may have been politically more excitable than Wordsworth in youth because for him republicanism was a visionary experience comparable to religious enthusiasm. In view of this probable difference between them, Wordsworth responds:

> And hence, O friend,
> If at the first great outbreak I rejoiced
> Less than might well befit my youth, the cause
> In part lay here, that unto me the events [of '89]
> Seemed nothing out of nature's certain course — (IX, 249–53)

It is thus just natural that a poet is a man speaking to men — that, although there is undeniably a hierarchy of intellect, "even the grossest minds" are "in kind / A brother of the very faculty / Which higher minds bear with them as their own" (MS. W., 16–22). Entailed in a vision of equality, though not in the long run a vision of political equality, is the belief that "there's not a man / That lives who hath not had his god-like hours" (III, 191–92).

It is on this account, and not just for the reason that Wordsworth can recall nothing about his own infancy, that the blest Infant Babe is evoked as a hypothesis about every mind at birth. Not only are all minds the same at that time as well as when the poet becomes a man speaking to men, not differing in kind but only in degree, but all minds in infancy likewise rely on Associationism to perceive external things as wholes, not parts (a mother, not a breast), perceiving sameness as well as being the same:

> Hence his mind,
> Even in the first trial of its powers,
> Is prompt and watchful, eager to combine
> In one appearance all the elements
> And parts of the same object, else detached
> And loth to coalesce. (II, 245–50)

This 1799 passage, wholly unrevised in 1805, was dropped altogether in 1850, replaced by some moving but philosophically less interesting lines about the spontaneous arousal of sympathy by natural beauty (II, 245–51). A growing squeamishness may have been involved, as the model "object" through which this habit of thought is to be learned is the maternal body, the key "element" of which, the breast, nourishing both the babe and its first intellectual tendencies, may in a Victorian climate have seemed a provocative fetish object, loth to coalesce with the rest of the mother beneath a decent drapery. The initial inclination toward unity in either version of the Infant Babe passage, however, is pointedly in contrast with "the false secondary power" — in itself a secondary tendency for which Wordsworth slyly enlists the unlikely disapproval of Coleridge — indicted a few lines earlier (II, 220–26).

In both the early and late passages what is at issue, Wordsworth claims, is the recognition of the "*active* universe" through feeling (II, 266; italics dropped 1850 [II, 254]). It is this conjectural pantheism, after all, which here and in many of his other best-known nature effusions Wordsworth introduces as a bridge of reconciliation with Coleridge's "One life within us and abroad." Books have been written about the Lake Poets' pantheism, a subversive article of faith encouraged by such works of "science" as Erasmus Darwin's *Zoö-nomia*, which indeed seems to have been presumed as part of their credo by many of their contemporaries and has contributed to a widespread definition of "romanticism" over the intervening two hundred years. But Coleridge was already uneasy with his pantheist conjectures — under the balefully orthodox eye of Gentle Sara — as early as "The Eolian Harp," and the fact that Wordsworth soon enough regretted having called himself a "worshipper of nature" has actually obscured from us the realization that, rhetoric apart, a sufficiently attentive reading of "Tintern Abbey" itself will show that he was not a worshipper of the active universe even then. Ironically enough, the repudiation of pantheism is precisely the point on which the two poets most closely agreed, albeit to contrasting ends. In Coleridge's definitions of the Primary and Secondary Imagination (*Biographia Literaria*, ch. 13), the "fixed and dead" natural world exists to be resurrected by the repetition in the finite human mind of divine creative life. For Wordsworth, the oneness figured most frequently by rocks and stones is inanimate, not animate: the unity of animate and inanimate things perceived through the mind's affinity with wholeness is plainest when all is tranquil as a dreamless sleep.

It has often been pointed out, for various evaluative purposes, that Wordsworth's nature descriptions are not as attentive to detail as Coleridge's more organicist renderings or, likewise, the more unadorned indexical notations of a John Clare or of Wordsworth's sister Dorothy's journal entries. Indeed, it is quite true that Wordsworth's bias in general is toward oneness at the expense of difference, a oneness of a different sort altogether from Coleridge's "multëity in unity." But sometimes he turns after all to a startling specificity of detail with an awareness that I think is not at all inconsistent with the abstraction in which he finds unity. Like a *pointilliste* or like such recent artists working with spots of color as Mark Tobey, Andrew Forge, or Chuck Close, he sees that vision coincides at the extremes of abstraction and atomism:

> gentle agitations of the mind
> From manifold distinctions, difference

> Perceived in things where to the common eye
> No difference is, and hence, from the same source,
> Sublimer joy. (II, 317–21)

This pleasure, exactly corresponding to its opposite, the "observation of affinities / In objects where no brotherhood exists / To common minds" (II, 403–04), tends likewise toward the one pivotal insight, couched here as a recollection of adolescence, hence conditionally flavored ("If this be error, and another faith / Find easier access to the pious mind" [II, 435–36]) by the rhetoric of pantheism:

> I was only then
> Contented when with bliss ineffable
> I felt the sentiment of being spread
> O'er all that moves, and all that seemeth still[.] (II, 418–21)

Until deleting the passage for 1850, Wordsworth here even calls back to Coleridge in his own language, like a Winandermere owl: "in all things / I saw one life, and felt that it was joy" (II, 429–30). By such means the autobiographer keeps just out of view the actual and opposite common ground of both poets: the universe of death.

The one life and the universe of death are never more difficult to distinguish than in those moments of vertigo with which Wordsworth feels such ambivalent fascination. Like Simon Lee reeling and stone blind, or like the exhausted dogs losing breath and eyesight in "Hart-Leap Well," Wordsworth finds in vertigo yet another form of insight through blindness. "Skating" offers this moment in its happiest form, no doubt, as does the dance preceding the Morning of Election in Book IV; but the same effect is produced by the whirl of the phantasmagoric, especially in the "blank confusion" of London, where "trivial objects" are "melted and reduced / To one identity by differences / That have no law, no meaning, and no end" (VII, 696, 703–05; in 1850 this is again a "perpetual whirl" at l. 725). Such dizzying moments in *The Prelude* may usefully be listed: "the year span round / With giddy motion" (II, 48–49); Wordsworth and Jones in France watched "[d]ances of liberty" and also themselves "formed a ring, / And hand in hand danced round and round the board" (VI, 381, 406–07); in London, "Pleasure whirls about incessantly," with "the quick dance / Of colours, lights, and forms" (1850; VII, 70, 154) and there is also St. Bartholomew's Fair, where one sees "children whirling in their roundabouts" (VII, 669). To "dance by the hour / In coronal, with Phyllis in the midst" (VIII, 421–22), or with Amaryllis in the shade, may be an aspect of pastoral conventions displaced by quotidian modern shepherds and soberer thoughts (as likewise in "Lycidas"), yet we have seen it return during Summer

Vacation, and in France. As a Paris *flâneur* at the time of his closest and also most ambivalent personal involvement with, as it were, the revolving of the revolution, like a moth near a flame he "coasted round and round the line / Of tavern, brothel, gaming-house, and shop" (IX, 51–52) — the lurid glow of the moment suffusing even the innocuous "shop." Fitting indeed in the circumstances that the scene of the recent massacre, near which he is drawn by the same magnetic attraction that is exercised by the enterprises abovementioned, is named the Place de Carrousel.

All these whirlings, increasingly urgent in the Paris of '93, arrive at the apocalyptic crescendo in which both outer violence and the inner torment of unsettled intellect and feelings result, by allusion to *Macbeth,* in the confusion of life, death, and its intermediary, sleep, which in all the registers of emotion remains the insight of blindness:

> "The horse is taught his manage, and the wind
> Of heaven wheels round and treads in his own steps;
> Year follows year, the tide returns again,
> Day follows day, all things have second birth;
> The earthquake is not satisfied at once" —
> And in such way I wrought upon myself,
> Until I seemed to hear a voice that cried
> To the whole city, "Sleep no More!" (X, 70–77)

Duncan is in his grave, as are all the revolving victims of revolutionary faction, martyrs to difference. After that fitful fever they sleep well, whirled round earth's diurnal course. But for the city that remains alive, as long as it enlists the false secondary power of reason as an object of festive worship in the cause of faction, the sleep of oneness has been murdered. To recall the profound comment of Cleanth Brooks in response to the concluding lines of the Westminster Bridge sonnet (written en route to France in 1802), Wordsworth puts the houses to sleep in order to make them seem alive.[20] He is always doing that to things.

# 8

## The Pastor's Wife and the Wanderer:
## Spousal Verse or the Mind's Excursive Power

Because a decent amount of insightful criticism has lately been written about *The Excursion,* it may no longer seem necessary for anyone taking it seriously to announce the rescue of Wordsworth's drowsy, frowsy poem from oblivion.[1] *The Excursion* has by now earned what it should never have lost: entitlement to careful reading. This is not to gainsay its many *longueurs,* or even to announce that it will "do" after all. No matter how thoughtfully we read its conversations, their prolixity endures; and no one can ignore Wordsworth's elephantine dispatch of narrative business. It is not easy to explain how verse as carefully tuned as Wordsworth's can lose effectiveness, except to say again that blank verse had better stay away from descriptive touches like "equipp'd with satchel." Yet even these safe-seeming remarks already presume too much about why *The Excursion* is the kind of poem it is. As I have argued elsewhere and will repeat in what follows, the diminishments of Wordsworth's verse in *The Excursion* are, for better or worse, accordant with his theme.[2] The task remains, though, to bring this theme into full view. It will have been the purpose of these companion chapters on Wordsworth's two completed long poems to argue that there is much still to be said about what motivates each of them — complicating the "philosophical" preference most feel for *The Prelude* — and to take my own turn working through these questions with the premise that Wordsworth's theme is never anything other than the function of poetry in human self-understanding. In *The Excursion,* the function of poetry does not change, nor is it merely eclipsed by religion in whatever form, but it does lose a measure of importance in the economy of human objectives. In *The Prelude,* poetry was subtly at odds with religion, but this tension was obscured at key moments by the sublimation of visionary experience as reflection. In *The Excursion,* the persistingly ontic function of poetry, entailing skepticism about the claims of reflection, promotes religion as long as it forswears its former arrogation of visionary power.[3]

The glimpses that Wordsworth's letters and criticism afford us of his sub-tlety as a close reader — especially of his own work — convince me that he would have admired some of the more ingenious modern readings of his work. I will admit again, however, that for the most part he would not have found my own approach convincing, least of all my approach to *The Excursion.*[4] To repeat, however: In order to come face to face with what is original and challenging in Wordsworth, we need to abandon presuppositions that Words-worth himself undeniably shared, or in any case found himself compelled to defend in keeping with the logic of his successive roles as leveling rural lyricist, psychological visionary, and Sage of Rydal Mount. It is a large part of *The Excursion*'s purpose to revisit such presuppositions by juxtaposing them, and surely this in itself suffices to explain Wordsworth's stylistically uncongenial choice of dialogic exchange for the composition of his poem. In saying this much I do feel that I would have his support, and that I have also convincingly explained why this poem is as much a detour from Coleridge's dream of a great philosophical poem as *The Prelude* was.

It is unwise, however, though certainly tempting, accordingly to distribute Wordsworth's three erstwhile *personae* abovementioned, with their diverse social, psychological, and philosophical leanings, among his three main char-acters: Solitary, Wanderer, and Pastor, respectively. Nor would it help to add a fourth preestablished role (though of course others could be added or re-aligned) and assign it to the Poet — who is plainly better suited in any case for the first role than the Solitary is. I think that there is discernible integrity in the Poet's viewpoint, even in Book I (where he is taken to be the foil or novice disciple of the Wanderer when his role is noticed at all), and I believe indeed that the Poet has the next to last word in the poem, with unexpected help from the cameo appearance of the Pastor's Wife. I do not believe, however, that the Poet's role exactly represents a past conscious viewpoint of Wordsworth, and I think this hybridity informs the other characters as well. The varied *doxa* that have sustained Wordsworth's poetic project from the beginning are not just juxtaposed here and for the first time confronted squarely *as doxa;* they are also reshuffled, bringing out hitherto unnoticed overlaps and points of allegiance. That is why there is one available retort against the complaint that all the characters sound alike, speaking the same timelessly stately blank verse with no relief to be had even from changes in tone. (Wordsworth's "with a faint sarcastic smile," "with a smile of triumph," "with a fond half-smile," "with some asperity," "with a complacent animation," and so on fail without exception to leave any trace on the speeches themselves, and what Geoffrey Hartman considers his vaguely purposeful exclamation points are as enigmatically distributed as ever.)[5] All the speeches *should* sound alike, one may say, because their viewpoints encroach upon one another more than over-sharp distinctions can acknowledge. The Solitary rarely *sounds* bitter, for example, though he says a number of disagreeably bitter things, and that is perhaps as it should be, signaling an appropriate balance between his reflexively misanthropic tendency to refuse festivities and the many evidences that he is far indeed from having relinquished all fellow-feeling.

In taking the Poet perhaps more seriously than anyone has yet taken him, I want to argue that in the years leading up to 1814 (years that include the final coordination of "The Ruined Cottage" and "The Pedlar" as Book I, entailing the reorientation of all their agendas as "early" texts),[6] Wordsworth finds a new way of expressing, in the voice of the Poet, the basic, nearly inexpressible insight about the community of human and inhuman things that motivates his writing from the beginning. That is to say, rather, he finds a new way of accommodating this insight to the cognitive and spiritual obligations (and assuredly not just those obligations imposed by Coleridge in sponsoring *The Recluse*) with which in the past, most dramatically in *The Prelude,* the intuition of somatic unity was sharply at odds. And this in turn is not to embrace the paradox that whereas fundamental divergences of viewpoint and emphasis exist in *The Prelude,* a monologue, they disappear in the dramatic form of *The Excursion.* Of course they do not disappear, and they need to be charted more rigorously than ever when they are once perceived somewhat to have bled into one another.

Setting more detailed and local points of dispute in the poem aside for the moment, we may say that the dialogic structure of *The Excursion* as a whole reflects and supports two sources of tension—fittingly reduced, however, by the uniformity of tone that offsets this structure. First there is the tension between what Wordsworth calls "spousal verse" in the "Prospectus" republished in the 1814 "Preface" to *The Excursion* and what the Wanderer celebrates, at the height of his exhortation to the Solitary in Book IV, as "the mind's *excursive* power" (1263). I shall make the incidental claim, building in part on the splendid rhetorical analysis of Alison Hickey, that this tension appears in the form of a chiasmus. The vertical thrust of the mind wedded to the ground is accomplished by the horizontal, aleatory, or Associationist trope of metonymy, whereas the horizontal sweep of the mind's excursus over and above the ground is accomplished by the vertical trope of metaphor.[7] Second, and largely dependent on the recognition of this first tension, there is the tension between poetry and religion, with prophecy — understood as the testimony of visionary witness — contested between them. It is just here that Wordsworth's decision to diminish the scope of his talent, perhaps even impair it, finds its sad yet scrupulous explanation. If the chiasmus that enables poetry in *The Excursion* newly allows for both excursive vision and spousal union, and preserves the metaphysics of reflection in the very critique of its transience, the claim of religion indicts this new poetics in turn as a kind of Cavellian skepticism that redeems doubt merely through its recovery of the ordinary: "the produce of the common day," "nothing more than what we are." Religion requires more, and the Pastor gets the last word.

*The Excursion* anticipates the logic of an important but nearly forgotten book by D. G. James, as High Church in its outlook as the Pastor could wish, called *Scepticism and Poetry.*[8] James argues that from the perspective of a religion whose deity is hidden and transcendent rather than immanent and manifest, any and all exercises of visionary imagination are noble heresies, arising from doubts about received truth, which nevertheless point the way to truth in acknowledging their own limits. This premise inspires what was then the best writing on *The Prelude* since A. C. Bradley, but it should have been reserved for *The Excursion,* about which James writes well in passing without coming to realize that the latter poem is, in effect, a rehearsal for his own book. Wordsworth calls Revelation "the written promise" long before the introduction of James's mild forerunner, the Pastor. There is the Bible (and Milton received as it were within it as an almost sacred text), and then there are other books, and Wordsworth's continued reservations about books, so powerfully if inadvertently recorded in *Prelude* 5 and concentrated here on Voltaire's hapless *Candide,*[9] now extend even to his own book, a self-consuming artifact or "inferior light." The hubris lurking in this modesty, as likewise perhaps in Prospero's, must not be overlooked. In announcing the relinquishment — not the loss — of his powers, the former torchbearer of visionary strength does not suppose himself to be offering the world a negligible book, but rather a final book, an encyclopedic screed containing everything that can be said in apocryphal form,[10] after which, the sun hidden behind the mountain, we shall be obliged to say that "the star of eve was wanting," and inferior lights shall appear in order serviceable.

Most of the social details that can be known about Wordsworth's characters have been sifted through in the recent commentaries, most often in support of arguments about the social, political, and economic determinations of the poem. The Wanderer's improbable vocation as a peddler in particular has been examined, though without establishing much consensus about whether or not it was then, or had been until recently, a plausible one.[11] The Wanderer and the Solitary themselves anticipate this topic at the beginning of Book VIII, and seem themselves not to be sure of the truth. Like modern readers demystifying Wordsworth's ideological blindnesses, such contemporaries as John Wilson, Coleridge, and Jeffrey (who expects the Wanderer to be "a person accustomed to higgle about tapes, and brass sleeve-buttons"), seemed to find the notion of a peddler-sage completely absurd, and this only in part out of loyalty to neo-classical standards of probability and propriety. Yet Wordsworth himself, who had never become inured to similar outcries against the "low" subjects of his earlier poetry, defensively cites not one but two different peddlers of his acquaintance as models for the role.[12] Interesting indeed that we still appear to have no way of knowing for sure whether one might have encountered an itinerant like the Wanderer in Wordsworth's day (or whether if one had one would have dismissed him without a hearing as a black-market rival of retail merchants, or as a "vagrant").[13] This is perhaps a token of how little objective knowledge we have even now of the "social circumstances" we compulsively attach and reattach to our various politicized images of the early nineteenth century. I hope, in any case, that my determination to ignore this entire issue will not be found too scandalous, especially when out from among all the interesting "suppressed details" I could have harnessed to a new-historicist view of this topic I seize upon only one, to which no one else to my knowledge —except De Quincey in "On Wordsworth's Poetry," indirectly—has attended. One of the two models Wordsworth mentions for the Wanderer, James Patrick of Kendal, was a married man related by marriage to Wordsworth's wife, Mary, and the guardian of his sister-in-law Sarah (beloved of Coleridge) throughout her childhood. In *The Excursion*, Margaret dies pining for her lost husband, the Solitary is aroused from the misery of losing his wife and children only by espousing (in those terms) the cause of Revolution, the Pastor is married to an exemplary helpmeet who makes an important late appearance, and nearly all the lives the Pastor recounts in the Churchyard involve memorable domestic circumstances. The Poet, though having withdrawn from "the passions of the world," pointedly rejoices in "the blessings of domestic love" (V, 59). *But the Wanderer has never married and has no dependents.*

There is, I think, a great deal to be made of this. I could imagine (though I have never heard) an argument couched in Christian imagery to the effect that the Wanderer's very celibacy is what entitles him to sing the great spousal verse that weds him to the created universe, an immaculate bridegroom. The philo-progenetive Blake probably had a dark suspicion of this sort in complaining about the fraudulence of Wordsworth's "fitting and fitted" in the "Prospectus." But Wordsworth himself was no celibate. If unconvinced by the Annette Vallon episode, we have only to read Wordsworth's correspondence with his wife to realize that for him—as for her—wedded bliss was not all tea and spinning wheels. But it is not just sex that binds Wordsworth to the earth. It should be brought out as part of the argument I have been making throughout this book that as a biographical figure Wordsworth was very much in all respects a creature of the body. His carefully nurtured "habits of temperance" —formed perhaps at least partly in reaction against Coleridge's excesses— must have been taxed somewhat on his frequent tea-time visits to the bibulous Joseph Sympson (viewed with equivocal interest by the Pastor in Book VI, and with strong disapproval by the Wanderer), and were easily overthrown, as he complains in his letters, during various rounds of dinners in London. Observe also what is eaten and drunk in his sister's account of their Scottish tours. The water-drinking bard sometimes had to settle for wine and whisky. And then, like everyone in his time and place (including the Child of "We Are Seven"), he had almost continuous contact with morbid sickness and corpses, yet even beyond these norms we know of his special fascination with funerary customs and his strong preference for keeping the corpse in plain view in transit from cottage to grave—all of which receives its due, and more, in the epitaphic *Excursion*. Consciousness itself in Wordsworth is sensuous and embodied.

Why then is it the Wanderer alone among Wordsworth's characters whose life has passed without immediate human ties? The better to make humanity his family, one again hears it whispered. Indeed, those to whom the Wanderer feels closest are "like a daughter," etc., and certainly the Poet hearkening back to their Hawkshead ties feels a filial bond. Critics make much of the discarded *Prelude* materials that partly comprise the Wanderer's biography in Book I, linking him to Wordsworth himself; but the differences (as told by the Poet) are telling, and all suggest a being among whose many virtues an aptitude for domestic life is wanting. I have more than once recalled the eighteen-year-old Wordsworth, scarcely in a state of sublimation until morning comes and the sea is laughing instead of his dance partners. Here by contrast is the Wanderer:

> And thus before his eighteenth year was told,
> Accumulated feelings pressed his heart
> With still increasing weight; he was o'erpowered
> By Nature; by the turbulence subdued
> Of his own mind; by mystery and hope,
> And by the first virgin passion of a soul
> Communing with this glorious universe. (I, 280–86)

He is ready to wed the universe, like Byron's Juan before he thinks of Donna Julia's eyes; but unlike Juan, he settles for nothing less.[14]

In stressing this issue I am of course joining the long line of readers, starting with De Quincey, who suspect the Wanderer of some slight deficiency in fellow-feeling,[15] but I must protest first that his moderate "distance from the Kind" ("Peele Castle") falls well short of habitual insensitivity. That he "never did anything for" Margaret is easily answered with "What could he have done?" He cannot have brought her husband back, nor, interestingly, can there be even a thought of taking her husband's place; he does at first talk her into better spirits; and we suppose him in his modest circumstances meanwhile to have been capable of only the smallest acts of charity—which in fact he performs in giving the child toys from his pack. And Margaret's poverty until the last phase of her descent to the grave is in any case an incidental matter, not yet acute, of which she seems scarcely conscious. (This is not to deny that her husband on the other hand was economically obsessed.) That the Wanderer cannot alter the course of Margaret's deepening melancholia, then, can scarcely be laid at his door. Hers is not a derangement for which an attendant would need to be summoned, but once it becomes inconsolability ("for my hope / It seemed she did not thank me" [I, 812–13]) it is chronic nonetheless, and additional visits interrupting the peddler's appointed rounds would have served only to add yet finer gradations to the declining arc of his story.

It is not this body of "evidence," then, on which I rely solely in choosing to echo De Quincey. Indeed, it is an undue focus on the matter of this first story (told as *The Ruined Cottage*, to which De Quincey responded) that prevents Wanderer-baiters from making a stronger case. Although it is the later signs that have for some reason been ignored, one may first review the other passages from Book I that have given pause. The first, again embedded in the Wanderer's early biography, is a reader's litmus test and has been read largely accordingly to preconception—as no doubt I do in my turn:

> there he kept
> In solitude and solitary thought
> His mind in a just equipoise of love.
> Serene it was, unclouded by the cares
> Of ordinary life; unvexed, unwarped
> By partial bondage. In his steady course,
> No piteous revolutions had he felt,
> No wild varieties of joy and grief.
> Unoccupied by sorrow of its own,
> His heart lay open. (I, 353–62)

Having thus budgeted his feelings, like the savings that have enabled a fairly early retirement from his job, he has emotional capital to spare:

> He could *afford* to suffer
> With those whom he saw suffer. (I, 370–71)

There is certainly no inadvertent suggestion here that the Wanderer lacks charitable instincts, or even strong sympathies. On the contrary, we are assured that he has them, as if to allay suspicion. What we are also told, however, is that he is definitely not Everyman, and this is in fact surprising. Wordsworth presumed that it was worthwhile talking about himself in *The Prelude* because a poet is a man speaking to men, not differing in kind but only in degree, hence in talking about himself must also be talking at least in some small measure about his readers. The Poet in *The Excursion* allows us to know that he himself is no stranger to the "wild varieties of joy and grief," and prompts us to wonder whether a life led without these ordinary passions (roads of excess overlooked in the poem by Blake) is in any sense exemplary. And to wonder, further, whether sympathy experienced by such a person can possibly translate into sympathetic understanding — the very endowment with which we are to suppose the sage Wanderer to be so generously possessed.

How can the Wanderer possibly put himself in the Solitary's shoes, and does he show any sign of having done so in his rather snide account of the Solitary's life? Surely the Solitary gets to tell his story again because the Wanderer's account is *unfair*. Otherwise the second narrative is largely superfluous: "perhaps it hath been said," says the Solitary, if not with resentment at least with the distrust we all have of having just been gossiped about (III, 964). But I anticipate. The Poet on hearing Margaret's story has been nearly overcome by the fraternal feeling of a fellow sufferer (his "one / Whom I had known and loved" and "brother's love" bring out by contrast the hint of distance in the Wanderer's solicitousness), and this excess is what the Wanderer endeavors to correct, as he likewise endeavors to correct the Solitary's despondency in Book IV. Breaking off his story at midpoint, the Wanderer appeals to "the calm of nature" (I, 604), and his expression of happy indifference mesmerizes the poet into an oblivious state (see I, 609–10). This cannot last, and upon being asked to resume his story the Wanderer warns against the "wantonness" of any "vain dalliance" with grief (I, 626, 628). When the story concludes, the Poet says, "I turned aside in weakness" (I, 919), and a certain Spenserian training in our makeup as readers keeps us from reading weakness as strength and girds us for correction: "My Friend! enough to sorrow you have given, / The purposes of wisdom ask no more" (I, 932–33). Yet is it wisdom, precisely, that the story of

Margaret can "afford"? Here in passing, though, one can point to the kind of overlap between characters that should keep our allegories at bay. The Poet too is soothed by "the calm oblivious tendencies / Of nature" (I, 928–29; indeed it is in character for him to be so, as we shall see), while the Wanderer for his part evokes the contiguity of death and life in a way that anticipates all the epitaphs to come (no more of them spoken by the Wanderer), yet remains utterly uncharacteristic, as we shall see, of its present speaker: "She sleeps in the calm earth, and peace is here" (I, 941). Peace is not in the earth but "here" just above it because the earth is nearby. Ironic indeed, yet also in keeping with the complexity of Wordsworth's investment in this poem, that the character who will finally be eclipsed, as I hope to show, by the sheer diversity of interest that reappears in Book IX, should be given an apt motto for Wordsworth's lingering somatism.

Because I wish only to argue that the Wanderer is but one spokesperson among others, not to discredit him or to saddle him with the deficiencies of the poem, I have been slow in coming to the evidences from later books, nearly always overlooked, that reinforce the cautionary notes sounded in Book I. But first, I cannot avoid mentioning the famous text, still in Book I, on which Shelley gleefully seized in the complex prose "Preface" to *Alastor,* as evidence that we need no longer pay heed (while paying him heed) to the atrophied Wordsworth. But the Wanderer, who says this in reverence to the dead, is the one who perhaps stands indicted: "Oh, Sir! The good die first, / And they whose hearts are dry as summer dust / Burn to the socket" (I, 500–02).[16] Indeed; and here he stands, gray-haired but in good health, as the Poet keeps admiringly pointing out. This is too pat, certainly in life as well as in the poem, and Margaret's protracted nine years of decline do not position her as the most striking contrast to the Wanderer's slow half-life of noble or ignoble aging (neither character quite fits the polar generalization); yet the ill-fated throw of the dice in the Wanderer's aphorism could certainly have been avoided.

In any case, as the Wanderer and the Poet approach the mountainous vale of the Solitary in Book II, the Poet somewhat gratuitously returns to the theme of the Wanderer's uninvolvement with others' emotions: "he was, himself, / To the degree that he desired, beloved" (II, 55–56). But no more. Approaching still more closely, the Wanderer having discouraged the Poet from having fun at a fair, the companions come upon the grotto that indicates in advance the Solitary's easy interaction, as a former loving parent, with children — a lesson not lost in the long run on the Wanderer, who later admires the Solitary's successfully avuncular relationship with the boy who helps serve the lunch. Yet the Wanderer fails the first spontaneous test. Realizing that the grotto is a fantasy ground for childish ingenuity, the Poet like Dante says, "Pleased with the sight, I could not choose but beckon to my Guide" (II, 428–29). Up comes the Wanderer as Virgil, and, "entering, round him threw a careless glance / Impatient to pass on" (II, 430–31).This indifference to the evidence of children's innocent pleasure is never rationalized, and will later be forgotten when we witness the Wanderer's popularity with the Pastor's daughter, but might it not be an instinctive residue of his Calvinist upbringing, burdened with Original Sin, and starkly at odds with Wordsworth's cult of the child? And finally there is the Wanderer's pious pleasure, at a time when all others present feel, at the least, the contemplative sadness earlier induced by the story of Margaret, following the Pastor's moving narrative of the Magdalene-like Ellen:

> —I noted that the Solitary's cheek
> Confessed the power of nature, — Pleased though sad,
> More pleased than sad, the grey-haired Wanderer sate;
> Thanks to his pure imaginative soul
> Capacious and serene; his blameless life . . . (VI, 1063–66)

—which leads the Wanderer to conclude: "Blest are they / Whose sorrow rather is to suffer wrong / Than to do wrong" (VI, 1069–71). But does not the underlying indifference that Wordsworth cannot conceal clearly reflect the simple fact, isolating in the extreme, that the Wanderer cannot fully empathize with domestic cares? In Books VIII and IX, belying his most unfeeling and reactionary speech of all, the one predicting that the friend of the Pastor's son is destined for a lower rank in life and will be content with it, a bond of affection between the son's "shy compeer" (IX, 431) and the son's sister, a "radiant Girl" (VIII, 493), is strongly hinted at. Whether or not his social views dovetail with Wordsworth's in this regard, the Wanderer's complete failure to realize that he may be prompting unhappy thoughts in several of his listeners by consigning the shy compeer to a humble future serves once more to show the blind spot in his understanding of human feeling.

The Wanderer as the Poet's Virgil, then, with a Beatrice still required to bring paradise into view: Enter the Pastor's wife, whose critique of the Wanderer strikes exactly the right note. Of course I do not mean the analogy to be a close one, as any special bond of feeling between this matron and the Poet is absurd to contemplate. But there remains to consider an anomalous detail, like the Wanderer's celibacy and like certain other details to be considered later: Why does the Pastor's wife make a point of falling back to confide in the Poet, having just been assigned the sole comment on the climactic reflection of the white ram in the pool? The "white ram Spot," a rejected *Prelude* fragment sharing with the sunset a pride of place here in the final Book comparable to that given the Ascent of Snowdon in *The Prelude*, will need later consideration. Suffice it here that we think it both an emblem of the Wanderer's imaginative mastery and of the validity of the reflection model of cognition on which that mastery is based. He has been talking steadily for 416 lines about the superior height (a metaphorical Snowdon) from which, in old age, no longer distracted by the buzzing of phenomena, he can achieve a transcendent overview. When he falls silent, the Pastor's wife, though she has not interrupted him, wastes no time ("No sooner had he ceased" [IX, 417]) suggesting a breath of fresh air and a picnic. The Wanderer will not speak another word for the rest of the poem. Then comes the reflected ram, the white patriarch "with his imperial front" (IX, 443) destined by self-reduplication solipsistically to civilize the entire world (each "the center of his own fair world" [IX, 448]) in the Wanderer's earlier harangues on education and empire. All gaze in silence, stunned alike by the orator and the after-image or vision of the white man's burden he appears to have conjured up. (One need only think of the "Victorian" skit in Woolf's *Between the Acts:* a fatuous patriarchal family on a picnic, talking of missionary work and bursting with Kipling's jingoism.) Again the Pastor's wife breaks the spell, and her theme is interruption:

> "Ah! What a pity were it to disperse,
> Or to disturb, so fair a spectacle,
> And yet a breath can do it!" (IX, 452–54)

A human breath, not a *spiritus,* and the "Lady" (*donna* in Dante) has used this human breath in whispering these lines (IX, 455). She continues to use this whispering breath, and contrast it with "spirit," in an aside addressed to the Poet alone, valedictory to the Wanderer, which incontrovertibly challenges the reflective model of human knowledge:

> Thence passing on, she said,
> In like low voice to my particular ear,
> "I love to hear that eloquent old Man
> Pour forth his meditations, and descant
> On human life from infancy to age.
> How pure his spirit! In what vivid hues
> His mind gives back the various forms of things,
> Caught in their fairest, happiest attitude!
> While he is speaking, I have power to see
> Even as he sees; but when his voice hath ceased,
> Then, with a sigh, sometimes I feel, as now,
> That combinations so serene and bright
> Cannot be lasting in a world like ours,
> Whose highest beauty, beautiful as it is,
> Like that reflected in yon quiet pool,

Seems but a fleeting sunbeam's gift, whose peace
The sufferance only of a breath of air!" (IX, 457–73)

We shall return to the Wanderer and his (metaphoric) power of visionary reflection. But for now, let us consider the Poet, the sole beneficiary of this judgment, who seems enlivened by it to the point of carrying forward the poem's momentum henceforth. Who is this boyish person who seems as obliviously bent on enjoyment as the boys themselves? "Eustace! Don't you see our guest wants to row?" "Oh, quite, Mama. Here, Sir, you take the oars." "Yes, love to, thanks awfully." (Instead of: "Oh no, no, you boys should row by all means." See ll. 478–83.) The Poet then evokes (as Wordsworth) the feats of youthful oarsmanship on Windermere that he recorded in Books I–II of *The Prelude,* including the moment when he did not just appropriate the oars of others but actually seized the oars of a stolen boat. But to what end, and why introduce these allusive recollections as a moment of social self-indulgence? Because, in a word, the Poet has been from the outset the poem's figure of un-self-consciousness — a portrait that almost requires, to be in keeping, an eternal boyishness. He identifies with a boy making a windmill — "the happiest he of all!" (III, 206; the Poet in his own voice uses the Virgilian *beatus ille* more often than anyone else); he loves fun, and tries unsuccessfully to lure the Wanderer from his steady course to visit a peasant festival (II, 138–40); he loves the *otium* of shepherd boys (again alerting our Spenserian antennae): "Ah! What a sweet Recess, thought I, is here! / Instantly throwing down my limbs at ease / Upon a bed of heath" (II, 349–51); he never indeed objects to ease in any form: "I, more impatient in my downward course, / Had landed upon easy ground" (II, 408–09) — happier here by far than when toiling across the bare wide common of Book I.

The Poet's enjoyment of ease accompanies an intellectual unambitiousness that is at once boyish and rustic, recalling many poems from the *Lyrical Ballads* period. It is the Poet who says, "they perhaps err least, the lowly class / Whom a benign necessity compels / To follow reason's least ambitious course" (V, 593–95). This is an unsurprising sentiment in a poem bent on refuting the Enlightenment sophistries of the Solitary, yet it is reserved for the Poet to say it, leaving to the Wanderer the more Coleridgean task of ascending the heights of metaphysics. All concur that, as the Wanderer says, "the mind's repose / On evidence is not to be ensured / By act of naked reason" (V, 560–62 — note how differently the word "naked" is here used than in *The Prelude*), yet the question remains whether the mind's repose can be ensured without an act of trans-rational visionary imagination; and here it is the Poet who seems to demur. The Poet alone among the three traveling companions never has nor ever had a vision, whether a Pisgah view or a composite figure for truth. On the contrary. In this he differs sharply from the autobiographer of *The Prelude,* who tried to play — because he felt that had no choice — the Poet, the Wanderer, and the Solitary by turns. What is reserved for the Poet of *The Excursion* now to adhere to unequivocally, then, is what throughout this book I have called a negative, anti-Coleridgean theory of the imagination — a faculty that perceives oneness by bracketing difference rather than shaping oneness in a symbolic gesture. The Poet speaks more than once of being unable to control his thoughts (as when he is advised to forget Margaret in Book I but then remembers her in spite of himself), and it is this very trust in the aleatory nature of thought that at the end of *The Excursion* recalls the opening strains of *The Prelude.* There, Adam (or Milton) disemparadised becomes Wordsworth going home, the world being all before his happily in-different gaze, which is ready to follow a twig in the stream; here, he feels likewise that he cannot go wrong: " 'Turn where we may,' said I, 'we cannot err / In this delicious region' " (IX, 503–04). Association, or metonymy, will get us by, especially if our prow has already been turned vicariously: "the Vicar said . . . 'my hand shall guide the helm' " (IX, 496).

Now we know why it is the Poet who has to be rowing. Much has been written about the oar-strokes in the Boat Stealing episode of *The Prelude,* sometimes suggesting sex, sometimes the regularity of poetic meter. There the poem, the making of the poem, was a masculine triumph signaling the rebellious heroism of an original vocation, or one that was stolen, as it were, from Milton. Here by contrast the vocation of poet conforms perfectly with the Poet's love of ease, and ease in love: "I dipped, with arms accordant, oars / Free from obstruction; and the boat advanced / Through crystal water, smoothly as a hawk"(IX, 489–91). He doesn't care if it rains or freezes, the Vicar is at the helm, poetry being now a pastoral *otium,* regularizing feeling as meter does (as in the argument of the 1800 "Preface"), free from the effort of sustaining vision (though figuratively aloft, like the "little boat" of *Peter Bell,* this boat is no eagle), and practiced under the sanction of religion. But this poetry is still sexual, still indeed a spousal verse enacting, through the repeated sameness of its iambic dipping, the union of all things both human and non-human. The Wanderer by contrast displays the mind's excursive power, and even "[t]he vision and the faculty divine," yet he is not a poet, "wanting the accomplishment of verse" (I, 79–80), as the Poet has been at pains to explain from the beginning. Possibly Emerson was the Wanderer's champion in saying that poetry is not meter but meter-making argument, and certainly Shelley's *Defense* (like Sidney's) is built around this distinction. But by the end of this poem, Wordsworth the Lost Leader has transvalued it; not as a stuffy sage, however, but as an older and wiser Idiot Boy, whose horse's relation to poetic meter I have discussed in Chapter 6. As verse, poetry is the return of the same.

Before turning back to the Wanderer, let us first see how closely the Poet works with his helmsman, the Pastor. Neither is a visionary, and both understand the world metonymically (vicarage being itself a sacred metonymy), but in representing the divine and the designification of material things, respectively, the Pastor and the Poet divide between them the two tendencies of metonymic thought. We have mentioned the Poet's attraction to simplicity, to which his occasional simple-mindedness should be added. So cozy is he on his bed of heath, for example, that he thinks the inhabitants of the Solitary's valley must be "uncalled upon to pay / The common penalties of mortal life, / Sickness, or accident, or grief, or pain" (II, 367–69) — and is mocked immediately in this musing by the coming of the funeral procession. Yet if we fail to allow this apparent wittol his point of view, we might as well let the Wanderer say everything. In such a place as this, we should reflect, the Poet does not deny the *existence* of mortality or accident; he only denies their appearance as distinct entities in a world of differences, preceded as that must be by the state he now imagines: "the pristine earth, / The planet in its nakedness" (II, 360–61). Here tellingly the word "naked," normatively discredited in this poem together with such *Prelude* keywords as "blank," "bleak," and "dreary," recovers the negative glory it enjoyed in the earlier poem. The Poet has just spoken of "a dreary plain, / With a tumultuous waste of huge hill tops / Before us; savage region! Which I paced / Dispirited" (II, 324–27). But despite participating to just this extent in the poem's tendency to wince away from the unity of the sublime and embrace the modulation of the beautiful, the Poet retains an openness to the zero degree of existential unity. What he instinctively distrusts — and in this comes closest to the speaker of *The Prelude* — is the false secondary power whereby we multiply distinctions. For this reason, the Poet remains silent during the Wanderer's encomium on education, so much at odds with *Prelude* 5, which is inspired by the Andrew Bell whom in real life we know Wordsworth for a few years to have admired and promoted. The Poet is more attuned to the continuousness of states of being than anyone except the Pastor. Of the oak-like woodcutter, for example, having said that his hair rings his temples "like ivy" (VII, 552), the Poet would never go on to say, with the Solitary, that his face "bears too much / Of Nature's impress" (VII, 559–60).

The Pastor's command of metonymy, however, is unrivaled in the poem, surely because it has a clear and definite rhetorical purpose. The Wanderer, we know, favors metaphorical clarity, being a devotee of Pisgah views (while encouraging the Solitary to cherish his own) from which all is clear and unified. The pretzel-like "mild respectful air / Of native cordiality" with which the Wanderer approaches the Pastor (and is received with "a gracious mien"), is probably not meant to remind us of Shakespeare's Osric or of the serpent bobbing and weaving in front of Eve, yet it does signal a surprising complexity in the encounter (V, 442–44). At least partly in *social* deference to the Pastor (it is hard to imagine him thinking himself intellectually or even theologically inferior, but in the Church of England there is of course an etiquette in deferring even to the unworthiest in holy orders), the Wanderer mentions the various heads of his dispute with the Solitary about human nature and requests enlightenment: "dispel this gloom" (V, 482). It would never occur to him, any more than to Coleridge, that wisdom, knowledge, and spiritual enlightenment are not coterminous. But the Pastor does not think that way. Wordsworth's "in mild reply" preceding the Pastor's response is coded elsewhere to mean that the previous speaker has given some offense that the next speaker chooses to overlook, so we are perhaps entitled to suppose that the Pastor has disapprovingly seen some way into the social and intellectual pretense of the Wanderer's atypical claim to be unenlightened, and to respond as follows, italicizing the "we" to make sure the Wanderer can make no sideways escape into visionary insight:

> "Our nature," said the Priest in mild reply,
> "Angels may weigh and fathom: they perceive,
> With undistempered and unclouded spirit,
> The object as it is; but, for ourselves,
> That speculative height *we* may not reach." (V, 485–89)[17]

Regardless whether Wordsworth knew anything at first hand about Kant, we have here to do with the *Ding an sich,* about which Coleridge is sure to have told him. The Wanderer has deferred to the Pastor most honestly in recognizing perhaps that his own metaphysic needs to be *grounded,* hence in requesting that the Pastor "[t]he mine of real life / Dig for us" (V, 630–31); but the Pastor is under no illusion about the power of epitome. Only in the Eternal Moment can statements of identity be made, and here below we need to build up knowledge through a chain of resemblances and gradations, resurrecting the somewhat outmoded Chain of Being (and angels with it!) of which the ontological leveling of Wordsworth's earlier poetic voices had been a critique.

This is clearly a complex matter, as I am hoping to show that the Pastor is an ally of the Poet, who for his part is capable of maintaining, with the Idiot Boy (and with Hegel), that there is a night in which all cows are gray. In the period at least between Hobbes and Hartley, the Chain of Being becomes an Associationist idea (like all others), hence neither a visionary synthesis *nor* an ontic indifference. It lends itself to Church hierarchies. I cannot imagine the Wanderer using the word "angels." Nothing overt is said about this, nor can be in a work that presents a unified front in attacking the Solitary's lapse from Christianity,[18] but there is an unspoken and perhaps unexamined tension between the Low Church Wanderer, with his Calvinist upbringing softened by visionary experience, and the High Church Pastor, whose distinguished social background placed him naturally in youth on the stage of urbane British culture, from which a deepening but never Enthusiastic sense of pastoral calling drew him to the comparative retirement of the Grasmere curacy. The Pastor in any case is, in the Poet's words, ideally suited to use the "fair trains of imagery" Wordsworth witnesses in the "Prospectus" when he thinks on man, on nature, and on human life ("Traynes" is Hobbes's word for the association of ideas): "Even such a Man. . ." (not *Ecce Homo* but vicariously linked)

> Before me stood that day; on holy ground
> Fraught with the relics of mortality,
> Exalting tender themes, by just degrees
> To lofty raised; and to the highest, last;
> The head and mighty paramount of truths, —
> Immortal life, in never-fading worlds,
> For mortal creatures, conquered and secure. (VI, 81–87)

Hence the "vesper-service" of the Pastor in the presence of the sunset begins by addressing God as "Power inaccessible to human thought, / Save by degrees and steps which thou hast deigned / To furnish" (IX, 615–17). The glory of the Pastor's technique is shown in his well-known comparison of human life to the eastern or western view of an April churchyard in the morning (viz. V, 526–57). You see it by degrees and from perspectives, yet the degrees can carry you to an opposite view. One thing leads by gradations to another: *Sub specie aeternitatis*, in other words, waiving the privilege of angels, the Pastor is a relativist, a skeptic about what we can know, and rather than pretending at any point to provide a whole picture, likens himself to a collector opening a cabinet of curios and displaying first one gem and then another (VIII, 20–30). He does not presume to "read" anything, even his own epitaphic stories (here in agreement with the Solitary's "*If* . . . every grave / Were as a volume" [V, 250–52; italics mine]), keeping his distance from the Book of Nature topos admired by the Wanderer and focused instead on "those truths . . . which the WORD, to the four quarters of the winds, proclaims" (V, 992–93).

This sense of the gradual — as opposed to the dialectical — moves the Pastor typically and in keeping with the Poet to speak the language of "Tintern Abbey," with its confusion of depth and height, distance and immanence, past, present, and future, all prefigured by the subtle indistinctness of its opening landscape. Calling attention to a certain dwelling, the Pastor points to a road that the eye can follow " 'till its line / Is lost within a little tuft of trees," proceeding then in "mazes serpentine" (the Miltonism lets us know that the resident, Mr. Sympson, is a less than perfect Vicar) toward its destination, verbally recalling the woods around Tintern:

> That little shady spot, that sylvan tuft
> By which the road is hidden, also hides
> A cottage from our view; though I discern
> (Ye scarcely can) amid its sheltering trees
> The smokeless chimney-top. (VII, 46, 48, 50–54)

The Pastor, who will perform his vesper-service in the presence of residual radiance when the sun is hidden ("Already had the sun, / Sinking with less than ordinary state, / Attained his western bound" [IX, 590–92]), like the Poet noting the absence of the Evening Star, characteristically speaks the language of things hidden or obliquely present — in contrast with the Wanderer, whose appeal to truths manifest and clearly reflected repeatedly speaks the language of the Intimations Ode, bringing out the close connection between that poem with its visionary gleam and the manifest Duty of the "Ode to Duty."[19]

The language of approximation, of contiguous reference, is the hallmark of the epitaph, and plays its most important part in describing the connection between the body in life and the body in death metonymically: "To a mysteriously united pair / This place is consecrate; to Death and Life" (V, 903–04), says the Pastor. All tacitly agree about this, even the Wanderer, who requests that the Pastor "pronounce, you can, / Authentic epitaphs" on "some of these / . . . from their lowly mansions hither brought" (V, 650–52). Of the house of the man with six daughters, still living but predeceased by his wife, the Pastor remarks: "Ye might think / That it had sprung self-raised from earth, or grown / Out of the living rock, to be adorned / By nature only" (VI, 1143–47). A deaf man is brought "to the profounder stillness of the grave" (VII, 468). The "pale" Solitary, whose death-in-life the poem addresses itself to revoke (thus far unsuccessfully), is mistaken for the corpse of another when the Wanderer and Poet enter his vale, which is "Urn-like . . . in shape, deep as an urn" (II, 333), and he is later seen in tableau as a churchyard monument emblematic of gradualist continuity: "The semblance bearing of a sculptured form / That leans upon a monumental urn / In peace, from morn to night, from year to year" (V, 215–17). It is indeed the challenge of metonymies evoking the death-wardness of life and time itself somehow to offset or cure the Solitary's death-wish, which had played its part in "Tintern Abbey":

> Night is than day more acceptable; sleep
> Doth, in my estimate of good, appear
> A better state than waking; death than sleep;
> Feelingly sweet is stillness after storm,
> Though under covert of the wormy ground! (III, 277–81)

(Wordsworth's use of enjambment and rhythm here is especially adventurous, a *gradus* vacillating between the collapse of boundaries in consciousness and the abruptness with which they are crossed in actuality.) Yet in this poem each speaker in his own way, certainly not excluding the Pastor with his hope elsewhere, the Poet with his love of oblivious states (happier he!), or even the Wanderer with his "peace is here," repeats the axiom of Freud, who read biology itself as a biodegradation: The aim of all life is death.[20]

What then is the cure? In the Wanderer's opinion, from which the Pastor's and the Poet's in this respect sharply diverge, the cure lies in the intimations of power, excursive power, experienced in intellectual mastery. Of the many Wordsworth passages the Wanderer would have written (had he been a poet), none is more central than Wordsworth's exultant announcement in the 1805 Spots of Time passage that there are

> passages of life in which
> We have the deepest feeling that the mind
> Is lord and master, and that outward sense
> Is but the obedient servant of her will. (*The Prelude*, XI, 269–72)

We may note in passing, if only to draw lines wherever they can be drawn, that in the 1850 *Prelude* these lines, duly qualified, would have been written by the Pastor: "those passages of life that give / Profoundest knowledge to what point, and how, / The mind is lord and master" (XII, 220–22). In the Wanderer, Coleridge's One Life ("an ebbing and a flowing mind" [I, 161]) seems to be given a Platonic (or Emersonian) turn — which is perhaps why the Intimations Ode also belongs to his canon. The "*active* Principle" of which he speaks in opening his last peroration is "the Soul of all the worlds," and is, he regrets to say, "reverenced least, / And least respected in the human Mind, / Its most apparent home" (IX, 3, 15, 18–20). It needs to be fixed in view, I think, that the Wanderer is the only transcendentalist in this poem. The mind can reflect, then (i.e., think in such a way that it mirrors itself, the world, and the truth), because it is what it sees. Knowledge of the object is identity with the object, a metaphor. This can occur only at a safe distance from mutability, aided by the lifelong avoidance of strong emotions we have emphasized, and finally achieves its fullest confirmation in the Pisgah view afforded by old age:

> For on that superior height
> Who sits, is disencumbered from the press
> Of near obstructions, and is privileged
> To breathe in solitude, above the host
> Of ever-humming insects, 'mid thin air
> That suits not them. The murmur of the leaves
> Many and idle, visits not his ear:
> This he is freed from, and from thousand notes
> (Not less unceasing, not less vain than these,)

> By which the finer passages of sense
> Are occupied; and the Soul, that would incline
> To listen, is prevented or deterred. (IX, 69–80)

This seems to me to be the Wanderer's finest moment, because of the justice it does to what it gives up. Unlike Keats, Wordsworth was only occasionally attuned to the Virgilian magic of insects humming (it is the Poet who unhappily fends off a swarm of them as the poem opens), but insofar as he is thus attuned, it is given to the Wanderer to sustain the motif ("this multitude of flies / With tuneful hum is filling all the air" [I, 596–97, and see IV, 445–48]); and unlike Coleridge and Shelley, Wordsworth did little to carry forward the "trope of the leaves" as markers of mortality that is hauntingly central in Homer, Dante, and Milton (not to mention Tennyson, Stevens, and Beckett). The song of the earth, however — or rather its sound — is more congenial, and the Wanderer has as much trouble calling it "vain" as Milton had had in banishing the pagan gods (probationally recalled by the Wanderer in Book IV). For Milton and the Wanderer alike, these are "the finer passages of sense," but sense has no place in the thin air of truth. It is the privilege of age not to be troubled by nature. (Contrast Keats's youthful sonnet, "How many Bards Gild the Lapses of Time.")

Now is the time to return to the early *Prelude* materials used for the Wanderer's biography in Book I. Like the boy Wordsworth, and like eighteenth-century theorists of the sublime, the Wanderer was stimulated in the solitudes of nature by fear. Yet on the Wanderer the effect of the sublime differs from its effect on Wordsworth. If for Wordsworth the experience of recoil from the bleakness and dreariness of nature's most forbidding moments modulates into the sense of undifferentiated oneness that inspires his poetry, for the Wanderer this same terror (I, 125–28), superimposed on the strictures of a gloomy religion, simply alienates him from the natural as such, or makes him feel in any case that his proper home is the transcendent imagination. He cultivates fear, like Collins in his ode, but does not use it — as the boy Wordsworth did — to reconcile himself to the bedrock of his living surroundings. On the contrary, in such a state he remains unvisited by precisely the song of the earth he is happy to tune out once more — if he has ever truly heard it — in Book IX, the passage quoted above which must surely recall this one:

> In his heart,
> Where fear sate thus, a cherished visitant,
> Was wanting yet the pure delight of love

— and one's hesitation in construal caused by the enjambment is I think telling —

> By sound diffused, or by the breathing air,
> Or by the silent looks of happy things. (I, 185–89)

To be sure, it would be absurd to claim that the Wanderer is not a nature enthusiast. Only Joanna and Peter Bell among all of Wordsworth's characters are not. In keeping his distance from the immediate experience of the natural, however, the Wanderer trains his excursive mind like a viewfinder on the world he passes through, a picturesque tourist in search not of well-framed scenery but of truth, or emblems of truth. Why — to halt before yet another anomaly — was he unable to teach school as a young man in need of a career? Because, in this important and literal sense, he lacked the direct experience he would have needed for influencing minds too unformed and closely confined for reflection. Such experience he does not so much gain in taking up a peripatetic trade as exchange for the advantages of reflection. He can only found, like the Plato he resembles in certain respects, a peripatetic school.

The excursive mind is not a schoolmaster, then, but lord and master, and this distinction is most interesting when we find the Wanderer freely exploring its social implications in the harangues of Books VIII and IX. He has the largely negative feelings any Wordsworthian character must have about the coming of industrialization, but uniquely in his case these feelings are tempered by his curiously Heideggerian fascination with the machine's imposition of authority — mastery — on the natural world:

> Yet do I exult,
> Casting reserve away, exult to see
> An intellectual mastery exercised
> O'er the blind elements; a purpose given,
> A perseverance fed; almost a soul
> Imparted — to brute matter. (VIII, 199–204)

Perhaps not even Wordsworth notices the inconsistency here in one who will soon insist that all things have an active principle, but it is an interesting one. Suddenly speaking the Enlightenment language that would one day provoke the critiques of Heidegger and of Adorno and Horkheimer, the Wanderer negatively transvalues the "brute matter" that has actually constituted Wordsworth's ontological ground from the beginning of his career — and the being together with which, in the many instances we have examined, is just what makes Wordsworth an important avatar of Heidegger. But here the Wanderer, like Heidegger, is of two minds, just as he appears to vacillate between two ideas of mind, an early Wordsworth in spite of himself. We can either harness the Rhine, "that brook converting as it runs / Into an instrument of deadly bane" (Wanderer, VIII, 257–58), or share Being with the river.[21] But as a social theorist, the Wanderer betrays the Coleridgean dream of a great philosophical poem transcendentally derived by extending the theme of mastery into a utilitarian dream of imperial Englishness:

Even till the smallest habitable rock,
Beaten by lonely billows, hear the songs
Of humanized society; and bloom
With civil arts, that shall breathe forth their fragrance,
A grateful tribute to all-ruling Heaven. (IX, 387–91)

The principle of colonized imitation is not at all the same as the active principle, but they have at least this in common: intellectual mastery.

This is the kind of mind that finds meaning wherever it looks, and the Wanderer begins his tutelage of the anti-intellectual Poet by telling him so: " 'I see around me here / Things which you cannot see' " (I, 469–70). Here meaning is not hermeneutic (though it often is for one who reads the Book of Nature) but mnemonic, as the Wanderer sees not concepts but absent "Things." Again the Poet's way of seeing the world may be contrasted. As readers, we find the poem's opening and closing descriptions uttered by the Poet to be allegorical. The difficult, shadow-strewn progress of the opening, accomplished with Milton's "languid steps," of course suggests to us the difficulty of life's journey, while the shadows across the ending suggest something similar; but the Poet himself never pretends to read what he says or sees. To him, the predominance of chiaroscuro in what he sees just accurately evokes things as they are, and his naïve joy in greeting moments of idyllic perfection shows how surprising he finds them. Far be from this Poet the concern of the author Wordsworth, sometimes underestimated, with the structure of this poem: the morning and sunset framing Book I repeated in the half of the poem that concludes Book IV and again at the end, Book V having begun with another morning of tedious walking; the Wanderer seen in tableau in Book I, the Solitary seen likewise in Book V, reflecting the symmetry between them to which I shall turn in a moment; the fundamental sequence of narrative — an excursion, a biography, an epitaph correcting despondency, a sunset — repeating the whole narrative in serial miniatures and vice versa. While the poet labors to unify things structurally, the Poet just knows that things are the same.

Until now I have spoken only incidentally of the Solitary, whose nihilism on the face of it sets him apart most sharply from the rest, joined as they are in hoping for his conversion. As I wish now to show, however, much of what needs to be said about him has been said already because, born in the same place, he is the alter ego of the Wanderer, a clinical exhibit of what happens when idealism fails. The symmetry is disturbed only in that the Solitary's idealism has never been transcendental, but has been invested instead in various hopes here below. This much is obvious, but bears closer examination, if only to bring out more fully the close interdynamic of these two characters in a poem in which neither the narrator nor the appointed voice of received religion are idealists. We may begin by considering the Solitary's preference for sitting home after lunch on a pleasant afternoon and drinking. The Wanderer, who will later sit in the vicarage after lunch on a pleasant afternoon and talk, here plays the Pastor's Wife and urges the Solitary outside to get some exercise — though talking had seemed good enough for him here too until the Solitary brought out the bottles. The bric-a-brac in the Solitary's abode should not be compared with the cabinet of curios from which the Pastor later figurally displays his gems. (By the way, Jeffrey notwithstanding, the notion of a ped-dler displaying wares from his pack is interestingly never expressed.) Rather than signaling the proper atomism of understanding, the Solitary's many abandoned intellectual hobbies are the sign of a disordered imagination, clos-est to Robert's ominously whimsical performance of tasks out of season in Book I, succumbing to the false secondary power after one has yielded up moral questions in despair. (Or, in Robert's case, yielded up wage labor ques-tions in despair.) Like everyone else, the Solitary needs an escape, a cure; and, judging from Wordsworth's mistaken impression in the Fenwick note that the dissenting preacher Joseph Fawcett had "fallen into habits of intemperance" (80), his cure is drink — as indeed in another poem it might have been Robert's cure too (one rather expects that turn of events in Book I, it seems to me).

I have already suggested that the water-drinking bard's contempt for this remedy, while earnest, is perhaps not as wholehearted as the Wanderer's. We need to remember that his affectionate condescension toward Benjamin the Waggoner is positively Burnsian, and that in later years he kept following the derelict behavior of Hartley Coleridge, whose talents he rated highly, with frustration yet also with a kind of sympathetic indulgence, thinking no doubt of Hartley's father but also perhaps of his own Solitary, modeled on Fawcett. It is easy to overlook the good-natured fastidious care with which the Solitary preparing lunch has spread the white cloth and set out his rustic "store / Of dainties," even including "cakes of butter curiously embossed," "Inviting us in glee to sit and eat," aided the while by the boy he has befriended, now in the role of Ganymede, "a willing Page, as he was bid, / Ministering to our need" (II, 672–88 *passim*). Not only is this festive setting scarcely what one expects in the house of a gloomy misanthrope, or even of a hermit ("You have regaled us as a hermit ought," the Wanderer inaccurately says later [II, 902]), it is given all the earmarks, generically, of the very opposite: the epicurean, pastoral, and Dutch realist touches actually move one to wonder, "Where's the wine?" (I can imagine the Poet looking around for it) and to approve, if anything, the Soli-tary's cordial and cheerful temperance.[22] Then the Wanderer makes him talk, and by the time he finishes telling the pensioner's tale the Solitary has been reminded, such is his sense of exclusion from the shining city on the hill he has witnessed, of his wish to die — though he is always at pains to explain that he is not suicidal. He now needs a pick-me-up, having had no wish to talk himself into this mood in the first place (see II, 730–32), yet in this moment, though the strain shows, we still find him playing the bountiful host, "with a blithe air of open fellowship." The "wine and stouter cheer" he brings out is still "cheer" offered in hospitality, the stale poetic diction is not avoided, and while Wordsworth no doubt here impugns the hypocrisy of drinkers pretending that a personal wish is a sociable one, he is very careful to admit, throughout this often surprising episode, that the pleasures of the table are indulged in for "cheer," for the purpose (vain and delusory like other purposes) of being happier.

The whole poem puts the question, how can we be happier? The Solitary — like Coleridge — wants to drink and talk, while the Wanderer — like Wordsworth — wants to walk and talk and forces the Solitary to join them, like Wordsworth and his sister with Coleridge in Scotland. With the Solitary once safely outside, the Wanderer later extols the healthy pleasures of exercise: "Quit your couch — / Cleave not so fondly to your moody cell" (IV, 481–82), partly to stay away from the bottle ("sink at evening into sound repose," IV, 504), and partly to put himself in the way of more visionary experiences like the shining city on the hill of which the Wanderer only now reminds him (IV, 471–74). Stasis and movement here seem to juxtapose distempered vision with visionary transport, but this is a somewhat unstable alignment. As many have pointed out and as the poem is itself at pains to show, wandering too is as often as not a dubious pastime, and has been ever since the river in Milton's Eden followed its mazy course. Yet in one sense or another wandering is what everybody does, and Wordsworth seems for the most part relatively uninterested in controlling the sometimes Spenserian or Miltonic ironies associated with the word. True, first Robert and then Margaret have "wandered much of late" (I, 754) and Margaret continues to do so until she dies, but as soon as her story ceases we find the Poet envying and hoping to emulate the medieval minstrel, "wandering on from hall to hall" (II, 2). In fact, we are to infer that, "ranging through the tamer ground / Of these our unimaginative days" (II, 23–24), the Poet and the Wanderer between them comprise a latter-day minstrel. The "mind's *excursive* power" (IV, 1263) has ceased to visit the high themes of Romance, but the Wanderer, the "obscure Itinerant" (II, 22), covers ground in a way that approximates — again — the aleatory metonymy of the ordinary, of nothing more than what we are. We shall return in the end to this reorientation of genre in assessing Wordsworth's revised opinion of the function of poetry, but it remains in the meantime to consider the Wanderer's own sense of his peripatetic vocation as an always-successful quest for significance.

As ever in Wordsworth, the rhetoric of "nothing more than what we are" cuts two ways. Peeping through the solemn grandeur of a David who proposes to enter into the lists with the Goliath Milton, unaided by pomp or epic machinery yet showing that "what we are" is a theme of cosmic as well as human proportions, the revolutionary insight that has been the main theme of this book continues to make its presence known. "Nothing" that is not there and the nothing that is: the sheer actuality of what we are, nothing more than what a stone is, or a sunset, still needs to be taken into account, but from a new perspective. We have seen the way in which the Poet and the Pastor tend to divide this perspective between them. The Poet inclines toward the quietly somatic pleasures of simplicity and ease, entailing the unambitious routines of rural custom (see VIII, 232–51), and seems largely indifferent to "the meaning of life." Like the speaker of a lyrical ballad, he makes his casual metonymic way among the beauteous and permanent forms of nature. The Pastor believes — has faith that — there is meaning, but presumes that the revelation of meaning is confined to a sacred book, and looks for meaning in the natural world not as though it were a parallel book but far more tentatively as though it might provide materials — in themselves nothing more than themselves — with which the animadverting mind can build up allegories to point a moral or adorn a tale. With eighteenth-century urbanity, he quietly distances himself from the secular revelations of the metaphoric imagination, treating it as though it were a distempered spirit.

As though it were the Solitary, that is, he who has had his Pisgah View. The Solitary is torn between believing his revelation to be significant, a promise from which his unworthiness excludes him (II, 875–76), and offering aggressively atheistic accounts of apparent marvels, accounts that require perhaps even more imagination than the Wanderer's well-practiced inferences from theodicy. These latter passages, somewhat maliciously meant by the Solitary to discomfit the Wanderer, are meant beyond this by Wordsworth to show how tortuous mechanistic explanations of origins must be. Books II and III gather together a variety of ways in which nature can be used to prove or disprove arguments of this kind. The most conspicuous disappointment is the Wanderer's, who has so very characteristically said "let us trace this streamlet to its source" (III, 30), expecting to reach a point, the spring, where "[t]he mountain infant to the sun comes forth / Like human life from darkness" (III, 34–35), only to find, with bushes in the way, that "such hope was vain" (III, 37) — an ironic backdrop to the continuing discussion of sources, causes, and origins.

The Solitary drives home his advantage soon enough, mocking the Hindus who "draw / Their holy Ganges from a skiey fount, / Even so deduce the stream of human life / from seats of power divine" (III, 254–57), confirming his own inclination to "decline / All act of inquisition whence we rise": "Our origin, what matters it?" (III, 234–35, 238). Still at lunch, and looking up at the twin peaks to be seen from his cell, the Solitary carefully demystifies any celestial overtones in the "music" to be heard from their summits, almost — but not quite — as vigilant against prosopopoeia as Paul de Man. It is strictly "nature's laws" that produce "a harmony, / So do I call it, though it be the hand of silence, though there be no voice" (II, 708, 710–12). But behind these expressions, as I have said, the poem still allows the voice of religion to whisper, "what strained paradoxes are these? Hands of silence indeed!" And so it is, at least intermittently, with the Solitary's account of his vision on the mountainside, here in the notorious language of Baron d'Holbach's *Système de la Nature:* "By earthly nature had the effect been wrought / Upon the dark materials of the storm / Now pacified" (II, 846–48). Again, having failed to find the source of the streamlet, the strollers arrive at what may or may not be a Druidic temple, only to have the Solitary insist gleefully: "The shapes before our eyes / And their arrangement, doubtless must be deemed / The sport of Nature, aided by blind Chance" (III, 124–26; cf. II, 139–40).

The Solitary never claims that nature is without significance, his strong reservation being however that its significance is of its own devising. The rather cramped circularity of this reasoning (there is no ghost in the machine, yet the machine is purposeful) is meant to remind us of those standard critiques of Lockeian materialism that still animate today's mind-brain discussions. For the Solitary, then, the Book of Nature is faintly written, intelligible yet neither theocentric nor even pointedly anthropocentric:

> "The strain of thought
> Accords with nature's language; — the soft voice
> Of yon white torrent falling down the rocks
> Speaks, though less distinctly, to the same effect." (VI, 523–26)

No accident perhaps that on this occasion he is called "the Sceptic." For the Wanderer by contrast, to understand the chain of being that composes the natural world, "the mighty commonwealth of things," not only improves the intellect but teaches us to "adore" (IV, 342, 349).[23] Habitually finding in all things not just any significance but a particular kind, the divine hand, mediated as "mind" or "spirit" — and this was indeed to be the lesson of "the great philosophical poem" — the Wanderer as I have said trusts in a reflective model of cognition. It remains to examine this premise more closely, and more particularly as it revisits the moments that sustain reflection in *The Prelude.*

Of all the materials in his autobiographical poem that Wordsworth seems most concerned to revisit in *The Excursion,* materials comparable in importance to the two versions of the paradise lost and regained plot miniaturized in "Tintern Abbey" and the Intimations Ode, none is more continuously on his mind than the climactic Ascent of Mount Snowdon. From the Solitary's vision upon emerging from mist in Book II (no doubt symbolically going downhill, though, rather than uphill) to the reflected ram and the reflected mountainscape in Book IX, Wordsworth keeps up a running allusion to the specular relationship between the imagination and the world to which the Snowdon scene apocalyptically lays claim. The moonlit spectacle of the mountaintops above the mist, the sea in one place visible and roaring up seemingly through that fissure (a splendid synaesthesia) somehow evoke "the imagination of the whole" and form, though it is not quite clear how, "[t]he perfect image of a mighty mind" (1805 *Prelude,* XIII, 65, 69). I have worried at this passage in the previous chapter, and need repeat here only that for all its glory Wordsworth's description can find no objective basis at all for its specular claim. Why should the mind, mighty or otherwise, look like *that,* we must ask, even while admitting with the benefit of anachronism that the light from above imposing form on the thrustings up of hills and sounds from below are a little like Paul Ricoeur's redemptive account of the Freudian dreamwork.

Now, in *The Prelude,* a figure of this kind becomes an emblem of the poem's intended madeleine-effect. Its very obscurity perpetuates it as an object of recurrent thought. The "meditation" that elaborates on what the climber has seen takes place only after "the scene / Had passed away" (ibid., 66–68), and thus becomes a last, sped-up version of the "two consciousnesses" in counterpoint that have haunted the entire poem. Reflection in a moment (the Spot-experience) gives rise to reflection across time, reflection on reflection. The two consciousnesses are an imperfect fit ("so wide appears / The vacancy between me and those days" [ibid., II, 28–29]), and the specularity of the Spots themselves perpetuates later reflection precisely in having been obscure in the first place; but for such losses the creativity of memory is an abundant recompense. In proportion as it is obscure, reflection can be sustained, and it is the office of poetry to do so, to forge a tenuous but all-important link between impression and understanding. In *The Excursion,* the theme of reflection, fostered almost exclusively by the Wanderer, is quite precisely the obverse of what it was in *The Prelude.* As the Lady so aptly points out, reflection under the Wanderer's sponsorship is persuasively lucid for a moment but cannot be sustained. The Solitary too has had a clear vision, much clearer than any Spot of Time, yet he doubts not only its staying power but also its authenticity. It is from the beginning an "appearance" (II, 834), "such as," but not to be ranked with, what "by Hebrew Prophets were beheld / In vision" (II, 867–68). The

Solitary will later compare this experience with the illusion of the "golden palace" (III, 714) that seemed to arise from the wreck of the Bastille. And in any case, he distrusts reflection in general, recalling now the illusion that replaced his disillusionment: "a troubled mind; / That, in a struggling and distempered world, / Saw a seductive image of herself" (III, 803–05). At least relatively speaking, the mountain vision is not evanescent — "The apparition faded not away" (II, 880) — but the Solitary's doubts as to its significance and his sense of exclusion even if it is significant turn him back to the task of getting the old pensioner down the mountain, and we have a glimpse of his isolation in history by the secularization of conscience, performing good works in a state of indifference to Revelation: "And I descended" (II, 881). To him, the reflection of his own life, which fully anticipates the still waters required for the reflections of Book IX, is a condition of useless stasis (in a passage that recalls the much more perturbed and vital water-gazing of *Prelude* IV):

> The tenour
> Which my life holds, he readily may conceive
> Whoe'er hath stood to watch a mountain brook
> In some still passage of its course, and seen,
> Within the depths of its capacious breast,
> Inverted trees, rocks, clouds, and azure sky:
> And, on its glassy surface, specks of foam,
> And conglobated bubbles undissolved,
> Numerous as stars; that, by their onward lapse,
> Betray to sight the motion of the stream,
> Else imperceptible. (III, 967–77)

What else, he says despairingly, can reflection be expected to reflect?

"[B]y happy chance we saw / A twofold image" (IX, 439–40), says the Poet of the White Ram reflection, joining forces here with the Lady in dispelling this climactic evocation of the Wanderer's imperialist harangue.[24] The moment is introduced by a clustering of fortuitous suspensions, a bridge (as from mind to object) in conjunction with the deep pool that interrupts an otherwise "hasty rivulet" (II, 438), but what is most important to notice is that the figure of reflection is not itself reflecting. The ram has its perfect counterpart in the water but is unaware of it — as is, of course, the reflection likewise: "Antipodes unconscious of each other" (II, 459), as if to recall the two consciousnesses in *The Prelude* that are able to bridge a far more extensive vacancy. Reflection then is a transitory trick of relation that cannot be reflected upon because it reflects no authentic working of the mind. Reflection is a trope, the more perfect as metaphor (Ram A is Ram B) the more vulnerable to the re-flexion of a breath. The ram's own "breathing" is part of the tableau, the point of dissolve between living original and fair copy, but the human breathing breathily sighed over and whispered about by the Lady is the loss of self-identity in time, and that loss invalidates any and all static models of cognition. It is hard to impute to Wordsworth an irony so sweeping, blunt, and even vulgar; yet it is just as hard not to notice, on reflection, that his culminating, imposingly handsome symbol of empire, patriarchal authority, and the triumph of human understanding is proverbially the stupidest and least self-willed of domestic animals. No wonder it just stands there.

But there is another reflection in Book IX, again commented on by the Poet: "That which the heavens displayed, the liquid deep / Repeated, but with unity sublime!" (IX, 607–08). This moment would appear to prefigure through the landscape the office of the Pastor, whose vespers are about to begin. Like the *dieu caché*, the light source of the reflection is absent ("the orb / Retired behind the mountain-tops or veiled / By the dense air" [IX, 593–94]), and in any case itself a diminished thing ("the sun, / Sinking with less than ordinary state" [IX, 590–91]), having lost some of its primitive potency as a symbol. These details correspond well to the way in which the Pastor's understanding of significa-tion works. He knows we have no direct access to understanding, and is willing thankfully to accept a relatively feeble type, "this local transitory type" (IX, 619), of the divine effluence, which is never to be confused with the divine itself. The reflection produced is a picture, composed into a "unity sublime" as it were by a Claudian hand, of which nature, without the handy Claude Glass of reflection, is incapable. The Wanderer has now long since fallen silent, and the eclipse of the visionary imagination he champions by the Pastor's know-ingly attenuated orthodox reflections restores the link, scorned by Words-worth in earlier years, between the vocation of wandering and Picturesque tourism. The "inferior lights" (IX, 762) that attend this vision would certainly seem to signal a change of intention, or heart, from the high-hearted "Pros-pectus" of years before, with its hope that "my Song / With Star-like virtue in its place may shine" (88–89).

"[T]he star of eve / Was wanting" (IX, 761–62). This is the last of many dismissals of the traditional genres, in this case the hesperidian idyll. Words-worth is of course closely associated in literary history with the "Romantic subjectification" of the genres, from the rejection of traditional pastoral and epic (the swerve from Milton modeled on Milton's swerve from classical mod-els) to the classifications devised for the 1807 edition of his poems.[25] In *The Excursion*, however, the outmodedness of the genres increasingly reflects the outmodedness of poetry itself, or at least of poetry understood as the primary vehicle of the most important truths. The most important genre newly rejected here is tragedy, on the grounds — frequently averred since Wordsworth's time

—that there can be no Christian tragedy. The Solitary thinks of himself as a modern tragic hero (for whom, as Arnold was to complain of such figures, "everything is to be endured and nothing to be done"), and he expects the struggle with destiny to be the theme even of the Pastor's epitaphs: "here the tragic Muse / Shall find apt subjects for her highest art" (VI, 551–52). The Pastor quickly responds, though, "these be terms / Which a divine philosophy rejects" (VI, 558–59). The story of Ellen, though movingly told with the help of Virgilian pathos, recalling the death of Lausus ("the green stalk of Ellen's life was snapped" [VI, 1000]), is reined in by the Pastor, not as a tragedy but rather under the redemptive aegis of *Paradise Regained:* "from these bonds released, she went / Home to her mother's house" (VI, 1005). Speaking like the tempted Son of that poem, which is attenuated with respect to *Paradise Lost* in just the way *The Excursion* is attenuated with respect to *The Prelude,* Ellen stills "with a prompt reproof" all consolation that is not sacred, "words of pity or complaint" (VI, 1044–45). The Pastor's is in general the voice raised against the traditional role of poetry, relying partly on Plato's argument that it feeds and waters the passions:

> "Noise is there not enough in doleful war,
> But that the heaven-born poet must stand forth,
> And lend the echoes of his sacred shell,
> To multiply and aggravate the din?
> Pangs are there not enough in hopeless love" (VII, 363–68) —

without the pastoral or anacreontic muse lending its aid? etc. What the poet can usefully do, he continues, still echoing Plato, is write hymns to divine goodness. As long, that is, as the snares of paganism are avoided: "As old bards / Tell in their idle songs of wandering gods, / Pan or Apollo, veiled in human form" (VII, 728–29).

It is not, finally, that we are to agree fully with the Pastor about the place of the poet in the Christian equivalent of Plato's republic. It should be recognized, though, that if the Pastor were the only spokesperson resisting the commitment of the Wanderer to visionary truth and the Solitary's futile apostasy from that same commitment, then Wordsworth in 1814 would have to be seen as agreeing that poetry can only now have a subordinately hymnic function, not perhaps unlike the epideictic ideal clung to by Sidney in his *Apologie.* But there is also the Poet, bard of "enfeebled Power" (IX, 783 — the Solitary's, of course, but how tempting as a motto!), who promises a sequel, more poetry. True, the aim is to convert the Solitary to an ideal of goodness that would displease neither Plato nor the Pastor. In fact, though, in actual practice, the resistance of this poem to the Solitary's conversion, and the doubt in all readers' minds whether an equally honest sequel would have made the difference, suggests that poetry however pious must always follow a different course from that of religious instruction. The personality of the Poet, *qua* Poet as we are now forced to realize, evincing a commitment to feeling and custom and a curious indifference to his companions' need for definitive truth, is after all the personality that has shone through Wordsworth's poems from the beginning. Despite the successive forms of utility to which his vocation has been prudently yoked, each in turn worthy and each in turn inadequate to explain Wordsworth's revolutionary position in literary history, he has always known and intermittently found ways of making plain the special niche from which poetry cannot be displaced by any sort of cognitive or fideistic claim. It is poetry that tells us of nothing more than what we are.

# 9

## Intimations Revisited:
## From the Crisis Lyrics to Wordsworth in 1817

In developing the argument of this book I have written only in passing about the central lyrics of the Great Decade, "Tintern Abbey" and the Intimations Ode. Nor have I extensively discussed "Resolution and Independence" and "Peele Castle," poems that unfortunately I shall not be able to consider at sufficient length here either. But in beginning with a few generalizations, I shall discuss the four poems as a group, a procedure that is justifiable in itself and that is warranted too by the fact that the retrospective odes of 1817 with which I shall conclude recall all four both openly and allusively, at times as though they were recalling a single poem. Written from 1798 to 1805, these variants on the Conversation Poem have often been called crisis lyrics, and one might think of them as Fortunate Fall lyrics, as the first two in particular announce their ambition in part by revisiting the Milton of *Paradise Lost* and "Lycidas." Two poems of the turn of the century that I will not discuss even briefly here likewise align Wordsworth's ambitions with Milton's: the conclusion of *Home at Grasmere* called "Prospectus to the *Recluse*" proclaims that "the mind of man" is subject matter sufficient for an epic profounder than Milton's; and *Michael* can be read, in view of this rivalry with Milton, as a complex reflection on poetic as well as property inheritance, a poem about the disappearance of a successor from his father's hills that is told without apparent irony "for the sake / Of youthful Poets, who among these hills / Will be my second self when I am gone." But the question for the reader of the present book remains: how can these crisis lyrics about paradise lost be understood in relation to the unique reorientation of the human to the natural in Wordsworth that has been my theme?

As all agree, each of these poems is about some form of compensation for a loss: the loss of glad animal movement and the haunting passion that succeeds it in "Tintern Abbey," the loss of the visionary gleam in the great Ode, the loss of the "gladness" of youthful poets in "Resolution and Independence," and the perhaps more acute loss of the belief, retained by the Intimations Ode speaker, that there ever *was* a "gleam . . . on sea or land" in "Peele Castle." Such losses are offset more or less convincingly by various sorts of "timely utterance." The usual approach to these poems, inclusive of the immense and insightful number of things that have been said about them, is to accept the premise that the rhetoric of before and after points to states of mind and modes of belief that differ sharply from one another in each case. Wordsworth *now* has the abundant recompense of hearing the still sad music of humanity; he has *now* reached the years that bring the philosophic mind; he *now* has the stay and help secure of the leech gatherer's example; and after the death of his brother, finally, he has *now* achieved "fortitude, and patient cheer" in social companionship rather than in solitude — which last version of gain after loss expands into *The White Doe of Rylstone* and drives the plot to redeem the Solitary in *The Excursion*.

In diverging from this consensus, what I want to argue concerning each poem is that when viewed from a certain angle their before and after states are only superficially altered states and reflect the persistence of Wordsworth's fundamental insight despite changes in vocabulary and context. I shall then argue that when in 1817 Wordsworth returns to these poems — especially but not exclusively the Intimations Ode — in a new set of odes, he surprises himself at certain moments with a more direct, less sublimated recognition of what the earlier poems had evasively disclosed, while at the same time deferring the poet's ontological calling to the religious framework found likewise in *The Excursion*. In some ways my argument concerning the Great Decade lyrics returns me to the themes of Chapter 6: What the animal and somatic impulses of human consciousness have in common with its spiritual and disembodied impulses is the revealed immanence of the nonhuman that reunites consciousness with the natural world from which anthropocentrism has estranged it. Nature as such and intimations of the spiritual *matter* to Wordsworth — they inhere in matter — because they sublate the alienation to which these crisis lyrics respond. In what looks in each case like a movement *from* nature to spirit, immanence to transcendence, the crisis is not so much a loss as a failure to understand that what seems to have been lost is always within reach. In itself unaltered, that which was lost returns in a form that makes it seem different, more consistent with the ethical humanism of mature reflection in response to suffering, yet still harboring Wordsworth's original insight as a poet.

More than any other freestanding lyric he composed (apart, that is, from many of the Spots of Time), "Tintern Abbey" reflects continuously on the somatism of the natural world in relation to death, though not with the emotional alienation of the poems to which I shall turn in conclusion.[1] That "Tintern Abbey" is not wholly candid about this downward pull, masking its preoccupation beneath the rhetoric of transcendence, is partly what made the early Empson, fascinated yet still disapproving, call the poem a "muddle." Critics have written about ascending patterns of transcendence in each of the poem's waves of exalted feeling;[2] yet Wordsworth — in keeping with the word "sublime" itself — points down just when one might expect him to point up: with "the deep power of joy, / We see into the life of things"; "elevated thoughts" turn out to be "a sense sublime of something far more deeply interfused" that dwells in "setting suns" and "in the mind of man"; this sense sublime "rolls through all things"; it is found in the "language of the sense" — the sensorium of Locke, that is, which holds down "my purest thoughts" as an "anchor." Yes, this is meant at least in part to be a pantheist poem written by a "worshipper of nature." But the poem forces the question, almost as a matter of chemistry, whether a divine spirit can be found anywhere other than in "all things"? Which is to say, bluntly, is this not a monistic poem straining rhetorically to find transcendence but finally anchored in materiality? Supposing the somatic world to be animate, can anything not belonging to that world be said to be animate as well?

These questions give rise to another, the question that haunts "Tintern Abbey," as I have indicated: from the standpoint of the contemplative askesis that is the poet's "abundant recompense" for the loss of glad animal movement and haunting passion, is the difference between life and death a matter of degree or of kind? It is worth rereading a well-known passage as the rather startling answer to this question: the revelatory feeling for which the poet is grateful arises in

> [t]hat serene and blessed mood,
> In which the affections [i.e., "affects"] lead us on, —
> Until, the breath of this corporeal frame
> And even the motion of our human blood
> Almost suspended, we are laid asleep
> In body, and become a living soul:

While with an eye made quiet by the power
Of harmony, and the deep power of joy,
We see into the life of things.

If this is visionary insight, and undoubtedly there is no great distortion in calling it that, it is nevertheless a state of mind that resembles a coma.[3] The poem's keyword is "deep," armed with which one returns to the first verse paragraph (which I read in Chapters 4 and 5 as an effacement of visual difference): the steep and lofty cliffs "impress / Thoughts of a more deep seclusion," as though they were stones pressing down from above. The speaker has returned to this spot to "repose" under a "dark" tree and look around at "plots," perhaps from his own plot. It is the language of the Graveyard School. Having firmly established his more deep seclusion, the speaker who is a year older than his sister finally turns to her as though from the grave, at least in experimental conjecture: "If I should be where I no more can hear / Thy voice." She is his Before, "what I was once"; he is his After, hence the need to pretend that the malingering of time ("five summers, with the length / Of five long winters!") has advanced him into old age, or beyond it, to the point of saying "remember me," like the ghost of Hamlet's father.

The poem's abundant recompense is the opportunity to hear the still sad music of humanity. It is while looking "on nature" that he hears this music (continuously or always hears, hears in spite of its silence). And it is "humanity" that he hears, synaesthetically, in the *appearance* of nature—just as the love of nature leads to the love of man in *Prelude* 8. But, here as there, how does this happen? Like the meanest flower that blows six years later, nature tells us something about the human condition that lies too deep for tears: that we are bodies, that we perish, and that being human means simply that we are the only bodies in nature that know their fate, and suffer accordingly in sadness. But after all, under the impossibly liminal sign of Wordsworth's materialistic pantheism, who knows what radioactive half-life may be in store for us in the state we call death? When the still sad music is understood to be immanent in the natural world while inaudible on any other plane of being, the countervailing happy undersong, Wordsworth's abundant recompense, declares that our alienation from our embodied life is now suspended. This alienation is nothing other than the Rousseauian state of society, leaving man "in city pent" to face the Miltonic political fate of "evil tongues, / Rash judgements," and the rest of it. Hence the New Historicists are right to argue that Wordsworth is bent on distancing himself from even the most marginal social conditions in this poem,[4] a process that requires delaying even the address to his sister and begins with the amazing oxymorons at the end of the first verse paragraph: the "notice" that is uncertain and may only seem to appear even as an uncertainty; the dwellers who are impossibly "vagrant" and in any case could scarcely dwell in woods that are "houseless," leaving only a possible hermit (who may not be there, so uncertain is the notice of the smoke) who "sits alone," the ultimate symbol of those anti-social impulses that Wordsworth explores again in the St. Gregory passage of *The Tuft of Primroses* that is recycled in *The Excursion*.

Only the hermit, encrypted in his cave, can hear the still sad music, "the din / Of towns and cities" being too remote from such a place for its static to interfere. To hear anything restorative for humanity, Wordsworth needs to reject the enlightenment definition of the human as a chattering animal whose "dreary intercourse" sustains the caprices of reason in history, including the allegedly "repressed" history of the French Revolution. That history is deliberately *sup*pressed, and it is only in insisting on this distinction that one differs from the New Historicists. Discourse enunciates difference and constitutes the difference of the human from other beings. The music heard by the almost insensate contemplative is the sound of being that reunites human beings with other beings in a common "dwelling" that really is houseless because it is in the light of setting suns. It is crucial, then, that the din of human voices and the still sad music of humanity not be confused with each other. Only a human voice, an ur-philosopher or messianic theologian, could *explain* "the burden of the mystery" (an expression the secondary sense of which is also verbal: a refrain). That would be to "lighten" the mystery with a powerful candle, a message of enlightenment, which is not at all what the reclusive poet, under a dark tree or in a cave, experiences. The poem is a "muddle" precisely because it must not overvalue language as a means of explanation, hence keeps ducking explanation in the perpetual flow of puns, antithetical meanings, subtexts, and other devices that we have intermittently noted.[5] No, this burden is not a darkness but a *weight*, a heavy load that could scarcely be lightened, lifted off our shoulders, by the catachresis of illumination. The rapt contemplative does not want an answer, a burden explained; he wants a respite from wanting an answer, a burden lifted; and in that respite he can hear music.

Here Wordsworth, rhetorically suggesting throughout that his serene and blessed mood entails some form of transcendence, uses Milton as a shield. "Nor harsh nor grating," the music he hears crushes yet once more the harsh berries of "Lycidas" (making "Tintern Abbey" itself a vocationally premature redemptive music) and is unlike the discourse of the bad shepherds whose songs "[g]rate on their scrannel Pipes of wretched straw." But more pointedly this music recalls *Comus*. The Elder Brother has been anxiously describing what happens even to the chaste body (Wordsworth's still sad music can "chasten and subdue") when it is defiled by lust, and the upshot of what he says is that when this happens, according to the platonic doctrine, you can no longer tell the difference between the body and the soul: "The soul grows clotted by contagion, / Imbodies and imbrutes" — resulting in the "muddle" of Wordsworth's poem. To this the Second Brother responds reassuringly by placing his trust in the wisdom given by such philosophy rather than brooding about it:

> How charming is divine Philosophy!
> Not harsh and crabbed as dull fools suppose,
> But musical as is *Apollo's* lute.

By association this makes the still sad music Pythagorean, a celestial music, and loosens the tie with the natural world that Wordsworth's embodying of the music has knotted so firmly. In an anechoic chamber one can hear the circulation of one's own body, otherwise "still," and that kind of soundproof box is what Wordsworth's poem aims for: the isolation that overcomes alienation.

So much then for the After, a way of grasping the unity of being that embraces human being in the absence of enlightenment distractions. The Before consists of two phases of development, both of them lost. The first, the "glad animal movements" when "like a roe, / I bounded o'er the mountains," reflects the unselfconscious redundancy of living energy that makes the child a hoofed being like those discussed in Chapter 6, tainted however by the first motions of guilt recorded in *Prelude* 1, "[f]lying from something that he dreads." Animal bliss, touched by fear and trembling. Then comes adolescence, the moment of the Morning of Election (see Chapter 5), when an indiscriminate eroticism is sublimated as an indiscriminate "appetite" for nature, "a feeling and a love, / That had no need of a remoter charm, / By thought supplied." However these phases may differ from each other, they have in common the absence of thought; they comprise "the hour of thoughtless youth" (Dorothy as the poem imagines her is still living in this hour) from which the mature poet claims now, deliberately protesting too much, to have unreluctantly graduated. This means, we take it, that he is now a thinker, as full of Platonism for example as the Elder Brother, he being Dorothy's elder brother. But this is why I have saved the Before and After issue for last. I hope to have shown already that, far from staking a claim as a thinker, the mature poet is dedicated to the avoidance of thought and its estrangements so as to register in a finer tone, as Keats would say, the very somatic immediacy that the then-now structure of the poem has staged as a "loss." What remains absolutely continuous across all three stages of Wordsworth's miniature autobiography is the immediacy of bodily circulation both to the mind and to the revolution of the earth. It is a condition differing from death only in degree, and by contrast defines life, the social life of the human species, as historical consciousness. It will be clear, I hope, that this way of reading the poem simply reverses, if I may so put it, the evaluative glove of the New Historicist readings.

"Ode: Intimations of Immortality from Recollections of Early Childhood"[6] turns directly to Plato rather than alluding indirectly to the display of divine philosophy in Milton; but the four strophes composed in 1802 do not yet bring in Plato. In that first effusion, the muddle of "Tintern Abbey," with its equivocation about how much the creativity of mind actually has to do with our perception of the earth's aura, remains in place. Coleridge was in no doubt about the continuity of doctrine between the two poems when he responded to them jointly in the successive drafts of "Dejection." In that poem Coleridge says that he too has lost the visionary gleam, and that he is more upset about it than Wordsworth is, but that in any case Wordsworth has identified the visionary gleam in the wrong way: it is not something we "half create, and half perceive," hence common both to the inner and the outer workings of our minds, but derives rather from the transcendentally given feeling that Coleridge calls "Joy" and renders synonymous with the imagination:

> Oh lady, we receive but what we give,
> And in our life alone does nature live.
> Ours her wedding garment, ours her shroud . . .

This is after all simply a transvalued way of expressing the insight Wordsworth shies away from: Nature in itself is just an inert body, and unless the imagination brings it to life by espousing its beauty, a yellow primrose will be nothing but a yellow primrose, as Peter Bell would say. As Coleridge sees it, the first four strophes of the Intimations Ode have done nothing to alter the materialism in Wordsworth's "natural religion" that has bothered him from the beginning of their interaction (see Chapter 2).

Indeed, in the 1802 text we must agree with Coleridge that there are no intimations of immortality at all. The "glory" of the first two strophes we know to be a technical term for a halo: an appearance of sacralization in natural objects that may or may not be divine. When it passes away it passes "from the earth," not from the growing child's mind as far as he himself is aware. In the second strophe, which haunts the opening lines of "Dejection," the mutable earth is still radiant, and even the rainbow, covenant of recurrence in the 1815 motto, "My Heart Leaps Up," still comes and goes, but now these luminous things are just the things that they are. They are naked lights, no longer clothed ("[a]ppareled") by any supplementary light. Having lost the glad animal movements of the birds, the lambs, the shepherd boy, and the

Babe that "leaps up" like his own heart, the poet "alone" feels this loss as a "thought of grief"; his is the sole human consciousness in the world's blithe springtime. What the "timely utterance" was that made him feel better for the moment remains a scholarly crux, and probably we will never identify it with confidence. Interesting, though, in view of the displacement of "language" (except that of "the sense") by music in "Tintern Abbey," that this brief cure is verbal, an explanation that seems to satisfy the poet while admonishing him not to be a spoilsport. Twenty-seven lines later, though, he is despondent again, and we may surmise that the utility of the timely utterance is ephemeral just because it *is* an utterance — the concluding pledge to be resolute in "Resolution and Independence," for example, which some have considered to be the timely utterance.

Or suppose it to be "My Heart Leaps Up," another leading candidate. That poem espouses the very "natural piety," or simple produce of the common day, that Coleridge had long found suspect, and it is in that altogether sublunary context, with no hint of Plato's Myth of Er, that "the child is father to the man." Wordsworth did not add this motto (or give the ode its full title) until 1815, which may seem rather surprising, as by that time one might think that the discrepancy between its naturalism and the Platonic ode for which he selected it as a gloss would have struck him forcibly. Indeed, perhaps he chose "My Heart Leaps Up" because after this considerable lapse of time he just wanted to indicate that it *was* the "timely utterance," composed the day before he began reflecting on the *limitations* of that utterance, hence could only take temporary solace from it as his reflections deepened. The four-strophe poem of 1802 concludes with a relapse. The details, like the "fields of sleep" and the timely utterance itself, remain somewhat enigmatic, though the "Pansy" is a happy touch, meaning "thought," that prefigures the "meanest flower" provoking thought with which the whole poem concludes in 1804. The singleness of things, when emphasized as here, is often perplexing in Wordsworth. It is tempting of course to think of the "Tree" as a composite Christian symbol, one that perhaps saddens him because he cannot feel the redemptive power of the symbolism, hence sees the tree — whichever tree it may have been that prompted this thought — as just a tree. Be this as it may, it seems likeliest that while looking at that particular tree he realized, worryingly like Peter Bell, that a yellow primrose is just a yellow primrose, as is the symbolism-neutral "single Field" that comes next.

I hope I have already shown that even in the short ode of 1802 there is the same continuity between Before and After, masked by the rhetoric of transcendence, that there is in "Tintern Abbey": first it is a joy to live an embodied life, then self-consciousness shows that the embodied life is our fate. Coleridge saw this clearly enough in "Dejection"—in one draft addressed to "William"—which was published in *The Morning Post* on the morning of Wordsworth's wedding, now addressed to Wordsworth's new sister-in-law. Partly in response to "Dejection," the grand strophes of 1804, founded on *Republic* 10, set about to establish a transcendental ground for Wordsworth's views more resolutely than anything he ever wrote before or after. Whenever Wordsworth discussed his expanded poem, he was moved to talk about his own bouts of childhood idealism, a topic that rarely comes up in any other context. The Fenwick note about having to grasp a tree or a wall as a child to escape "the abyss of idealism" is the best known, but there are also the reports in Christopher Wordsworth's *Memoirs* that repeat the Fenwick recollection of *"clasping a tree"* and recall the "'all-soulness'" of his childhood.[7] In a letter of 1815 commenting on the poem Wordsworth speaks of a "childhood indisposition to bend to the law of death," in a vein similar to the citation in the Fenwick note of the child's denial of death in "We Are Seven."[8] Undoubtedly Wordsworth must have had such feelings as a child, or must have recalled having them; it is surprising, though, first that the child of "We Are Seven" seems *not* to have had them, as I have argued, and second, that Wordsworth seems to find the experience of idealism unsettling even in retrospect: an "abyss of idealism." And not just in prose: the intimations of immortality in the Ode itself are "blank misgivings." As is also clear at the beginning of *Prelude* 5, Wordsworth finds it unpleasant to contemplate a state of being in which the "garments" of earthly existence are absent and irrelevant.

From this evidence one might well infer not that Wordsworth is more comfortable with the dualism of conventional Christianity, but that in fact immaterialism of any kind gives him vertigo. The Christian promise for him must then have been precisely the promise of being reunited with our bodies at the end of time. Most readers agree that the Platonism of the Intimations Ode is foreign to Wordsworth, and express uneasiness that his most famous poem, the one he always accorded its special place in arranging his successive editions, is also so idiosyncratic. I do not pretend that it is easy to explain away this problem if one builds on the premise, like the "Cambridge" Wordsworthians Empson, Basil Willey, and Hugh Sykes Davies, that Wordsworth is a monistic empiricist in the tradition of Locke.[9] A possible explanation, though, could take two forms. First, as I have suggested all along, Wordsworth could never bring himself to see clearly how fundamental his disagreement with Coleridge not only was but had always been: hence the declared idealism in the later versions of the Spots of Time passage in *Prelude* 11 and the attempt at idealism in the strategically placed Simplon and Snowdon narratives; hence the suddenly Coleridgean account of the imagination in the 1815 "Preface";

and hence, finally, Wordsworth's 1804 response, in the rest of the Intimations Ode, to Coleridge's response to him in "Dejection." No, Wordsworth protests, I am not a materialist. The theme is announced in the opening lines of the fifth strophe, and then explored. Needless to say, once more, there must have been some sense in which Wordsworth believed in his intimations and felt the urgency of proclaiming them. As Simplon and Snowdon also suggest, it was a matter of *achieving heights* (not the depth of "Tintern Abbey"), and for that reason the metaphor comes easily when one speaks of the Intimations Ode as a high point in Wordsworth's career, to be highlighted in any new edition as a pinnacle of accomplishment, a poem of the transcendental imagination *par excellence.*

There is another way of understanding the important yet anomalous status of the Intimations Ode, however, this time returning us not so much to the passages mentioned above as to the dissonances of "We Are Seven" and of the reflections on perishable books in *Prelude 5.* Very possibly the doctrine of idealism, or at least the premise that the soul "cometh from afar," seems to Wordsworth simply irrefutable. After all, Berkeley, Coleridge, and others had cogently pointed to the difficulty of assigning either agency or creative ideation to a mind that has only a single faculty, the empirical understanding, at its disposal. Insofar as Wordsworth is likely to have thought about the matter philosophically, then, he may have been convinced by such arguments, arguments that he nonetheless not only found intuitively irrelevant to his own sense of what it means to be a human being among other beings, but also found uncanny and alienating: "Haunted for ever by the eternal mind," the child is addressed as:

> Thou, over whom thy Immortality
> Broods like the Day, a Master o'er a Slave,
> A presence which is not to be put by;

— and he is said to have experienced the "abyss of idealism":

> those obstinate questionings
> Of sense and outward things,
> Fallings from us, vanishings;
> Blank misgivings of a Creature
> Moving about in worlds not realized.

Immortality and its patriarch may have browbeaten the child and his adult spokesperson into accepting their reality, but this does not mean that either the child or the adult can accept them without rather severe discomfort. It is just here that the Before and After effect of this poem starts to seem less marked.

Much of the time, though, Wordsworth can deploy the rhetoric of transcendence with enthusiasm because he is not contrasting it with his hallmark unitary state of being at all, but rather with the very same inauthenticities of social and cognitive distinction that were his foil in "Tintern Abbey." The "prison-house" that closes on the child is felt as a smothering by the human ties (the "pleasures" and "yearnings" that socialize) and social rituals ("weddings," "festivals," "funerals") that are reviewed in the sixth and seventh strophes; it is, indeed, a prison house of language, Jameson's as much as Hamlet's. That the vision splendid is actually succeeded at least in part by something *other* than these milestones of life, by the quotidian that is the very focus of celebration in Wordsworth's more characteristic verse, is kept as much as possible out of view: "At length the Man perceives it die away, / And fade into the light of common day." Here is the irreducible difference: before there was a gleam, now there is none. Yet what more or less covertly remains the same, as in "Tintern Abbey," is the dwelling of toddling child and sober adult alike in unitary experience, indifferent to the Aristotelian, anti-Platonic insistence that life is role-playing. Still, it is his predictable dissatisfaction with this unflattering view that makes any evidence of transcendence more appealing than it would be otherwise. Conning parts, the six-years' Darling of a pigmy size disregards the critique of poetry that precedes the Myth of Er in Book 10 of the *Republic* and becomes an Aristotelian playwright:

> Filling from time to time his 'humorous stage'
> With all the persons, down to palsied Age,
> That Life brings with her in her equipage;
>     As if his whole vocation
>     Were endless imitation.

These lines, a sketch of little Hartley Coleridge, are warmly affectionate, hence differ sharply from the attack on urban mores in "Tintern Abbey," but the prison house they point toward forces a revaluation of the keywords "custom" and "life" (the latter of which specifically means *social* life both here and in what follows): "And custom lie[s] upon thee with a weight [akin to the "burden" of "Tintern Abbey"], / Heavy as frost, and deep almost as life!" This gloom makes even the blank misgivings of the next strophe, "be they what they may," equal in attraction to the "most worthy" animal movements expressing childhood's "[d]elight and liberty." The "worlds not realized" under the influence of idealism here take on the role of the minatory presences in nature that were fostered by superstition in "Tintern Abbey" and *Prelude* 1, and cause the troubled child to "tremble like a guilty Thing surprised." Yet all these negatives, under their grimly gendered "master light," can still seem far preferable to what is made rhetorically to seem like the only alternative: "Our noisy years," comparable here to the plight of being "in city pent" in other poems. Yet the actual site from which we can revisit the intimations of childhood in the poem's climactic lines is not "noisy": while it is as "inland far" as urban life may be, hearing the mighty waters rolling evermore requires "a season of calm weather" that the noisy years will not afford. It is like listening to the conch shell one has kept for years after a childhood trip to the beach. In just such a shell the dreamer of the Dream of the Arab hears "an ode, in passion uttered" — a part of *Prelude* 5 that was written at much the same time as the great Ode, along with the lament for the perishable garments of books.

This comparison, which to me at least seems irresistible, reveals the fragile artifice with which the Before and After structure of the poem has been preserved. Both in the "calm" of the present and as witness to the joyousness of the past, the poet can hear the sound of being, and that sound, like the earlier blank misgivings — "be they what they may" — may not even transcend the immanence in the natural world that Wordsworth's oceanic metaphor, for all its magnificence, seems to insist upon. Idealism may turn out after all to be one of the childhood superstitions that Wordsworth's autobiographical poems always document. That seems certainly to be the drift of "Peele Castle" in any case — by which time the power of the sea perforce assumed a very different role in his imagination. Having recorded the sound of mighty waters, perhaps his favorite oceanic figure until 1805, Wordsworth with his "philosophic mind" reverts to the themes of "Tintern Abbey," with no further intimations. The mighty waters become the still sad music of humanity, shifted to the visual register:

> The Clouds that gather round the setting sun
> Do take a sober colouring from an eye
> That hath kept watch o'er man's mortality.

Under the leveling, the wonderful dying fall, of these closing lines, the last word is given to the small celandine or daisy about which so many poems had been written at the time of the 1802 strophes. The pathos of "the meanest flower that blows" is that it exists in time, and may exist at the end of time.

A remark or two about the two remaining poems is in order before turning to the 1817 group. As I argued in my Introduction, the leech-gatherer makes the poet resolute not because of what he says (the speaker notoriously fails to focus his attention on that) but because of what he *is:* a composite of all orders of being, from stone to cloud, who levels these normally hierarchical orders and thereby discloses that unity of being in which the youthful poet had reveled when beginning in "gladness," like the hare of the first stanza. The poet as man is able to persevere, avoiding despondency and madness, because he sees that the poet as child, joyously at one with otherness, was right. "Peele Castle" is a very different sort of poem from the three others because it begins by declaring that the child, or in this case a naïve younger self, was wrong. Shattered by his brother's death at sea, Wordsworth rethinks the continuity between child and man without — as he may seem to do — abandoning it. As we shall see, this continuity had hitherto resided in the true basis of social ties, of the "little nameless, unremembered acts" mentioned in "Tintern Abbey," through a paradoxical and — in our own time — much-maligned escape from the social in order to grasp, sympathetically, what is fundamental to all human life. But now Wordsworth associates the somatic nature of existence in the absence of human sympathy with the walls of the castle in the storm as painted by Beaumont, an "unfeeling armor." Hence, no longer escaping society, "at distance from the Kind," he pledges to return to society (or at least to the community of an extended domestic circle) and to realize within it the same commonalty of existence in suffering that he had always intuited before in the philosophic calm of solitude. Thus whereas the blithe youthful sojourner on the Lancashire coast had felt harmony with his natural surroundings, the mature elegist who sees the minerality of existence with unblindered eye nonetheless feels *this same* harmony, only now it subsists within the human species in its most abstractly generic form: "the Kind." The education of the speaker during the course of "The Pass of Kirkstone" will take the same form.

Wordsworth told Isabella Fenwick that "Vernal Ode," the first of the 1817 series with which I shall conclude, was "[c]omposed to place in view the immortality of succession where immortality is denied, as far as we know, to the individual creature" (17). While I think the poem is about a good many other things as well, this account of it is the first of many signs that he had wished at that time to revisit the crisis lyrics in this and several other poems. It repeats the message of the meanest flower that blows, whose mode of existence is in time but may recur at the end of time — although it is not in this case a flower but a bee that illustrates the motto from Pliny: *Rerum natura tota est nusquam magis quam in minimis.* This poem, probably composed in April, is the first of a series of "personal" odes (as their Cornell editor Carl Ketcham calls them)[10] that succeed the series of political odes in response to the Battle of Waterloo in 1816. No doubt then one may see in this two-year experiment with the ode a miniature *après-coup* of Wordsworth's "apostacy" during the French Revolution: the movement from radical politics to radical inwardness repeated now as a movement from conservative politics to religiously tempered private thoughts. Introducing this latter transition, the "Vernal Ode" may be vernal in part because England itself is reborn; but the suggestion is remote, except when the angelic visitant seems in his own lineaments to con-firm and endorse the national identity threatened by Napoleon:

> Firm as some old Tower
> Of Britain's realm, whose leafy crest
> Waves high, embellished by a gleaming shower!

Even here, though, the primary frame of reference is not national but personal: the unfeeling armor of Peele Castle is varnished with the gleam of the Intima-tions Ode, the gleam denied to the mature painter of Peele Castle.

Yet this is an angel, not an image of the natural world. In many of the 1816–17 odes, Wordsworth is as much preoccupied with the angels of Genesis 6 who descend to find mates among mortal women as was the Byron of *Heaven and Earth* four years later. Or more precisely in Wordsworth's case it is in part such an angel, who descends to admire mutable things and seems to share the wish of Keats's gods to die into life (of this more below), and in part the angel who is the tutelary spirit of Tobias in the Book of Tobit. The complexity that attaches to Wordsworth's angel as first described is, again, that he is himself an evening version of the visionary gleam (a "bright effulgence" resembling the setting sun, softened as he approaches earth), while at the same time he admires the earth as it appeared on the glorious mornings of the Intimations Ode and "Resolution and Independence": "all the fields with freshest green were dight." The angel in short half creates and half perceives what he both is and observes. This odd elision of the spectator's viewpoint—that of the speaker who takes over again when the angel stops talking—to some extent merges the angel with the world he has descended to admire; his superior nature, like his superior position on a "summit," is not compromised by this device, yet the device may still be a necessary part of the speaker's repertoire, as we shall see.

Wordsworth first composed the ensuing speech in his own voice, but on second thought he distances himself from a role he can more comfortably assign to a superior being. It is difficult on the face of it to say why he would do this, yet explaining why may hold the key to understanding the exact orienta-tion of this poem and its immediate successors toward the lyrics to which they continuously allude. The first thought any reader is likely to have who has noted the persistent leveling of orders of being in the earlier Wordsworth is that his growing insistence on the importance of social hierarchy and his increased subordination of human understanding to religious mystery must have erased the theme of ontic unity altogether. The angel comes into this and other poems in the same way that personifications and classical machinery come in at the same period, heralded possibly by the Wanderer's celebration of the dawn of Greek and other polytheistic religions (*Excursion* 4). The angel is there to reopen Wordsworth's personal vision to the broad world-historical horizons of culture that he had hitherto excluded programmatically in the course of finding a rhetoric to mask and temper his insight; but this is precisely to say that that vision is not thereby eclipsed. The poet-speaker of this poem is our old friend the feckless and simplicity-loving Poet of *The Excursion,* but the angel provides a perspective that is available to none of the *Excursion* speakers (angels alone can know what we humans cannot know, as we have observed the Pastor to say). A survey of the rest of the poem should clarify these generalizations — which might not seem quite so abstract were this ode and its successors better known.

The angel argues that there are two kinds of immortality. There is that of his own unchanging "native habitations," the "imperial palace" of the Intimations Ode, and then there is a state which is not quite the same, that of the seemingly immutable stars and other natural symbols of permanence that are placed before mankind to inspire thoughts of absolute transcendence. But these features of season and cycle, which at least seem to recur endlessly (they are "endlessly renewed," says the angel), have special attractions even for those stationed in paradise:

> "Mortals, rejoice! The very Angels quit
> Their mansions unsusceptible of change,
> Amid your pleasant bowers to sit,
> And through your sweet vicissitudes to range!"

Note that in being allowed at least to witness change, if not to participate in it, the angel is given a sideways escape, or at least reprieve, from that which is "unsusceptible of change"; but this is simply to say that the mansions themselves, the many in my Father's house, *cannot* change. In speaking of eternity, sublunary language forces one to speak of limits, determinations, rather than of freedom. By this means, then, Wordsworth can now assign to the angel the feelings of regret and anxiety that had crept into his personal conception of immortality in the Intimations Ode.

Of course poetry throughout its history had nearly always found enjoyment in the aesthetics of impermanence, but it had also supposed, under Christian influence, that *not having to be eternally dead* is a small price to pay for the loss of pleasurable variety. Spenser's Mutabilitie is attractive (in effect if not in person), but we are never in doubt about the desirability of escaping her. Even before death comes into the world, Milton's benevolent Raphael, whose name is also that of the tutelary angel in Tobit, subtly condescends toward the human sphere, which is a luxuriant picturesque garden that is too irregular for his taste. Blake's angels in *Poetical Sketches* are distinct in outline, as for him all imagined beings must be, but they are also *genii* whose "influence," like that of Collins's personifications, permeates their locales. This more closely anticipates Wordsworth in 1817, but in the "Vernal Ode" we find a shift in sympathy toward that which is mutable, the telltale sign of which is not necessarily the day-tripping angel *per se*. Whether it arises from Genesis 6 or not, the theme of the strayed yet unfallen angel is of course an old one, as for example in the concluding lines of Dryden's "Ode for St. Cecilia's Day," but it remained for Keats and to a lesser extent Byron to bring out the full metaphysical and psychological implications of hating and fearing death yet preferring it to the monotony of eternal life. Whether those two mockers of *The Excursion* were prepared to admit it or not, Wordsworth's blank misgivings when faced with immortality anticipate their feelings, just as Wordsworth's disclosure of being in and through nature anticipates Keats's more sensuous but also more morbid naturalism.

Such misgivings likewise anticipate the feelings of the "Vernal Ode," contemporaneous with the hated Byron at the height of his fame (see the "Address to a Noble Lord" co-authored by Wordsworth with Mary Barker two years earlier) and with the composition of Keats's *Endymion* (begun April 1817). Only now, as I say, Wordsworth gives these feelings authority by assigning them to the angel. We see, in other words, that the reintroduction of ontological hierarchies to Wordsworth's verse has just the opposite purpose from what it may seem to have. Yes, now there is definitely more than one order of being, not just the myth of a second, imperishable order borrowed experimentally from Plato, a myth in which the emphasis still falls on the successive *changes* of body through which the soul passes; yet the purpose of the second order is primarily to affirm the worth of the first. The rest of the poem, the angel having fallen silent, brings out this purpose fully, with preternaturally Keatsian results:

> Wrapped in a fit of pleasing indolence,
>
> . . . . . . . . . . . . .
>
> To lie and listen — till o'erdrowsèd sense
> Sinks, hardly conscious of the influence —
> To the soft murmur of the vagrant Bee.

Certainly verse of this kind owes much to Coleridge's "solitary humble bee" that "[s]ings in the bean-flower" — to which Keats too is indebted — and all these writers, like Tennyson after them, are alert to the play on words in what I have elsewhere called the "hum of being." But lines like these also suggest another way of expressing the argument of this chapter: Wordsworth moves closer to Keats just when he is supposed to have moved farther away from him.

This speaker is the wisely passive poet whose "tired lute hangs on the hawthorn-tree," even though he is not exiled like the Children of Israel but snugly at home in the world. He purports not to understand why it is he who has been allowed to hear the angel instead of the votaries of Urania, the Miltonic muse he had earlier rivaled, or Clio, who might well have inspired the "Thanksgiving Ode" of the previous year. Happier far to celebrate the bee, no longer just a trivial creature, a small celandine or green linnet reserved for Wordsworth alone to notice, but also a classical object of attention and admiration for all, including the Pliny of the poem's motto. With Pliny, the poet marvels at the microcosmic complexity of the bee (*nusquam magis quam in minimis*), supposing that in prelapsarian times it had no sting, and by this means introduces the lament for the golden age with which he concludes. Like all of his poetic gestures in recent years, these final lines are at once more traditionally pious and more openly earthbound than the high-wire act of the crisis poems, with their "glimpse and shadow" of something ineffable, and they confirm the blank misgivings of the angel: "The golden years maintained a course / Not *undiversified* through smooth and even [italics mine]." Because there was no abyss between the mutable realm and that of the angels who "mixed familiarly with men," all was "a universal heaven!" In short, all orders of being, however exalted, conformed to earthly standards, and realized the unity everywhere that today is discernible in natural things and is the original subject of Wordsworth's "mild pastoral Muse." The bee as it turns out is both classical and personal, like all the other bits of traditional machinery in the later Wordsworth: it is a microcosmic emblem or symbol of intelligent design, yet it is also just another of the meanest flowers that blow (to which, with its "laden thigh," it is metonymically linked), a figure for the ontic unity of non-human and human things.

The "Ode to Lycoris" begins where the "Vernal Ode" leaves off, aligning the visionary gleam of the poet's own childhood, to the tune of "There was a time" in the Intimations Ode, with the world-historical vision of a golden age:

> An age hath been when Earth was proud
> Of lustre too intense
> To be sustained.

But the theme of this poem, or in any case its main argument, is quite different. At least to my ear, this chiastic theme, to which Wordsworth returns in the third strophe of "Composed upon an Evening," is oddly inconsequential, or is so in any case if one disregards the symbolism of Christian hope that neither poem is at pains to emphasize. If in youth — so runs the argument — if in the springtime of our lives we affectedly seek out evening, nocturnal, and autumnal scenes and moods, as in Wordsworth's juvenilia from *The Vale of Esth-waite* to *Salisbury Plain*, then it behooves us as we age to favor matitudinal and vernal scenes and moods — more for the simple symmetry of the thing than for any other reason, as I've said, though of course nothing prevents reading the conclusion, "as we nearer draw to life's dark goal, / Be hopeful Spring the favourite of the Soul!," as a Christian homily.

A few more links to the earlier crisis poems may help to explain what purpose this argument serves for Wordsworth. First, we understand "Lycoris" to be Dorothy. One might think that Mary too could be a candidate, but this poem does refer us to the period of youth, a period that must end well before either the Intimations Ode or Wordsworth's marriage with Mary in 1802. In 1798, when Wordsworth most famously addresses Dorothy (whom he had likewise addressed in *An Evening Walk*), although he is no longer a youth he is still an evening poet who favors "the light of setting suns"; and Dorothy, with her wild eyes, reflects yet an earlier taste, with nature still haunting her like a passion, and Wordsworth imagines her therefore against a moonlit backdrop. In turning to her again now, he tells her that — at least within the history of his poems — neither of them have done justice to nature's happier faces, and that both should remedy the imbalance in the time remaining. All this, then, is expressed in the context of converting the privately experienced visionary gleam into a seasonal event that is available to all. Note the language in which the "Guest" called Spring (making it like the angel of "Vernal Ode," or one of Blake's) is greeted:

> Then welcome, above all, the Guest
> Whose smiles, diffus'd o'er land and sea,
> Seem to recall the Deity
> Of youth into the breast.

"Peele Castle" laments "the gleam, / The light that never was, on sea or land." "Ode to Lycoris" by allusion not only restores this gleam but also *diffuses* it, a joy in widest commonalty spread, indicating that the throes of grief are as unjust to seasonal variety as the exotic tastes of youth. For the moment one may say simply that the evenness with which the gleam is diffused corresponds to the poet's recommended even-handedness in the treatment of times and seasons.

A final allusive context may lend substance to this covert idea. The nominal occasion for the poem was the sight of two white clouds reflected in a lake. Again, the connection between this sight and the rest of the poem seems oddly inconsequential, as indeed it plays no further role after the first strophe. Be-lated with respect to the golden age (and youth), the "bard of ebbing time, /

and nurtured in a fickle clime" (with "Clouds that gather round the setting sun") witnesses the reflection that prompted the poem:

> These swan-like specks of mountain snow,
> White as the pair that slid along the plains
> Of heaven, when Venus held the reins!

The clouds are anything but clouds; they are snow and swans, both local swans in resemblance and classical swans in fancy, with all these images dissolved, *like* clouds, on the glassy surface of the water. Here is an instance of that leveling of being, with its orders made interchangeable through metaphor, that Wordsworth in his 1815 "Preface" had singled out as an important function of the imagination, using as his example the commingling of stone, sea-beast, and cloud when the leech-gatherer is envisioned in "Resolution and Independence." This is the context, I believe, in which Wordsworth's cloud-snow-swan image, doubled in reflection, needs to be understood. The inclusive balance of things, whether the contrasting but equal-opportunity seasons or the imaging of diverse yet linked entities, is the guiding thread that carries us through the poem and lends it consequence. The poem is thus about "[a] skill—to balance and supply," to diffuse feeling evenly, so that the Before and After premise that seems to shape all these odes no longer weighs in the balance.

The second "Ode to Lycoris" ("To the Same") I will mention here only to point out that its particular point of recollection, perhaps inspired similarly by the renewed address to Dorothy, is "Tintern Abbey." Associating sublime vistas with a Napoleonic "contempt" for quotidian life spread out below, "[a]s in a map," Wordsworth and his companion turn instead to the cave imagined but not visited in "Tintern Abbey." Having rejected the sublime as a flight from social ties dictated by "Ambition," proclaiming that instead " 'tis the *heart* that magnifies this life," brother and sister choose a retreat of their own to hear the still sad music. They hear it together, merging the solitude of "Tintern Abbey" with the companionship of "Peele Castle," but it is unmistakably what Wordsworth heard nearly twenty years ago. Together, he and his sister are engaged in:

> The sighs of Earth
> Interpreting; or counting for old Time
> His minutes, by reiterated drops,
> Audible tears.

Clearly there is more of the hermeneutic in this moment than in that of Wordsworth's earlier audition, and its pathos is far more allusively literary. The tears, one may imagine, are those of Dante's Man of Crete, and one feels also the presence of Richard II sitting upon the ground and telling sad stories of the death of kings:

> Music do I hear?
> Ha — ha — keep time! How sour sweet music is
> When time is broke and no proportion kept! (V, v, 41–43)

Perhaps, though, Wordsworth's " or [rather] counting" here dismisses the conceit of "[i]nterpreting," with its focus on the explanation avoided in "Tintern Abbey," returning us instead to the theme of meter, which tells time as well as keeping it. The change is only in the eye, not in its object. Dorothy's "wild eyes" are no longer wild; she has joined Wordsworth in the After state, with its sober vision, and her "eye" becomes as "calm as water when the winds are gone." What she sees, though, as always when it is no longer in focus, is the human condition.

"Enough of climbing toil!" begins "To the Same" (the second "Ode to Lycoris"), and Wordsworth may have in mind his recent poem about climbing through the rugged pass north of Grasmere. Readers of that ode, "The Pass of Kirkstone," such as there may be, are likely to concentrate on what would seem to be the on-the-spot education of the speaker, who first denies the presence of man in the landscape, and then, having passed through a volatile mood-change or two, comes to accept it. There is a letter of Dorothy Wordsworth's from long before (1804), concerning a pass to the northwest, that perfectly captures the mood of this opening and its revision:

> there was neither a stone fence nor hedge, nor any work of men but the Road for a considerable way before us between the hills, a milestone and a wall upon the sloping ground at the foot of the mountain built by the shepherds in the form of a cross as a shelter for their sheep — it is so strange that so simple a thing could be of so much importance, but the mountains and the very sky above them, the solitary mountainvale all seemed to have a reference to that rude shelter — it was the very soul of the place. (*CL*, I, 507)

This alteration would make the Before and After movement take place in the present time of the poem rather than as a contrast between a remembered past and the present. Be this as it may, the subject of man's genial presence keys the poem to its most important antecedent, "Peele Castle." If the earlier poem began by stripping away the shiny varnish we inexperienced painters superimpose on existing things, this one begins by showing how "strong fancies" superimpose meaning on things, unsignifying in themselves, where there is "no appanage of human kind." Already, though, the human is difficult to keep at bay because the very rocks seem "cognizably shaped," both reminding us of our own artifacts and seeming to have been put to use by humans in the distant past: merely seeming, that is, in the case of the Egyptians, who cannot have been there — but, well, why *not* the Druids, who were as likely to have been there to perform their sacrifices as were the Romans on their march in the third strophe? This apposition of the Egyptians and the Druids is difficult to understand, because it undermines the presumably intended contrast, supported by the Romans' known presence, between the speaker's initial demystification of human referents in nature and his later acceptance of such referents as signs of habitation. Once again, that is — as a possible explanation — Before and After are destined to merge.

The second strophe is the strangest, because its peevish attack on human settlements and enclosures along the slopes of the pass — akin to the Daniel Boone attitude that today we would identify as "anti-growth" — amounts to an unmotivated contradiction of the claim in the first strophe that there are no signs of humanity in that same pass at all. In recovering from this bad mood, the speaker reverses his claim at ll. 7–10 that the human masks the natural by claiming that nature in the form of a veiling mist can mask the "care" and "guilt" that attend upon humanity. That is, the unmotivated contradiction mentioned above results in a chiastic balance, an equilibrium of elemental relations (nonhuman-human / human-nonhuman), comparable to the balance of ages and seasons in the first "Lycoris" and "Composed upon an Evening" (youth-evening / age-morning). With this balance established, the rest of the poem can explore the relation of the human to the nonhuman as a coexistence rather than a contrast. On the one hand the cliff can acceptably become the "churchlike frame" that "[g]ives to this savage Pass its name," while on the other hand the appearance of the nonhuman can acceptably become illusory: "Though habitation none appear, / The greenness tells, man must be there." Rather than choose between solitude and domestic solace, as in "Peele Castle," the speaker deliberately echoes "Peele Castle" — "Farewell, thou desolate Domain!" — in order to show that here in this pass, first during the steep climb (up the steepest road in the Lake District) and then in descent to "the cultured plain," the nonhuman and the human pass into one another without conflict, as in the word "Kirkstone" itself.

The concluding lines readmit personifications, alongside the new classicizings of other poems, as part of Wordsworth's broader reconsideration of "poetic diction." What once seemed to him artificial, distancing language from personal feelings that all would share if not blinkered by such language, now presents itself as another and more traditional kind of common denominator that links personal feeling to this same language, understood now as a body of conventions sanctioned by time and literary history. Just so, the child's verbally rudimentary "shouts" while experiencing a gilded nature in 1802 can merge in 1817 with the immemorial topos, ceremoniously recalled, of a golden age in the childhood of history. There was a time, an age hath been; the child is father to all. In saying this, I seem to be writing a critic's Intimations Ode, balancing Before and After states in the development of Wordsworth's poetics. No doubt, but in my own imitation of his ode structure I would likewise insist on the underlying continuity I have been emphasizing. Both his early and his late poetics are searches for the universal or "common." If the 1800 "Preface" must equivocate between the antithetical senses of the word "common," localizing a diction that is supposed to reflect sentiments common to all, the later apologies for his return to poetic diction equivocate comparably about the tenuously synecdochic relation between "classical" myth or archetype, conventionally evoked, and sentiments common to all. In each case Wordsworth aspires to be the medium uniting part with whole, in keeping with his unaltered intuition that the restoration of indiscriminate phenomenal unity to consciousness is the innovative purpose of his poetry.

The most obvious difference between effulgences vouchsafed to the poet in the earlier lyrics and those he witnesses in 1817 is that evening has replaced morning, except when morning is abstracted into a golden age. Wordsworth was now forty-seven, had lost a brother and two children, and could scarcely anticipate living another thirty-three years. The sunset that inspired "Composed upon an Evening of Extraordinary Beauty and Splendour," a better-known poem than its companions, resembles the one that graced the conclusion of *The Excursion*.[11] Like that one, this sunset passes away, with the evening star likewise wanting: "the visionary splendour fades; / And night approaches with her shades." The point of the later conclusion is not however the identification of a more modest scope for poetic ambition with "inferior lights." Rather it is death that is coming, as in all the 1817 odes, and the most urgent business of the poem, as the "NOTE" now openly admits, is to revisit the movement from the visionary splendor of childhood's spring morning to the dying fall at sunset of the Intimations Ode. The mediation of *The Excursion* is important. The protracted sunset is not now a manifestation of divine presence somewhere between nature and the mind, but has become, rather, as it is for the Pastor, a sign of something other than itself: "What is? — ah no, but what *can* be!"

This first strophe then offers Wordsworth's last reinterpretation of "the gleam." As a covenant rather than a theophany, the gleam can now become what it was not before: the revisionary symbol of death in relation to, or even as equivalent to, the philosophic calm of Wordsworth's After state: "The shadow—and the peace supreme!" This group of thoughts already circulates through "Tintern Abbey," but there the deathlike moment in which the burden is lifted still largely occurs in the vicinity of the darknesses and depths, still perhaps even tinged with horror-gothic, that the speaker of the first "Ode to Lycoris" has repudiated (only to revisit such scenes in "To the Same," making the two addresses an ode and a palinode). The gleam retains all its other recent associations, especially recalling again the golden age when "fervent Angels sang / Their vespers in the grove," "strains suitable to both" angels and men for reasons I have stressed; and when in other poems the gleam has been "diffused" on land and sea, here it is diffused in time, "endued with power to stay," so that it is no longer just a glimpse or intimation, the sort of moment that once inspired "blank misgivings" and would now have been uncomprehendingly witnessed with "blank astonishment." This sunset stays long enough to inspire meditation.

The rather beautiful second strophe evokes a radiant mountain landscape in leading up to an insistent second revision of "what we half create, and half perceive," a subject-object compromise in which, to Coleridge's distress, there was no necessarily implied transcendent source. Now Wordsworth, addressing this landscape, expresses faith in such a source:

> As long as god-like wish, or hope divine,
> Informs my spirit, ne'er can I believe
> That this magnificence is wholly thine!

Building on, or rather constrained by, the prior insistence that the gleam is not a visitation but a covenant standing in the place of the *deus absconditus* of mainstream Christianity, these lines are pointedly faith-based rather than cognitive, however. The speaker wishes and hopes, but no claim is being made for visionary *insight,* and this new modesty is quite in keeping with the silencing of the Wanderer as I have interpreted it in *The Excursion.* From this modesty, strengthened in a narrower but less muddled vocation, there emerges a moment of bardic confidence that fuses the incantatory rhythms of the Intimations Ode with the pious nationalism of *The Excursion:*

> —From worlds not quickened by the sun
> A portion of the gift is won;
> An intermingling of Heaven's pomp is spread
> On ground which British shepherds tread!

In a sense the angels have returned and revived a world "suitable to both," impressively repeating the later Wordsworth's introduction of vertical, evermore comprehensive elements to his continued leveling of being, repeated in the "hazy ridges" ascending upward in the ekphrasis of Washington Allston's

*Jacob's Dream* in the next strophe. The tone and rhetoric of this passage, which has much about it of Collins's "How Sleep the Brave" and seemingly nothing of the earlier Wordsworth, should not conceal the fact that these shepherds can be found among the protagonists of *Lyrical Ballads*. The setting is the same, the gleam has returned — in the sky, certainly, but at this moment on the "ground." Even as he thinks of Jacob wrestling with an angel and ascending the ladder (for Wordsworth the great chain of being is always softened into upward gradations), Wordsworth deliberately remains grounded: "Wings at my shoulders seem to play; / But, rooted here, I stand and gaze." It is this grounding that makes piety possible, though at the expense of knowledge: the poet now believes that what is elsewhere is not here (is not, that is, ontically comparable to the descent of angels to men), but only represented here in its absence. It is, again, a covenant: "Come forth, ye drooping old men, look abroad, / And see to what fair countries ye are bound!"

He is a drooping old man himself in the fourth and last strophe, now openly recalling the Intimations Ode with its stern companion the "Ode to Duty" thrown in ("From THEE if I would swerve"), and rethinks the grounding from which the rhetoric of the third strophe springs aloft: "My soul, though yet confined to earth, / Rejoices in a second birth!" That is, he is again a joyous child, and has found an answer to his perplexed question, "This glimpse of glory, why renewed?" It is renewed to show him what remains the same under all the flashes of difference. It is a sameness that is problematic at either extreme. For material being, it is the sameness of death (which gets the last word here owing to the security of the poem's achieved piety); for spiritual being it is the sameness of eternity that troubles the Intimations Ode, returns to trouble the 1817 odes, and is still diversified here as a plurality of "countries," the many mansions of my Father's house.

Neither of these samenesses, either distinct or meeting its opposite *as* the same, is or can be the theme of Wordsworth's poetry, though both do play an important role in defining the nonhuman. Nor would there be any interest in the poetry if they were its theme. They are, again, the nonhuman in the human. What Wordsworthian poetry achieves, both in theme and texture, is the disclosure of sameness in what is splendidly various, like a morning or evening. That the unity of things that exist is their existence itself: this theme can be disclosed, under the veil of difference, the "cognizable shape" of what we know, and it can disclosed by poetry even in the midst of human life. I have not mentioned Shelley until now, but by 1817 we will have arrived at him, just as it has been possible to show, surprisingly, that we have arrived at Keats and Byron. Wordsworth's business as a poet is to lift the painted veil which those who live call Life.

# Afterword: Just Having It There Before Us

As I remarked in Chapter 4, one of Wordsworth's shrewdest early twentieth-century debunkers was Irving Babbitt, whose New Humanist attack on the "primitivism" of the romantics forms the theme of his then highly influential *Rousseau and Romanticism*. From our retrospect, it is easy enough to see that Babbitt had a long pedigree, traced back to Matthew Arnold by T. S. Eliot (who was mainly irritated by the New Humanists' non-religious appeal to Christian ethics),[1] but visible still farther back if the lines are drawn more closely to those that shape this book. Hazlitt then looms into view, with his equally withering scorn for Rousseau's "*Voila de la pervenche!*" — extended forward to his many remarks on Wordsworth coloring everything he saw with his subjective impressions.[2] Hazlitt in turn inspires Keats's "Wordsworthian or egotistical sublime," probably the single most tyrannical notion governing preconceptions about Wordsworth to this day. Virtually no one who has written about Wordsworth works free of this preconception altogether, and many critics flourishing today accept it as given that not just Wordsworth but romanticism *tout court* (including Keats) can be summarized and dismissed with that catch-phrase. Thus we celebrate all the "non-canonical" authors of the period because they seem unaffected by the egotistical sublime; and in that spirit, I would suggest that a still more obvious precursor to Babbitt is Francis Jeffrey, to whom I have devoted a chapter.

My own view, which in this one respect I have may not have sufficiently emphasized despite my deliberate repetitiousness, is wildly at variance with this consensus about "romanticism."[3] Although in person Wordsworth was undoubtedly an egotist who left everyone outside his immediate circle wondering whether anything like the give and take of conversation was possible, I want to insist that his attention to objects in his poetry and his theory of poetry is an almost monastic discipline aimed at *effacing* the ego. "Sure, other peoples' egos," one might respond, but I hope I have shown that his poems and much of his prose are aimed as rigorously at his own pretensions to superior explanatory power as at anyone else's. Not that Rousseau at that one moment in the *Confessions* ridiculed by Hazlitt actually differed in this respect: "There are the periwinkles!" is indeed a truly Wordsworthian exclamation. What it means is: the periwinkles are there as much, and in the same way, as I am here. As doctrine or insight, that is severely self-curtailing, whatever one may be able to retort about its being self-promoting as rhetoric or as a "professional" gambit.

The egotism (or solipsism) canard aside, then, one still needs to ask, what is involved in the gesture, whether ascetic or self-admiring, of saying that things, including human things, are just there? The answer in my view is to be found in the analysis of the hermeneutic circle by Martin Heidegger, Irving Babbitt's contemporary, and can be worked through in reflecting on the following passage from *Being and Time:*

> When we have to do with anything, the mere seeing of the Things which are closest to us bears in itself the structure of interpretation, and in so primordial a manner that just to grasp something *free*, as it were, *of the "as,"* requires a certain readjustment. When we merely stare at something, our just-having-it-before-us lies before us *as a failure to understand it any more.* This grasping, which is free of the "as," is a privation of the kind of seeing in which one *merely* understands. It is not more primordial than that kind of seeing, but is derived from it. If the "as" is ontically unexpressed, this must not seduce us into overlooking it as a constitutive state for understanding, existential and *a priori.*[4]

What Heidegger points out here is that what I have variously called the ostensive or ontic moment of lyric, the moment that becomes focal for the first time in Wordsworth, is *not* the inaugural or "primordial" moment of perception. Primitivists think that it is; primitivists were thick on the ground in the Twenties, much to Babbitt's disgust, and Heidegger in 1927 knew he risked being considered one himself. (In the long run, what Adorno called his jargon of authenticity converted him into one.) That such a moment inaugurates consciousness and perception had been the supposition of much traditional phe-nomenology, including Hegel's; but in this as in many other respects Heidegger descends more directly from Kant and the hermeneutic tradition. To see some-thing, Heidegger says, is always already to see it *as* something. To fail "to understand it any more" is actually then a belated, decadent moment of per-ception that is achieved through a concentration of the will.

I look out the window and see a tree, a chimney, a street lamp. The street lamp in daylight has a strange, encased shape, not identifiable in itself, and I see it from the third floor of my house rather than looking up at it; yet I see it as a street lamp nonetheless, because I cannot stop knowing that it is one without effort. Furthermore, if there really were an anomalous shape in my field of vision that I could not identify (there appears to be one: what may be a piece of paper or plastic caught in the tree that looks from this distance like a bird or animal), the hermeneutics of identification would still be in play from the outset; my observation would still be inseparable from conjecturing that it was something in particular: a piece of paper or plastic, a bird or animal. It is not that my first impression is necessarily accurate; I see the tree as a tree, not an oak, the chimney as a chimney, not a functional chimney, and so on. My first glimpse is a conjecture or hypothesis that I then fit more and more closely to the object through studying it, arriving thereby at whatever degree of interpre-tive precision suits the occasion. But now I look again at the tree with the nagging awareness that, being human, I just happen to call it a tree and under-stand its attributes as a tree in a certain way, unlike the squirrels and birds that are more at home in it than I but call it nothing and understand it very dif-ferently. I don't want either my bias or theirs, though; I want to "just have it there before me." Perhaps I can do so if I empty my mind, as we say, and if I fail—I am in fact failing as I try to conduct the experiment—at least I have now recognized in myself both the desire to bracket my knowledge of things, to escape interpretation into being, and also the possibility that perhaps I could do so by exerting more discipline. Whence arises this desire? Partly to offset the biases of knowledge, if only for a moment, and partly to *suspend* the workings of the ego.

But wait: Have I not been arguing all along in this book that Wordsworth recovers things from their forms and names? That where others see their distinct natures from a subjective/objective distance, he sees their common existence and eclipses the subject-object relation that is grounded in reflection and merges with that common existence? Yes, that is precisely what I have been doing, but I hope to have shown that for Wordsworth this gesture is no more primordial than it is egotistical. It is the afterthought of lyric, not primordial in itself but constituted as the disclosure of the primordial. It is not childhood experience, furthermore, but the constructed memory of childhood experience that makes unreflected being seem prior to self-consciousness. Memory is precisely the invention of that priority. The poet is father to the child who is father to the man; and if another, rather obvious way of talking about Wordsworth's originality is to say that he invented childhood, I think it more circumspect to say that he *disclosed* childhood (with other marginal states) as the moment in which the priority of "just having it there before us," the oneness of the nonhuman felt as prior to the semeiosis of the human, was an efficacious illusion.

# Notes

## Chapter 1: Introduction: Wordsworth's Originality

1. William Butler Yeats, *The Poems of W. B. Yeats*, ed. Richard Finneran (New York: Macmillan, 1983), 348. A note here on my system of quotation from Wordsworth's poems: Whenever the argument hinges on a choice of text, I quote from the appropriate Cornell Wordsworth volume or from the Norton *Prelude*, as indicated. Otherwise I quote without pagination or line indicators — except for longer poems — from my teaching text of long standing: *William Wordsworth: The Poems*, ed. John O. Hayden, 2 vols. (London: Penguin Classics, 1989).

2. See Chandler, *Wordsworth's Second Nature: A Study of the Poetry and Politics* (Chicago: University of Chicago Press, 1984).

3. Thompson, *The Romantics: England in a Revolutionary Age* (New York: The New Press, 1997), esp. 41–57.

4. Samuel Taylor Coleridge, letter to George Coleridge, *Collected Letters of Samuel Taylor Coleridge*, ed. E. L. Griggs, 6 vols. (Oxford: Clarendon, 1956), I, 238.

5. I.e., from *The Spirit of the Age*, *The Complete Works of William Hazlitt*, ed. P. P. Howe, 21 vols. (New York: AMS, 1967), XI, 87.

6. See Bewell, *Wordsworth and the Enlightenment: Nature, Man, and Society in the Experimental Poetry* (New Haven: Yale University Press, 1989), 21–22, 24–29, 45–47.

7. I would not oppose a loose way of arguing for an implicit analogy between equality in politics and in the natural world, along the lines proposed by Carl Woodring in "On Liberty in the Poetry of Wordsworth" (*PMLA* 70 [1955]: 1033–48).

8. See Bromwich, *Disowned by Memory: Wordsworth's Poetry of the 1790s* (Chi-

cago: University of Chicago Press, 1998); and Liu, *Wordsworth: The Sense of History* (Stanford, Calif.: Stanford University Press, 1989).

9. Coleridge, letter to John Thelwall, *Letters,* ed. Griggs, I, 215–16.

10. Empson, *Seven Types of Ambiguity* (1930; London: Chatto & Windus, 1949), 151–52. This issue has of course been constantly revisited, most systematically by Empson's fellow Cantabridgean Basil Willey in his two "Background" books. For a recent reconsideration, see Keith G. Thomas, *Wordsworth and Philosophy: Empiricism and Transcendentalism in the Poetry* (Ann Arbor: UMI Research Press, 1989). A subtle recent alignment of Wordsworth with Locke, to some extent following the lead of Alan Grob's *Wordsworth's Philosophic Mind* (Columbus: Ohio State University Press, 1973) is Laura Quinney, "Wordsworth's Ghosts and the Model of the Mind," *European Romantic Review* 9 (1998): 293–301. For a relatively recent argument couched in philosophical terms and defending the presence of the transcendent in Wordsworth, see Melvin M. Rader, *Wordsworth: A Philosophical Approach* (Oxford: Clarendon, 1967).

11. See his January 1815 letter to Catherine Clarkson, *The Letters of William and Dorothy Wordsworth,* ed. Ernest de Selincourt, Chester L. Shaver, Mary Moorman, and Alan G. Hill, 8 vols. (Oxford: Clarendon, 1967–93), 3, 188. Throughout this book, all quotations from Wordsworth's letters are cited parenthetically from this edition as "*CL.*"

12. See Chapter 2 for a discussion of the intermittent presence of this topos in the poetry before 1796. The passage in the letter to Catherine Clarkson cited above (ibid.) shows clearly that Wordsworth now again believes in, and believes himself to have put into "Tintern Abbey," "innumerable analogies and types of infinity" that he has "transfused into that Poem from the Bible of the Universe as it speaks to the ear of the intelligent." Many readers take for granted that Wordsworth never abandons this topos, which is an aspect, as Jonathan Arac points out, of Herbert Lindenberger's approach to *The Prelude* (see Arac, " 'The Prelude' and Critical Revision," *Post-Structuralist Readings of English Poetry,* ed. Richard Machin and Christopher Norris (Cambridge: Cambridge University Press, 1987), 239.

13. Apart from the essay on Wordsworth and Coleridge cited above, the following of my essays are relevant: "Clearings in the Way: Non-Epiphany in Wordsworth" and "The Absent Dead: Wordsworth, Byron, and the Epitaph," together with a number of other sustained comments on Wordsworth in *A Defense of Poetry: Reflections on the Occasion of Writing* (Stanford, Calif.: Stanford University Press, 1995); "The Diligence of Desire: Critics On and Around Westminster Bridge," *WC* 23 (1992): 162–64.

14. See, e.g., Giorgio Agamben, *Infancy and History: The Destruction of Experience,* trans. Liz Heron (London: Verso, 1993), 1–63.

15. In the passage from the third "Essay upon Epitaphs" that lent Frances Ferguson's first important book its title, Wordsworth endorses the deconstructive position, but with a crucial proviso: "Language, if it do not uphold, and feed, and leave in quiet, like the power of gravitation or the air we breathe, is a counter-spirit, unremittingly and noiselessly at work to derange, to subvert, to lay waste, to vitiate, and to dissolve." *Wordsworth's Literary Criticism,* ed. W. J. B. Owen (London: Routledge & Kegan Paul, 1974), 154 (cited hereafter as *Criticism*).

16. Agamben, *The Coming Community,* trans. Michael Harte (Minneapolis: University of Minnesota Press, 1993).

17. The best account of this intellectual context in Wordsworth, especially as it informs the "primitivism" of the 1800 "Preface," remains that of M. H. Abrams, *The Mirror and the Lamp: Romantic Theory and the Critical Tradition* (New York: Oxford University Press, 1953).

18. For these views, see Iser, *Prospecting: From Reader Response to Literary Anthropology* (Baltimore: Johns Hopkins University Press, 1989), 262–84; and Iser, *The Fictive and the Imaginary: Charting Literary Anthropology* (Baltimore: Johns Hopkins University Press, 1993), passim.

19. *The Fenwick Notes of William Wordsworth*, ed. Jared Curtis (London: Bristol Classical Press, 1993), 67.

20. See *Criticism*, 79, on the intractability of specialized knowledge in poetry.

21. Stephen Gill is aware of this in emphasizing contemporary critics' reactions to the Duddon sonnets that were focused on "the barbarous name of an insignificant river" ("Wordsworth and *The River Duddon*," *Essays in Criticism* 57 (2007): 26). For an excellent essay on why "things" matter in Wordsworth, see Brooke Hopkins, "Wordsworth, Winnicott, and the Claims of the 'Real,'" *SiR* 37 (1998): The corporeal "is what makes the child 'feel real' or alive" (185).

22. *Journals of Dorothy Wordsworth*, ed. Ernest de Selincourt, 2 vols. (London: Macmillan, 1959), I, 63.

23. Hartman, *The Unremarkable Wordsworth* (Minneapolis: University of Minnesota Press, 1987), 8.

24. Mayo, "The Contemporaneity of the *Lyrical Ballads*," *Wordsworth: A Collection of Critical Essays*, ed. M. H. Abrams (Englewood Cliffs, N.J.: Prentice-Hall, 1972), 67–74; and the effort at rebuttal by Charles Ryskamp, "Wordsworth's *Lyrical Ballads* in Their Time," *From Sensibility to Romanticism*, ed. Frederick W. Hilles and Harold Bloom (New York: Oxford, 1965), 357–72. Unrelated to this dispute, or rather bracketing it, is the indispensable work of Mary Jacobus, *Tradition and Experiment in Wordsworth's "Lyrical Ballads"* (Oxford: Clarendon, 1976).

25. Weiskel, *The Romantic Sublime: Studies in the Structure and Psychology of Transcendence* (Baltimore: Johns Hopkins University Press, 1976), 17.

26. The critic who has written best, recurrently, on the vocabulary of blankness in Wordsworth is Harold Bloom, especially in *The Breaking of the Vessels* (Chicago: University of Chicago Press, 1982), 75–107.

27. See *CL*, III, 2, 178: "the range of poetic feeling is far wider than is ordinarily supposed, and the furnishing new proofs of this fact is the only *incontestable* demonstration of genuine poetic genius."

28. For the pioneering and in some ways still the best account of the phenomenology of the Spots of Time, see Jonathan Bishop, "Wordsworth and the 'Spots of Time,'" *ELH* (1959): 50, 62.

29. For a comparable reading of this passage with "Slumber," see Jonathan Wordsworth, *William Wordsworth: The Borders of Vision* (Oxford: Clarendon, 1982), 56.

30. This wave of the hand is not meant solely to dismiss McGann, Levinson, and more measured readers like Johnston and Bromwich from consideration as arbiters of the antisocial Wordsworth in "Tintern Abbey." I have in mind as well the more agenda-neutral, overtly philosophical claim of Frances Ferguson, which repeats the Kantian-Cavellian argument of her whole book, that the poem is framed (especially by the first verse para-

graph) to deny the existence of other minds—i.e., "independent consciousness" (Ferguson, *Solitude and the Sublime: Romanticism and the Aesthetics of Individuation* [New York: Routledge, 1992], 126). A relevant essay that curiously combines the emphasis on other minds and the otherness of things with my preoccupation with things in themselves is Seamus Perry, "Coleridge, Wordsworth, and Other Things," *TWC* 29 (1998): 31–41.

## Chapter 2: Wordsworth in the Rime

1. Of the many biographies, I mention only the most recent distinguished examples in each case: Stephen Gill, *William Wordsworth: A Life* (Oxford: Clarendon, 1989), and Richard Holmes, *Coleridge: Early Visions* (New York: Viking, 1989). Works focusing on verbal allusion are: Mary Jacobus, *Tradition and Experiment in Wordsworth's "Lyrical Ballads"* (Oxford: Clarendon, 1976); Gordon Thomas, "Rueful Woes, Joyous Hap: The Associate Labor of 'The Idiot Boy' and 'Christabel,'" *TWC* 14–15 (1983–84): 84; Neil Fraistat, *The Poem and the Book: Interpreting Collections of Romantic Poetry* (Chapel Hill: University of North Carolina Press, 1985), 41–94; Lucy Newlyn, *Coleridge, Wordsworth, and the Language of Allusion* (Oxford: Clarendon, 1986); Paul Magnuson, *Coleridge and Wordsworth: A Lyrical Dialogue* (Princeton, N.J.: Princeton University Press, 1988); and Susan Eilenberg, *Strange Power of Speech: Wordsworth, Coleridge, and Literary Possession* (New York: Oxford University Press, 1992). Studies ranging in between these emphases are: H. M. Margoliouth, *Wordsworth and Coleridge, 1795–1834* (Hamden, Conn.: Archon, 1966); A. S. Byatt, *Wordsworth and Coleridge in Their Time* (London: Nelson, 1970); William Heath, *Wordsworth and Coleridge: A Study of Their Literary Relations, 1801–1802* (Oxford: Clarendon, 1970); Thomas McFarland, *Romanticism and the Forms of Ruin: Wordsworth, Coleridge, and the Modalities of Fragmentation* (Princeton, N.J.: Princeton University Press, 1981); Jonathan Wordsworth, *William Wordsworth: The Borders of Vision* (Oxford: Clarendon, 1982); Richard Gravil, "Imagining Wordsworth: 1797–1807–1817," *Coleridge's Imagination*, ed. Gravil, Lucy Newlyn, Nicholas Roe (Cambridge: Cambridge University Press, 1985); Raimonda Modiano, "Coleridge and Wordsworth: The Ethics of Gift Exchange," *TWC* 20:2 (1989): 113–20; Gene Ruoff, *Wordsworth and Coleridge: The Making of the Major Lyrics, 1802–1804* (New Brunswick, N.J.: Rutgers University Press, 1989); Adam Sisman, *The Friendship: Wordsworth and Coleridge* (New York: Viking, 2006).

2. Paul H. Fry, *A Defense of Poetry: Reflections on the Occasion of Writing* (Stanford, Calif.: Stanford University Press, 1995), 101–03.

3. I leave *Peter Bell* aside for now, simply because it did not appear in *Lyrical Ballads,* but there is little doubt that indeed it is this poem that is Wordsworth's concerted and systematic response to the *Rime.* See Margoliouth, *Wordsworth and Coleridge,* 29, and Newlyn, *Coleridge, Wordsworth, and the Language of Allusion,* 50–51. For reasons less easy to justify, I shall also have nothing to say in this context about "Hart-Leap Well," which features the blighting of the natural world ensuing upon the shooting of an innocent animal. For pertinent comments, see Jonathan Wordsworth, *William Wordsworth* (137–38).

4. See E. L. Griggs, ed., *Collected Letters of Samuel Taylor Coleridge,* 6 vols. (Oxford: Clarendon, 1956), I, 215–16. See also I, 192–93, for passages attacking the materiality of Priestley's God.

5. As Stanley Cavell points out, Coleridge in the *Biographia* criticized Wordsworth for calling the child a "philosopher" in the Intimations Ode (*In Quest of the Ordinary: Lines of Skepticism and Romanticism* [Chicago: University of Chicago Press, 1988], 42). "I believe most steadfastly in original Sin," writes Coleridge in March 1798, "that from our mothers' wombs our understandings are darkened" (*Collected Letters*, I, 396).

6. E. E. Bostetter, "The Nightmare World of *The Ancient Mariner*," *SiR* 1–3 (1962): 241–54; William Empson, "Introduction," *Coleridge's Verse: A Selection*, ed. David Pirie (New York: Schocken, 1973); McGann, *The Beauty of Inflections: Literary Investigations in Historical Method and Theory* (Oxford: Clarendon, 1988), 135–72; Matlak, "Forty Questions to Ask of the Ancient Mariner," *Approaches to Teaching Coleridge's Poetry*, ed. Matlak (New York: MLA, 1991), 102–09; Warren, *New and Selected Essays* (New York: Random, 1989), 335–423.

7. Note that in the dedicatory epistle (1819) to *Peter Bell*, Wordsworth stresses that the imagination has no need of the supernatural. See McFarland, *Romanticism and the Forms of Ruin*, 74. As Lawrence Lipking reminds us in this context, Coleridge promised to preface the *Rime* with an essay on the supernatural ("The Marginal Gloss," *Critical Inquiry* 3 [1977]: 76).

8. Of course it was Coleridge himself, not Wordsworth, who was the programmatic Hartleyan through much of the 1790s, and it was he, too, who believed at one time that he could prove that every aspect of thought was what we would now call neurophysiological. One may suspect, though, that were it not for the enthusiastic theism of Part Two of the *Observations on Man*, Coleridge could never have been a Hartleyan even for a moment; and while the aggressive disavowal of Hartley that culminates in the *Biographia* cannot yet be said to have begun (any more than the open disagreement with Wordsworth had begun), Coleridge's discovery of Berkeley at the end of 1796 had already made him a different sort of monist, one who puts matter into mind rather than the other way around. Wordsworth on the other hand held less programmatic views of the basis of thought in the senses, views to be found in Locke and others, and never stopped holding them. For good accounts of this issue, see Walter Jackson Bate, *Coleridge* (New York: Macmillan, 1968), 32; and James D. Boulger, "Introduction," *Twentieth-Century Interpretations of the Rime of the Ancient Mariner*, ed. Boulger (Englewood Cliffs, N.J.: Prentice-Hall, 1969), 15–16. For the contrary insistence, elaborated in detail, that Coleridge remains a Hartleyan when writing the *Rime*, see Dorothy Waples, "David Hartley in 'The Rime of the Ancient Mariner,'" *JEGP* 35 (1936): 337–51.

9. On the contrasting symbolizations of marriage in Wordsworth and Coleridge, see Milton Teichman, "The Marriage Metaphor in the 'Ancient Mariner,'" *Bulletin of the New York Public Library* 73 (1969): 45.

10. In this same letter (*Collected Letters*, I, 599), Coleridge also focused on revisions for the 1798 "Withouten wind, withouten tide" (l. 161), suggesting that at this point magic currents were much on his mind (see Martin Wallen, ed., *Coleridge's "Ancient Mariner": An Experimental Edition of Texts and Revisions, 1798–1828* [Barrytown, N.Y.: Station Hill, 1993], 28). Again, note the conflict between the strong wind that reaches the ship in 1798 and the loud wind that does not reach the ship in 1800 (ibid., 51).

11. See James Butler and Karen Green, eds., *"Lyrical Ballads and Other Poems, 1797–1800 by William Wordsworth* (Ithaca, N.Y.: Cornell University Press, 1992), 283.

12. Empson, "The Ancient Mariner," 1964, in *Argufying*, ed. John Haffenden (Iowa

City: University of Iowa Press, 1987), 300 ("the darker Albatross mentioned in the anecdote of Shelvocke . . . does, I am told, make a tolerable soup that would keep off scurvy").

13. The most important recent revision of the way in which we think about this passage, especially in relation to Wordsworth, is that of Jonathan Wordsworth ("The Infinite I AM: Coleridge and the Ascent of Being," *Coleridge's Imagination,* ed. Gravil). In insisting, though, that the religious function of the primary imagination gives it greater importance than critics focused on the aesthetic have believed, Jonathan Wordsworth somewhat underplays the remaining fact that the secondary imagination alone is capable of producing poetry (see 46ff.).

14. The best account of the Mariner's cry as a textbook synecdoche is that of Eilenberg, *Strange Power of Speech,* 283–85. Eilenberg cites (6n.) the passage from Coleridge's *Miscellaneous Criticism* (ed. T. M. Raysor [London: Constable, 1936], 99) in which Coleridge gives "sail" as an example of synecdoche.

15. Or nearly always. Coleridge is not always enthusiastic even about the symbol. In the *Notebooks* (ed. Kathleen Coburn [New York: Bollingen, 1957], II, 2998), he speaks of "the inadequacy of Words to Feeling, of the symbol to the Being" (cited also in this context by Raimonda Modiano, "Words and 'Languageless' Meanings: Limits of Expression in 'The Rime of the Ancient Mariner,'" *MLQ* 38 [1977]: 42).

16. This famous passage from *The Statesman's Manual* is best known to modern readers from the discussion of it by Paul de Man in "The Rhetoric of Temporality," *Blindness and Insight: Essays in the Rhetoric of Contemporary Criticism,* 2nd ed. (Minneapolis: University of Minnesota Press, 1983), 192.

17. Reed convincingly elaborates this argument, which hinges on his reminder that, having removed nearly all the archaisms from the poem, Coleridge retained the spelling of "Rime" even in 1817 ("The Mariner Rimed," *Romanticism and Language,* ed. Reed [Ithaca, N.Y.: Cornell University Press, 1984], 168).

18. McFarland points out (*Romanticism and the Forms of Ruin,* 68) that in looking forward to the Discharged Soldier, the Drowned Man, and the Leech Gatherer, the Mariner is "a projection from the psycho-dramatic center of Wordsworth's fantasy more than from that of Coleridge."

19. Warren saw that the Hermit's religion is close to the soil: he is "both priest of God and priest of nature" (*New and Selected Essays,* 379). This passage has not gone unobserved by the speculative—from Kenneth Burke deducing vaginal fear from "prayer-above-moss-hiding-rot" (*The Philosophy of Literary Form* [New York: Vintage, 1957], 194) to the inference of castration from the stump by Donald Ault in his "Foreword" to Wallen's *Coleridge's 'Ancient Mariner'* (xiii).

20. The character Leslie Brisman has dubbed "Porlock" ("Coleridge and the Ancestral Voices," *Romantic Origins* [Ithaca, N.Y.: Cornell University Press], 1978, passim) comes closest in existing commentary to the figure I am linking with Wordsworth. With his "genial, natural accents" (37), Brisman's Porlock must be "made to confront the undisturbed 'one life' that it is his nature to interrupt" (43). Because "the primacy of the natural voice is Porlock's great claim" (51), the Ancient Mariner necessarily "goes about seeking out the Porlocks, interrupting marriage feasts for whatever increase in vision his power of voice can impart" (52). In an excellent reading of the poem, Paul Magnuson

points out that the Hermit is "something of a poet" (*Coleridge's Nightmare Poetry* [Charlottesville: University of Virginia Press, 1974], 73).

21. For the necessary contextualization of Coleridge's exchange with Barbauld, see Frances Ferguson, "Coleridge and the Deluded Reader," *"The Rime of the Ancient Mariner,"* ed. Paul H. Fry (Boston: Bedford / St. Martin's, 1999), 120–22.

22. Wordsworth got the colors for the thorn from Dorothy Wordsworth's Alfoxden Journal, as James Holt McGavran points out ("Darwin, Coleridge, and 'The Thorn,'" *TWC* 25:2 [1994]: 121), but the parallel with Coleridge's colors is still noteworthy. See, e.g., Warren Stevenson, "The Case of the Missing Captain: Power Politics in 'The Rime of the Ancient Mariner,'" *TWC* 26:1 [1995]: 13.

23. For other remarks connecting the *Rime* and "The Thorn," see Susan J. Wolfson, "The Language of Interpretation in Romantic Poetry: 'A Strong Working of the Mind,'" *Romanticism and Language,* ed. Reed, 23ff.

24. In 1836 Wordsworth told Henry Crabb Robinson that Coleridge had written the first four lines of "We Are Seven." I would suggest only that even with such evidence in hand one must appeal to the asymmetry of motive alleged above. See Mark L. Reed, "Wordsworth, Coleridge, and the 'Plan' of the Lyrical Ballads," *UTQ* 34 (1965): 250.

25. For comments on this parallel, see Peter Larkin, *"Lyrical Ballads:* Wordsworth's Book of Questions," *TWC* 20:2 (1989): 107.

## Chapter 3: *Jeffreyism, Byron's Wordsworth, and the Nonhuman in Nature*

1. For an account of the origins of this term, or at least its elements, in the first sentence of Jeffrey's 1807 review of Wordsworth, see Peter A. Cook, "Chronology of the 'Lake School' Argument: Some Revisions," *Review of English Studies* 28 (1977): 175–81. Despite what is often said, the term does not appear in the 1802 review of Southey's *Thalaba.*

2. Wordsworth understood the bringing together of four figures (including Lamb) by the critics under this heading, yet he still quite rightly remarked in 1804 that "it is scarcely possible that a greater difference should exist between any set of men or Authors" (*CL,* I, 434).

3. For a comparable view of Byron's underlying approval of Jeffrey, see Muriel J. Mellown, "Francis Jeffrey, Lord Byron, and *English Bards, and Scotch Reviewers,"* *Studies in Scottish Literature* 16 (1981): 81.

4. A recent editor of a Jeffrey selection has also argued that the Alison review provides a basis for Jeffrey's critique of Wordsworth. He points, however, to Jeffrey's insistence at the end of the essay that poets have a special responsibility to be sure that their associations are not merely personal but universal. I take it, though, that this particular complaint had been a commonplace in Wordsworth reviews ever since 1798. See Peter F. Morgan, in Morgan, ed., *Jeffrey's Criticism: A Selection* (Edinburgh: Scottish Academic Press, 1983), 169.

5. Francis Jeffrey, *Contributions to the Edinburgh Review* (1843; Boston: Phillips, Sampson, and Co., 1856). Cited parenthetically as *Contributions.*

6. An interesting brief discussion of this matter, and of the moderately Liberal politics of the *Edinburgh,* appears in Leslie Stephen, *Hours in a Library,* 3 vols. (London: Smith, Elder, & Co., 1909), II, 226–28.

7. A youthful essay on Beauty from the period 1791–92 already reflects Alison's Associationist principles and the key discussion of the imagined beautiful and sublime landscapes to be discussed below. For a surviving passage, see Henry Thomas Lord Cockburn, *Life of Lord Jeffrey,* 2 vols. (Edinburgh: Adam and Charles Black, 1852), I, 42–43.

8. That Jeffrey likewise says nothing of Hume in any version of the essay is more surprising, in that "Of the Standard of Taste" is surely the main source of Alison's Associationist aesthetics. In Hume, too, one finds a full exposition of Alison's and Jeffrey's relativism qualified by social consensus — not surprisingly, as no other conclusion can be drawn from Associationist views that is not inferred, like David Hartley's, from divine providence.

9. For an account of the negligible role played by form and structure in Wordsworth's view of nature, see Chapter 4.

10. *The Edinburgh Review* 23 (Nov. 1814), 2. I cite this and the other "Lake Poets" reviews from the facsimile reprints in Jonathan Wordsworth, ed., *Jeffrey on the Lake Poets* (Poole, U.K.: Woodstock Books, 1998), but I shall refer parenthetically to *ER,* etc., when citing these and other articles.

11. Also emphasizing Jeffrey's anthropocentrism is W. H. Christie, "Francis Jeffrey's Associationist Aesthetics," *British Journal of Aesthetics* 33 (1993): 260.

12. While it is irresistible to compare Jeffrey here with Mary Crawford in *Mansfield Park* ("I am like the famous Doge at the court of Lewis XIV; and may declare that I see no wonder in this shrubbery equal to seeing myself in it" [Signet edition, 1964, 164]), it should be clear that sorting out the conflicting ideological implications brought to light by the comparison would require an article in itself.

13. One turns eagerly to James A. Greig's ultra-Jeffreyan *Francis Jeffrey of the Edinburgh Review* (Edinburgh: Oliver and Boyd, 1948), which devotes three chapters to Jeffrey's attacks and much of the rest of the book to laying a groundwork for those chapters; but its only real purpose is to issue in Jeffrey's behalf (and, perhaps, in Scotland's) a *tu quoque* to Wordsworth and his modern admirers by saying that in person Jeffrey was more pleasant and tolerant than Wordsworth.

14. See Jonathan Wordsworth, "Introduction," *Francis Jeffrey on the Lake Poets,* passim (no pp.).

15. See Claude Lévi-Strauss, *Structural Anthropology,* trans. Claire Jacobson and Brooke Grundfest Schoepf (New York: Anchor Books, 1967), 211–12.

16. See Ernst Robert Curtius, *European Literature in the Latin Middle Ages,* trans. Willard R. Trask (1948; Princeton, N.J.: Bollingen, 1973), 319–26.

17. Greig points this out in *Francis Jeffrey of the Edinburgh Review,* 220.

18. Greig (ibid., 221–22) suddenly awakens here to the source of disagreement, noting "the poet's concentration of interest on the doe instead of on the human characters and situations."

19. *The White Doe of Rylstone; or The fate of the Nortons,* ed. Dugas (Ithaca, N.Y.: Cornell University Press, 1988), 60.

20. See Wu, "Rancour and Rabies: Hazlitt, Coleridge and Jeffrey in Dialogue," *British Romanticism and the Edinburgh Review: Bicentenary Essays,* ed. Massimiliano Demata and Wu (London: Palgrave Macmillan, 2002), 174.

21. *The Works of Lord Byron. Letters and Journals,* 6 vols., ed. R. E. Prothero (London: John Murray, 1901), V, 102. Cited parenthetically as *LBLJ.*

22. As Charles Augustin Sainte-Beuve remarked in "What is a Classic" (1850; trans. Elizabeth Lee), Byron, who slighted even Shakespeare, "never denied Pope, because he did not fear him; he knew that Pope was only a *low wall* by his side" (W. J. Bate, ed., *Criticism: The Major Texts* [San Diego, Calif.: Harcourt Brace Jovanovich, 1970], 493).

23. *The Prose Works of William Wordsworth,* ed. W. J. B. Owen and Jane Worthington Smyser (Oxford: Clarendon, 1974), 142.

24. A number of commentaries could be cited that stress the importance of "The Thorn" in Byron's prose introduction, but *The Excursion* in this context goes virtually ignored. See especially Gordon K. Thomas, "Wordsworth, Byron and 'Our Friend the Story-Teller,'" *Dutch Quarterly Review* 13 (1983), 200–212; Jerome J. McGann, *Don Juan in Context* (Chicago: University of Chicago Press, 1976), 161–63.

25. Byron cleverly stations himself in this tableau as one of the two "travellers" at a slight distance from the narrator and his auditors. Recalling his trek through the Sierra Morena of 1809, Byron here listens to the narrator's tale, while his companion Hobhouse admires an Andalusian maid. Vis-à-vis *The Excursion,* Byron is the Poet, the Narrator is the Pedlar, and the "Curate of the hamlet" is the Pastor. *Lord Byron: Don Juan,* ed. T. G. Steffan, E. Steffan, and W. W. Pratt (New Haven: Yale University Press, 1982), 38. This text is cited parenthetically as *DJ.*

26. Ll. 40–41, 65–66, 57–58 quoted by Wordsworth in the prose preface to *The Excursion* that Byron would have read in 1815 (*William Wordsworth: The Poems,* 2 vols., ed. J. O. Hayden [Harmondsworth: Penguin, 1977], II, 38–39). See *The Poetry and Prose of William Blake,* ed. David V. Erdman (Garden City, N.Y.: Doubleday Anchor, 1970), 656.

*Chapter 4: Green to the Very Door? The Natural Wordsworth*

1. See, e.g., Geoffrey Hartman, who cites the Isabella Fenwick Intimations Ode note to this end in his 1977 essay "A Touching Compulsion" in *The Unremarkable Wordsworth* (Minneapolis: University of Minnesota Press, 1987), 20.

2. De Man, *The Rhetoric of Romanticism* (New York: Columbia University Press, 1984), 16. This is one of de Man's earliest formulations of the issue using the linguistic terms of his later work.

3. Liu, *Wordsworth: The Sense of History* (Stanford, Calif.: Stanford University Press, 1989), 104. Liu's position gains its subtlety from the consciousness of reformulating without restructuring the purportedly hegemonic forms of antinaturalism in Wordsworth studies in order to redirect the course of interpretation. Marjorie Levinson somewhat comparably speaks of her political demystifications as "deconstruction" (*Wordsworth's Great Period Poems: Four Essays* [Cambridge: Cambridge University Press, 1986]), while Tilottama Rajan elaborates a more complex compromise formation in arguing that deconstruction would have taken a different turn had it attended to narrative rather than lyric elements in Wordsworth (see her "The Erasure of Narrative in Post-Structuralist Representations of Wordsworth," in *Romantic Revolutions: Criticism and Theory,* ed. Kenneth R. Johnston, Gilbert Chaitin, Karen Hanson, and Herbert Marks [Bloomington: Indiana University Press, 1990], 350–70).

4. See Bate, *Romantic Ecology: Wordsworth and the Environmental Tradition* (London: Routledge, 1991), 9.

5. See my "Wordsworth's Severe Intimations," in *The Poet's Calling in the English Ode* (New Haven: Yale University Press, 1980), 133–61. See also my *A Defense of Poetry: Reflections on the Occasion of Writing* (Stanford, Calif.: Stanford University Press, 1995), 91–107, 159–80, together with "The Diligence of Desire: Critics on and Around Westminster Bridge," *TWC* 23 (1992): 162–64.

6. See Arthur Beatty (who cites Tinker's 1922 *Nature's Simple Plan*), *Wordsworth: His Doctrine and Art in Their Historical Relations* (Madison: University of Wisconsin Press, 1922), 122.

7. See Joseph Warren Beach, *The Concept of Nature in Nineteenth-Century Poetry* (New York: Macmillan, 1936), 118.

8. Basil Willey, *The Seventeenth-Century Background: Studies in the Thought of the Age in Relation to Poetry and Religion* (London: Chatto & Windus, 1949), 304.

9. H. W. Piper, *The Active Universe: Pantheism and the Concept of Imagination in the English Romantic Poets* (London: Athlone, 1962), 115.

10. William Wordsworth, *Home at Grasmere*, ed. Beth Darlington (Ithaca, N.Y.: Cornell University Press, 1977), MS. D., 816–18, 810 (105).

11. Walter Pater, "Wordsworth," in *Selected Writings of Walter Pater*, ed. Harold Bloom (New York: Signet, 1974), 128, 130, 131. Pater almost certainly has in mind the passage in "Resolution and Independence" making the Leech Gatherer a mediatory figure between a stone, a sea beast, and a cloud—the passage Wordsworth cites in the 1815 "Preface" to illustrate the workings of the imagination.

12. William Hazlitt, *Lectures on the English Poets*, in *Lectures on the English Poets and The Spirit of the Age* (New York: Everyman, 1960), 163.

13. See Matthew Arnold, "Wordsworth," in *Poetry and Criticism of Matthew Arnold*, ed. A. Dwight Culler (Boston: Riverside, 1961), 343.

14. F. R. Leavis, "Revaluations (VI): Wordsworth," *Scrutiny* 3 (1934): 235.

15. See William Empson, *Seven Types of Ambiguity* (1930; rev. ed. London: Chatto & Windus, 1949), 153–54; and Empson, *The Structure of Complex Words* (Ann Arbor: University of Michigan Press, 1967), 304. That there appears to have been a "Cambridge School" of Wordsworth criticism, with Empson, Leavis, Willey, and Hugh Sykes Davies its chief exponents, has not to my knowledge been remarked. For de Man's opinion, see *The Rhetoric of Romanticism*, 88.

16. Basil Willey, *The Eighteenth-Century Background* (London: Chatto & Windus, 1940), 253.

17. Irving Babbit, "The Primitivism of Wordsworth," *Bookman* (USA) 74 (1931): 3, 10.

18. Hartman, *Beyond Formalism: Literary Essays, 1958–1970* (New Haven: Yale University Press, 1971), 311.

19. A. C. Bradley, "Wordsworth and the Sublime," in *Discussions of Wordsworth*, ed. Jack Davis (Boston: D. C. Heath, 1964), 47–62; G. Wilson Knight, *The Starlit Dome* (1943; rpt. New York: Barnes & Noble, 1960), 16; D. G. James, *Scepticism and Poetry* (1937; rpt. New York: Barnes & Noble, 1960), 141–69.

20. John Jones, *The Egotistical Sublime* (London: Chatto & Windus, 1954), 48. See Hartman, *Wordsworth's Poetry, 1787–1814* (1965; rev. ed. Cambridge, Mass.: Harvard University Press, 1987), 349.

21. See Hartman, *The Fate of Reading and Other Essays* (Chicago: University of Chicago Press, 1975), 277.

22. Lionel Trilling, *The Liberal Imagination* (New York: Anchor, 1953), 140.

23. For the obvious truth of this fact, with its non-Marxist implications, one need look no farther than the *National Geographic* for August 1994 for a gruesome article on pollution in the former USSR, "Lethal Legacy" (70–115). Interestingly, the lead article in this issue, "England's Lake District," reflects Bate's Ruskinian view of that region: "Wordsworth called it 'a blended holiness of earth and sky.' Today this poetic rolling landscape receives 12 million visitors each year — and feels the strain."

24. Anna Bramwell, *Ecology in the Twentieth Century: A History* (New Haven: Yale University Press, 1989). In support of Bate's (and Bramwell's) celebration of a specifically British grasp of the politics of nature, elaborated in Bramwell's chapter called "Back to the Northland," one might add that during the vogue among intellectuals for mountain climbing in the early twentieth century, the typifying charismatic figure in England was the leftist journalist Michael Roberts, friend of Richards and others, whereas in Germany the comparable figure was Leni Riefenstahl.

25. P. D. James, *Devices and Desires* (New York: Knopf, 1990), 61–62.

26. I should say that in Bate's best chapter, "The Naming of Places," there are touches of an ontological perspective. See, e.g., the fine description of "Michael" on 105.

27. Alfred North Whitehead, *Science and the Modern World* (New York: Mentor, 1948), 80.

28. High praise, on this criterion, to Marshall Brown, "Wordsworth's Old Gray Stone," in *Preromanticism* (Stanford, Calif.: Stanford University Press, 1991).

29. See John Stilgoe, "The Kayak Elite, the String Bikini, and the Indoor Child," *Harvard Alumni Magazine*, Special Supplement (Summer 1994): 3–12.

30. See Alan Bewell, *Wordsworth and the Enlightenment* (New Haven: Yale University Press, 1989), 202.

31. Cf. Carol Jacobs, "The Unimaginable Touch of Time: Wordsworth's 'Tintern Abbey,' Crossing the Alps, and 'Intimations of Immortality,' " *Telling Time* (Baltimore: Johns Hopkins University Press, 1993), 161. Thomas McFarland, commenting on Marjorie Levinson's treatment of these visual circumstances as products of Enclosure, launches his alternative reading of the poem in *William Wordsworth: Intensity and Achievement* (Oxford: Clarendon, 1992), 34, 52.

32. Wordsworth's objection to whitewashed houses in the *Guide to the Lakes* reaches this conclusion: "the safest colour, for general use, is something between a cream and a dust-colour, commonly called stone colour; — there are, among the Lakes, examples of this that need not be pointed out" (*Guide Through the District of the Lakes in the North of England* (Malvern: Tantivy Press, 1835), 70).

## Chapter 5: The Novelty of Wordsworth's Earliest Poems

1. Quoted from *Letters of William and Dorothy Wordsworth: The Early Years, 1787–1805*, ed. Ernest de Selincourt, rev. ed. Chester L. Shaver (Oxford: Clarendon, 1967), 327–28.

2. *An Evening Walk*, ed. Averill (Ithaca, N.Y.: Cornell University Press, 1984); *Descriptive Sketches*, ed. Birdsall (Ithaca, N.Y.: Cornell University Press, 1984). Unless it is

otherwise specified, I shall quote these poems from Averill's Reading Text of the former (1794), and Birdsall's Reading Texts of the latter (either 1793 or 1836, as indicated). Other juvenilia I quote from Hayden. The liveliest pages to date on *An Evening Walk* are in Alan Liu, *Wordsworth: The Sense of History* (Stanford, Calif.: Stanford University Press, 1989), 203–08.

3. Hartman, *Wordsworth's Poetry, 1787–1814* (1965; rev. ed. Cambridge, Mass.: Harvard University Press, 1987), 79. In his reading of *Descriptive Sketches*, Hartman anticipates me more closely in stressing the "powers and presences" in the poem (103), but he sustains this emphasis in keeping with his great theme, the *tension* between nature and the mind's transcendent impulses.

4. Pfau, *Wordsworth's Profession: Form, Class, and the Logic of Early Romantic Cultural Production* (Stanford, Calif.: Stanford University Press, 1997); Siskin, *The Work of Writing: Literature and Social Change in Britain, 1700–1830* (Baltimore: Johns Hopkins University Press, 1998).

5. I shall return to these critics, but concerning *Descriptive Sketches*, see Johnston, "Wordsworth's Revolutions, 1793–1798," *Revolution and English Romanticism,* ed. Keith Hanley and Raman Selden (Hemel Hempstead: Harvester Wheatsheaf, 1990), 182.

6. Empson, "Basic English and Wordsworth," *Argufying: Essays on Literature and Culture,* ed. John Haffenden (Iowa City: University of Iowa Press, 1987), 237.

7. Wimsatt, *The Verbal Icon: Studies in the Meaning of Poetry* (New York: Noonday, 1964), 103–16.

8. *The Poetical Works of Mark Akenside,* ed. Alexander Dyce (1845; New York: AMS, 1969), 249. For reasons related to the present argument, this poem has drawn the attention of Geoffrey Hartman in *The Fate of Reading and Other Essays* (Chicago: University of Chicago Press, 1975), 147–50, and I have returned to it twice already: Fry, *The Poet's Calling in the English Ode* (New Haven: Yale University Press, 1980), 114–15, and *A Defense of Poetry: Reflections on the Occasion of Writing* (Stanford, Calif.: Stanford University Press, 1995), 91–93.

9. Duncan Wu's agnostic treatment of this text has nothing to say, either, about the Cornell editors' open window for the first line, but all scholars admit that it could have been composed as late as 1802, the year of the sonnet's publication in the *Morning Post* (Wu, *Wordsworth: An Inner Life* [Oxford: Blackwell, 2002], 58–59).

10. This and other Virgilian conventions of eighteenth-century description are subtly evoked by Christopher R. Miller, *The Invention of Evening: Perception and Time in Romantic Poetry* (Cambridge: Cambridge University Press, 2006), esp. 17–20.

11. See especially Ronald Paulson, *Literary Landscape: Turner and Constable* (New Haven: Yale University Press, 1982), James A. W. Heffernan, *Re-creation of Landscape: A Study of Wordsworth, Constable, and Turner* (Hanover, N.H.: University Press of New England, 1985), and Karl Kroeber, *Romantic Landscape Vision* (Madison: University of Wisconsin Press, 1975).

12. See Barrell, *The Dark Side of landscape: The Rural Poor in English Painting, 1730–1840* (Cambridge: Cambridge University Press, 1980), esp. 151–52.

13. Quoted from *Evening Walk,* ed. Averill, 302.

14. Quoted from *Descriptive Sketches,* ed. Birdsall, 300.

15. Birdsall in nonetheless right to remark that "the decaying 'lilly of domestic joy'" (723) is well excised from 1793 (ibid., 20).

## Chapter 6: Hoof After Hoof, Metric Time

1. See, e.g., Bloom, *A Map of Misreading* (New York: Oxford University Press, 1975), 38.

2. Cameron, *Lyric Time: Dickinson and the Limits of Genre* (Baltimore: Johns Hopkins University Press, 1979), 203, 205.

3. *Wordsworth's Literary Criticism*, ed. W. J. B. Owen (London: Routledge & Kegan Paul, 1974), 72. By 1810, when he wrote his three essays "Upon Epitaphs," he appears to have been more comfortable with the girl's position despite his even more overtly pious perspective, and wrote of "the wholesome communion between living and dead which the conjunction in rural districts of the place of burial and the place of worship tends so effectually to promote" (ibid., 137).

4. I continue not to annotate Wordsworth's poems unless there is some difficulty identifying editions or lines, but I shall quote Lyrical Ballads from *"Lyrical Ballads" and Other Poems, 1797–1800*, ed. James Butler and Karen Green (Ithaca, N.Y.: Cornell University Press, 1992).

5. The best remarks to date on this poem include a lively account of its attention to numbers. See Frances Ferguson, "Historicism, Deconstruction, and Wordsworth," *Diacritics* 17 (1987): 40–42.

6. Marilyn Butler is right to imply a politics in those who ignore Wordsworth's political links to his contemporaries in favor of connecting him with Stevens among other successors, but perhaps what she dislikes is best considered a holiday from politics (see Butler, "Plotting the Revolution: The Political Narratives of Romantic Poetry and Criticism," *Romantic Revolutions: Criticism and Theory*, ed. Kenneth R. Johnston, Gilbert Chaitin, Karen Hanson, and Herbert Marks (Bloomington: University of Indiana Press, 1990), 137).

7. *"Lyrical Ballads,"* ed. Butler and Green, 322.

8. Hartman, *Wordsworth's Poetry, 1787–1814* (1965; rev. ed. Cambridge, Mass.: Harvard University Press, 1987), 24.

9. For every aspect of meter in Wordsworth, see Brennan O'Donnell, *The Passion of Meter: A Study of Wordsworth's Metrical Art* (Kent, Ohio: Kent State University Press, 1995).

10. *The White Doe of Rylstone*, ed. Kristine Dugas (Ithaca, N.Y.: Cornell University Press, 1988), 104.

11. It is interesting at least to me that Wordsworth at one point thought about publishing three of these poems in a cluster (see Dorothy Wordsworth's letter to De Quincey of 1 May 1809, *The Letters of William and Dorothy Wordsworth, 1806–1811*, ed. Mary Moorman [Oxford: Clarendon, 1969], 325).

12. *The Fenwick Notes of William Wordsworth*, ed. Jared Curtis (London: Bristol Classical Press, 1993), 10. Wordsworth had been told that an idiot near Alfoxden had said this, but his sister's journal for 1802 would suggest that at least part of this passage could be felt as a continuous experience: "The owls had hooted 1/4 of an hour before,

now the cocks were crowing" *Journals of Dorothy Wordsworth*, ed. Ernest de Selincourt, 2 vols. (London: Macmillan, 1959), 160.

13. See his letter to John Wilson, *Wordsworth's Literary Criticism*, ed. W. J. B. Owen (London: Routledge & Kegan Paul, 1974), 107. A commentator who recognizes much of what I stress here but nonetheless insists on Wordsworth's comic distancing throughout the poem is John F. Danby, *The Simple Wordsworth: Studies in the Poems, 1797–1807* (London: Routledge & Kegan Paul, 1960).

14. I shall quote this poem from *Benjamin the Waggoner*, ed. Paul F. Betz (Ithaca, N.Y.: Cornell University Press, 1981).

15. Quoted ibid., 26.

16. This poem too I quote from the Cornell edition: *Peter Bell*, ed. John E. Jordan (Ithaca, N.Y.: Cornell University Press, 1985).

17. Wordsworth guards against even Peter's ascription of supernatural agency to the ass, however, in canceling a passage from MS. 2 (45v): "oft deeming him as you will guess / A supernatural beast" (*Peter Bell*, ed. Jordan, 22).

18. "In the woods of Alfoxden I used to take great delight in noticing the habits, tricks, and physiognomy of asses" (quoted from the Fenwick note in *Peter Bell*, ed. Jordan, 4).

19. In another version of this passage from the same notebook, which may have been meant for *The Ruined Cottage*, Wordsworth' s lingering but I think intermittent pantheism appears. There he speaks, extending his domain of reference to "forms inanimate," of "objects such as have no power to hold / Articulate language. In all forms of things / There is a mind." See *"The Ruined Cottage" and "The Pedlar,"* ed. James Butler (Ithaca, N.Y.: Cornell University Press, 1979), 121–22.

20. *Fenwick Notes*, ed. Curtis, 33.

21. Christopher Wordsworth, *Memoirs of William Wordsworth*, 2 vols. (London: Edward Moxon, 1851), II, 311.

22. Wagner, *A Moment's Monument: Revisionary Poetics and the Nineteenth Century English Sonnet* (Madison, N.J.: Fairleigh Dickinson University Press, 1996).

23. As Thomas McFarland says, Wordsworth "could set even the sonnets to streaming" (*William Wordsworth: Intensity and Achievement* [Oxford: Clarendon, 1992], 41).

24. See my article, "The Diligence of Desire: Critics On and Around Westminster Bridge," *TWC* 23 (1992): 162–64, for a summary of the ways in which this poem has been read.

25. Williams, *The Country and the City* (Oxford: Oxford University Press, 1973).

26. *Journals of Dorothy Wordsworth*, ed. Ernest de Selincourt, 2 vols. (London: Macmillan, 1959), I, 173.

27. Vendler, "The Experiential Beginnings of Keats's Odes," *SiR* 12 (1973): 591–606.

## Chapter 7: The Poem to Coleridge

1. The working text from which I shall quote *The Prelude* is *The Prelude 1799, 1805, 1850*, ed. Jonathan Wordsworth, M. H. Abrams, and Stephen Gill (New York: Norton, 1979). Quotations are from 1805 unless otherwise specified. Anyone facing the task today of citing even the very most important commentators on this poem might well turn faint. The pioneering sustained readings are by Hartman in *Wordsworth's Poetry, 1787–*

*1814* (1965; rev. ed. Cambridge, Mass.: Harvard University Press, 1987), Herbert Lindenberger (*On Wordsworth's Prelude* [Princeton, N.J.: Princeton University Press, 1963]), M. H. Abrams (*Natural Supernaturalism: Tradition and Revolution in Romantic Literature* (New York: Norton, 1971), and the brilliant feminist and historicist work of Mary Jacobus in *Romanticism, Writing, and Sexual Difference: Essays on "The Prelude"* (Oxford: Clarendon, 1989). The apotheosis of deconstructive approaches, especially to the Spots of Time, is in the special issue of *Diacritics* devoted to Wordsworth (17 [1987]). I can only try to cite an indebtedness or two in later notes. Two commentaries that have afforded me precise ways of thinking about the Spots of Time are Jonathan Bishop, "Wordsworth and the 'Spots of Time,'" *ELH* (1959), whose phenomenological account included the key question, "What do they appear to be *about?*" (46), and Thomas Weiskel, whose concept of "the overdetermination of the signifier" in *The Romantic Sublime: Studies in the Structure and Psychology of Transcendence* (Baltimore: Johns Hopkins University Press, 1976) enables much that follows. For important discussions of the epigraph to this chapter, see Jonathan Wordsworth, "As with the Silence of the Thought," *High Romantic Argument: Essays for M. H. Abrams,* ed. Lawrence Lipking (Ithaca, N.Y.: Cornell University Press, 1981), 58–64, and Mary Jacobus, "Apostrophe and Lyric Voice in 'The Prelude,'" *Lyric Poetry: Beyond New Criticism,* ed. Chaviva Hosek and Patricia Parker (Ithaca, N.Y.: Cornell University Press, 1985), 176–77.

2. Siskin, *The Work of Writing: Literature and Social Change in Britain, 1700–1830* (Baltimore: Johns Hopkins University Press, 1998), 112.

3. I quote the poem from *Samuel Taylor Coleridge: the Complete Poems,* ed. William Keach (London: Penguin, 1997), 339. The variant is quoted from the Wordsworth Library MS in ibid., 573.

4. Abrams, "The Correspondent Breeze: A Romantic Metaphor," *English Romantic Poets: Modern Essays in Criticism,* ed. Abrams (New York: Oxford University Press, 1960).

5. Caruth, *Empirical Truths and Critical Fictions: Locke, Wordsworth, Kant, Freud* (Baltimore: Johns Hopkins University Press, 1991).

6. Empson, *The Structure of Complex Words* (Ann Arbor: University of Michigan Press, 1967), 294–95. For a valuable update on this issue, see Kerry McSweeney, *The Language of the Senses: Sensory-Perceptual Dynamics in Wordsworth, Coleridge, Thoreau, Whitman, and Dickinson* (Montreal: McGill-Queen's University Press, 1998).

7. Paul de Man, *The Rhetoric of Romanticism* (New York: Columbia University Press, 1984), 11–17; David Ferris, *Theory and the Evasion of History* (Baltimore: Johns Hopkins University Press, 1993), 135–82.

8. Alan Liu, *Wordsworth: The Sense of History* (Stanford, Calif.: Stanford University Press, 1989), 22–31.

9. Weiskel, *The Romantic Sublime,* 17.

10. See *Journals of Dorothy Wordsworth,* ed. Ernest de Selincourt, 2 vols. (London: Macmillan, 1959), II, 259. See the photograph of this oppressive, eight-story-high structure, the Kaspar Stockalper Spittal, which was destroyed by a flood in 2000, in Donald E. Hayden, "Wordsworth's Gondo: Gone," *TWC* 32 (2001): 117.

11. Hartman too acknowledges that the imagination on Snowdon is figured in natural imagery (*Wordsworth's Poetry,* 187).

12. I am anticipated in doubting the transcendence of the mind in the Spots by Brooke Hopkins, "Wordsworth, Winnicott, and the Claims of the 'Real,'" *SiR* 37 (1998): 190–91.

13. Letter to J. H. Reynolds, 3 May 1818, *Letters of John Keats,* ed. Robert Gittings (Oxford: Oxford University Press, 1970), 95.

14. Fry, *A Defense of Poetry: Essays on the Occasion of Writing* (Stanford, Calif.: Stanford University Press, 1995), 91–107.

15. The point is made by the editors of the Norton *Prelude,* 152n.

16. This was established by Jane Worthington Smyser, "Wordsworth's Dream of Poetry and Science," *PMLA* 71 (1956): 269–75. For important comments on this episode, see Timothy Bahti, *SiR* 18 (1979): 601–27, and Simon Jarvis, *Wordsworth's Philosophic Song* (Cambridge: Cambridge University Press, 2007), 74–79.

17. Among the intricate readings of this passage, that of David Collings (*Wordsworthian Errancies: The Poetics of Cultural Dismemberment* [Baltimore: Johns Hopkins University Press, 1994]) should not be overlooked.

18. With this emphasis one is bound to be haunted by the well-known passage from the third "Essay upon Epitaphs" that inspired the path-breaking book of Frances Ferguson, *Wordsworth: Language as Counter-Spirit* (New Haven: Yale University Press, 1977): "Language, if it do not uphold and feed, and leave in quiet, like the power of gravitation or the air we breathe, is a counter-spirit, unremittingly and noiselessly at work to derange, to subvert. To lay waste, and to dissolve" (*Wordsworth's Literary Criticism,* ed. W. J. B. Owen [London: Routledge & Kegan Paul, 1974], 154).

19. For a fine reading of this passage, see Robert Griffin, "Wordsworth's Horse," *The Wordsworthian Enlightenment: Romantic Poetry and the Ecology of Reading,* ed. Helen Regueiro Elam and Frances Ferguson (Baltimore: Johns Hopkins University Press, 2005), 129–45.

20. Brooks, *The Well-Wrought Urn* (New York: Harcourt, 1947), 3–7.

*Chapter 8: The Pastor's Wife and the Wanderer:*
*Spousal Verse or the Mind's Excursive Power*

1. Most notable are Alison Hickey, *Impure Conceits: Rhetoric and Ideology on Wordsworth's "Excursion"* (Stanford, Calif.: Stanford University Press, 1997); William Galperin, *Revision and Authority in Wordsworth: The Interpretation of a Career* (Philadelphia: University of Pennsylvania Press, 1989); Kenneth R. Johnston, *Wordsworth and the Recluse* (New Haven: Yale University Press, 1984), 9–19 (on the role of Coleridge); Esther H. Schor, *Bearing the Dead: The British Culture of Mourning from Enlightenment to Victoria* (Princeton, N.J.: Princeton University Press, 1994); David Simpson, *Wordsworth's Historical Imagination* (New York: Methuen, 1987); Susan Wolfson, *The Questioning Presence: Wordsworth, Keats, and the Interrogative Mode in Romantic Poetry* (Ithaca: Cornell University Press, 1986). Earlier — apart from the first monograph on the poem, Judson Lyon, *The Excursion: A Study* (New Haven: Yale University Press, 1950) — there is lively commentary by Cleanth Brooks, "Wordsworth and Human Suffering: Notes on Two Early Poems," *From Sensibility to Romanticism,* ed. Frederick W. Hilles and Harold Bloom (New York: Oxford, 1965); Geoffrey Hartman, *Wordsworth's Poetry,*

*1787–1814* (1964; rpt. Cambridge, Mass.: Harvard University Press, 1987), 292–323; Frances Ferguson, *Wordsworth: Language as Counter-Spirit* (New Haven: Yale University Press, 1977), Reeve Parker, " 'Finer Distance': The Narrative Art of Wordsworth's 'The Wanderer,' " *ELH* 39 (1972): 87–111, and most recently Sally Bushell, *Re-reading "The Excursion"* (Aldershot: Ashgate, 2002). Specifically on *The Ruined Cottage*, the most challenging interpretations are those of Jonathan Wordsworth, *The Music of Humanity: A Critical Study of Wordsworth's Ruined Cottage* (London: Nelson, 1969), and Alan Liu, *Wordsworth: The Sense of History* (Stanford, Calif.: Stanford University Press, 1989), 311–58. Like me but with a very different end in view, Liu dwells at length upon the charge against the "inhumanity" of the poem's responses to suffering, especially the Wanderer's, and views this weakness as an effect (New Critical by way of Brooks) of privileging an "economy" of imagery such as the spear grass over the narration of economic circumstances.

2. Fry, "The Absent Dead," *A Defense of Poetry: Reflections on the Occasion of Writing* (Stanford, Calif.: Stanford University Press, 1995), esp. 160–67. In this essay, first published nearly thirty years ago, I argue, as I shall here, that the self-curtailment of *The Excursion* follows the logic of metonymy. Referring mainly to the Churchyard Books (V–VII), I point to a pattern, especially in the Pastor's discourse, on which I shall be elaborating here.

3. A passage from a letter of 1811, saying that he would like his own poems had he read them as another's, and likes them well enough in any case, but can no longer feel any "personal interest" in them, would suggest that the importance of his vocation, if not its purpose, is losing ground (see *CL*, II, 1, 471).

4. Geoffrey Hartman sees in advance the movement of my approach as the danger risked by the poem: "Wordsworth's separation of visionary and visual results usually in the atrophy of both" (*Wordsworth's Poetry*, 293). Yet Wordsworth himself, it should be admitted, never gave up the sense that any good poetry was implicitly religious, and he associates this idea, in a letter to Landor of 1824, with the sense of the oneness of things that I have emphasized in this book: "those passages where things are lost in each other, and aspirations are raised" (*CL*, III, 1, 245). For the view that Wordsworth had been Christian all along and broke no new ground in *The Excursion*, see William Ulmer, *The Christian Wordsworth, 1798–1805* (Albany: SUNY Press, 2001), 183–85.

5. See Hartman, "Reading and Representation: Wordsworth's Boy of Winander," *European Romantic Review* 5 (1994): 94.

6. Without wishing to discredit the intricate research that has established the provenance and interconnection of these many texts (one of the most impressive accomplishments of the Cornell-Dove Cottage project), I shall suppose Wordsworth by 1814 to have made Book I continuous with the rest of the poem (which is also of course a coordinated patchwork), and read it accordingly, referring to earlier materials only when wishing to point to a particular contrast.

7. Here I wish to point out, in qualification of deconstructive readings of Wordsworth, from de Man to Caruth, the mere inevitability with which the necessarily material referents of tropes of transcendence drag them back to earth. This "what did you expect?" response must, I think, shadow my reading of the Snowdon episode in the previous chapter, and I follow Hickey, whose demands as a reader comparably risk this sort of

emptiness, in candidly quoting John Hodgson: " 'The language of Wordsworth's transcendental passages contains immanent, phenomenal figures. But what alternative is there? Can there be such a thing as a noumenal figure? No—by definition, as it were' " (*Impure Conceits,* 197n., citing Hodgson, review of Keith Thomas's *Wordsworth and Philosophy, TWC* 21 [1990]: 152).

8. James, *Scepticism and Poetry: An Essay on the Poetic imagination* (London: Allen & Unwin, 1960).

9. Quite apart from the Wanderer's opinion of Voltaire, what other poet would celebrate the child's happy indifference to learning by making a book a building block, a prop? Even the Bible was a prop for the head of the sleeping Ann Tyson in *The Prelude,* but there, while the Greuzeian tableau once again deemphasizes reading, we recognize that the Gospel secures us all in Abraham's bosom by whatever means. No secular author can do that, but any book makes a good cornerstone for a makeshift playhouse. Better that than "the task / Of puzzling out the faded narrative" from which the Poet is later glad to be relieved (V, 206–07). In this poem, books are tattered, torn, and (except for the Wanderer's Milton) neglected, as if to recall the wish for some more durable form of expression at the beginning of *Prelude* 5.

10. Consider what he says about *Paradise Lost* in the 1815 "Essay, Supplementary" of the same period: "Take ... those who wished to possess the Poem as a religious work, and but few I fear would be left who sought for it on account of its poetical merits" (*Criticism,* 200). Poetry loses little value because it is now clearly distinct from theology. See also *CL,* VII (III), 4, 43.

11. See Liu, *Wordsworth,* 344, and Celeste Langan, *Romantic Vagrancy* (Cambridge: Cambridge University Press, 1995).

12. *Fenwick Notes,* ed. Curtis, 79.

13. The most interesting discussion of this mercuric concept is that of Celeste Langan, *Romantic Vagrancy.*

14. Here is where I would clearly distance myself from Kenneth Johnston's ingenious eroticization of Margaret and the Wanderer in Book I as simply misplaced—there being no objection at all, in my view, to that way of reading other texts: "Nutting," for example. Johnston's interest in Wordsworth and sex is much more to the point, I think, than F. W. Bateson's earlier focus on incest in *Wordsworth: A Re-Interpretation* (London: Longmans, Green, 1954).

15. Thomas De Quincey, "On Wordsworth's Poetry," *Tait's Edinburgh Magazine* 12 (1845): 545–54.

16. The Wanderer is not the only speaker who says "Sir" in the poem, and it may just be a question of filling out the meter, but I wonder if I am the only reader brought up short by the note of unctuous deference on these occasions. By Wordsworth's time Dr. Johnson's invariant mode of address was used much as it is now, in real or pretended deference. Shelley probably never used this term in speaking to anyone, and it is a tacit compliment to Wordsworth that he does not drive the nail in still farther by quoting "Oh, Sir!" along with the rest of the passage. But does not Wordsworth as well find this a subtle means (wasted on his contemptuous public) of keeping his peddler-sage's social inferiority before us in the proper degree? If the Wanderer has been a kind of upstairs servant to the

Poet, as his address would indicate, and if the Poet was himself an obscure schoolboy put out to board when he knew him, class relations have here been pegged strikingly downward without ceasing to be vertical.

17. See Hickey, *Impure Conceits*, 93–94. See also Lyon, *The Excursion: A Study*, 81.

18. From the beginning Wordsworth had to fend off readers, misled perhaps by the defense of superstition with its pretty piece of paganism in Book IV, who claimed that *The Excursion* was not Christian enough, and the notorious changes of 1845 (Margaret ever mindful of the Cross, and so on) were his final response to them. Some modern readers seem to have taken their cue from these readers in arguing that the poem is at most antinomian, just not as inspired as the doctrinally evasive *Prelude*. Perhaps it is a certain alertness in the presence of exotic states of mind arising from my own total irreligion, but I find this reaction shockingly counterintuitive. Although it is not part of Wordsworth's intent to explain the history of Church doctrine in this poem, as he does in the *Ecclesiastical Sonnets*, surely the structure of *The Excursion* leaves no doubt that it is meant to celebrate the social and religious aspects of the Church of England with equal fervor. To do this and to convert the Solitary (from whose Dissenting pulpit the slippery slope to agnosticism had fallen away) are the same. Like Chaucer in the General Prologue (the excellent comparison is Kenneth Johnston's [*Wordsworth and "The Recluse,"* 297–98]), he gives us several "priests" to choose from: an urbane good man (the Pastor), a worldly but genial and competent place-holder (the Sympson portrait), and an otherworldly saint (the Robert Walker portrait); and the result is not blasphemy or anticlericalism but what Dryden in this context called "God's plenty."

19. I relegate these passages to a footnote because I have to say of them only that they are all spoken by the Wanderer during his effort to wean the Solitary from despondency. See IV, 83–86, 110–25, 205–08, 1132–42. His presumption is — and this is one of the strongest evidences for my contention that the Wanderer and the Solitary are the obverse and inverse of a single coin — that the Solitary has lost the visionary gleam without having acquired philosophic calm, or Duty.

20. Hartman writes: "I doubt that there exists another poem of such length in which death and tragic mutation become so literally the ground of the whole" (*Wordsworth's Poetry*, 296; see also 300). As Lyon points out, much of the poem was composed in the aftermath of the death of two children (*The Excursion: A Study*, 14).

21. Martin Heidegger, "The Question Concerning Technology," *The Question Concerning Technology and Other Essays*, trans. William Lovitt (New York: Harper, 1977), 16.

22. The so often faintly praised Lyon is the only one to have tried, indirectly, to account for this scene. He rightly calls attention to Coleridge's 1799 letter urging Wordsworth to write a poem chastising the anti-social habits — among them " 'an almost epicurean selfishness' " — of those disillusioned with the French Revolution. Perhaps that is what Wordsworth is attempting here, but he fails to make the Solitary act like an Epicurean, throwing all the emphasis on his "glee" and warmth of hospitality. Still, Lyon's balanced treatment of the Solitary's character and Wordsworth's motives in modulating it as he does is one of the best things written on this topic, and deserves rereading (*The Excursion: A Study*, 62).

23. Wordsworth himself believed that he had now returned to the Book of Nature

topos, pointing to "the innumerable analogies and types of infinity" that "I have trans-
fused into [*The Excursion*] from the Bible of the Universe as it speaks to the ear of the
intelligent" (*CL*, III, 2, 188).

24. See Hickey, *Impure Conceits*, 160.

25. Stuart Curran's thesis offsetting that of, e.g., M. H. Abrams in *The Mirror and the
Lamp* and Earl Wasserman in *The Subtler Language*, as well as of Wordsworth himself in
subjectifying generic distinctions in the arrangement of his work in 1807, is not meant to
deny that genres are transformed by romanticism, only to restore a balance. See Curran,
*Poetic Form and British Romanticism* (New York: Oxford University Press, 1986),
esp. 250n.

### Chapter 9: Intimations Revisited:
### From the Crisis Lyrics to Wordsworth in 1817

1. Strikingly alert to the deathwardness of this poem viewed as an aspect of the
relation between psychology and vocation is Thomas Pfau, *Wordsworth's Profession:
Form, Class, and the Logic of Early Romantic Cultural Production* (Stanford, Calif.:
Stanford University Press, 1997), 130. An especially sensitive confrontation with the fact
that even childhood in Wordsworth can be read as a kind of blissful being-dead is that of
Willard Spiegelman, *Wordsworth's Heroes* (Berkeley: University of California Press,
1985), 60–64.

2. Especially strong on this pattern is the splendid essay by Albert S. Gérard, "Dark
Passages: Wordsworth's *Tintern Abbey*," *English Romantic Poetry* (Berkeley: University
of California Press, 1968), 89–117.

3. A critic who sees this clearly is Jonathan Wordsworth, who writes in a book whose
very title reflects such an emphasis, here apropos of this passage among others, "It is
when his functions are 'silently sealed up' . . . that the p[oet] is most aware of the song of
the One Life" (*William Wordsworth: The Borders of Vision* [Oxford: Clarendon, 1982],
4). See also ibid., 10, 26; during the course of this brilliant opening chapter, however,
Jonathan Wordsworth moves gradually from his then unprecedented focus on somatic
and marginal states to modulations of these states into transcendent registers.

4. The first new historicist essay on "Tintern Abbey," from which modern scholars get
most of their information about the charcoal burners and their smoke in the village of
Tintern, the homeless persons in the Abbey a few miles away, and so on, was that of J.
Bard McNulty, "Wordsworth's Tour of the Wye, 1798," *MLN* 60 (1945): 291–95. The
most influential work in this vein, building on remarks by Jerome McGann in *Romantic
Ideology*, is that of Marjorie Levinson, "Insight and Oversight," in *Wordsworth's Great
Period Poems* (Cambridge: Cambridge University Press, 1986). The issues she raises are
interestingly revisited by Charles Rzepka, "Pictures of the Mind: Iron and Charcoal,
'Ouzy' Tides and 'Vagrant Dwellers' at Tintern, 1798," *SiR* 42 (2003): 155–85. Perhaps
the most subtle and comprehensive account of these issues is that of Kenneth Johnston,
"The Politics of 'Tintern Abbey,'" *TWC* 14 (1985): 6–14. The best discussion directing
the politics of the poem toward Wordsworth's feelings about the French Revolution and
the English response to it is that of David Bromwich in *Disowned by Memory: Words-
worth's Poetry of the 1790s* (Chicago: University of Chicago Press, 1998).

5. To me, one need go no farther than Keats and Empson to be aware of Wordsworth's verbal evasiveness in this poem, but among the modern deconstructive essays I would single out Carol Jacobs, "The Unimaginable Touch of Time: Wordsworth's "Tintern Abbey," Crossing the Alps, and 'Intimations of Immortality," *Telling Time* (Baltimore: Johns Hopkins University Press, 1993), 159–87.

6. Except concerning my discussion below of "the abyss of idealism" in the Fenwick note, I find that what I say here does not significantly overlap with what I wrote about this poem thirty years ago in *The Poet's Calling in the English Ode* (New Haven: Yale University Press, 1980). I find myself curiously anticipated here from an unexpected source: Cleanth Brooks, "Wordsworth and the Paradox of the Imagination" (*Wordsworth: A Collection of Critical Essays,* ed. M. H. Abrams [Englewood Cliffs, N.J.: Prentice-Hall, 1972]), who writes: "The continuity between child and man is actually unbroken" (186).

7. *Fenwick Notes,* ed. Curtis, 61, and Christopher Wordsworth, *Memoirs of William Wordsworth,* 2 vols. (London: Edward Moxon, 1851), II, 476, 480.

8. *The Letters of William and Dorothy Wordsworth, 1812–1820,* ed. Mary Moorman and Alan G. Hill (Oxford: Clarendon, 1970), 189. It is in this same letter (188) that we find one of Wordsworth's apologies for having said he was a worshipper of nature in "Tintern Abbey."

9. It is remarkable how fully Davies confirms this tendency as a school of thought in *Wordsworth and the Worth of Words,* rpt. ed. John Kerrigan and Jonathan Wordsworth (Cambridge: Cambridge University Press, 1986).

10. I shall quote throughout the remainder of the chapter from the Reading Texts supplied in this edition: *Shorter Poems, 1807–1820,* ed. Ketcham (Ithaca: Cornell University Press, 1989). *Op. cit.,* 12–14.

11. One should point out that Wordsworth in Grasmere, with "high mountains" to the west, was deprived of sunsets for the most part (see *CL,* II, 1, 93).

*Afterword: Just Having It There Before Us*

1. Eliot, "The Humanism of Irving Babbitt," *Selected Prose of T. S. Eliot,* ed. Frank Kermode (New York: Harcourt, 1975), 277–86.

2. Hazlitt quotes the *Confessions* [I, 6]) in his "On the Character of Rousseau" (quoted from *Criticism: The Major Texts,* ed. W. J. Bate (New York: Harcourt, 1970), 301. See also his second essay "On Genius and Common Sense" (ibid., 328).

3. A voice recently raised in this cause, invoking one aspect of Geoffrey Hartman's work in turn, is Gerald Bruns, "Poetic Knowledge: Geoffrey Hartman's Romantic Poetics," *The Wordsworthian Enlightenment: Romantic Poetry and the Ecology of Reading,* ed. Helen Regueiro Elan and Frances Ferguson (Baltimore: Johns Hopkins University Press, 2005), 112–28.

4. Heidegger, *Being and Time,* trans. John Macquarrie and Edward Robinson (1927; New York: Harper & Row, 1962), 190.

# Index